Theatre in
a Media Culture

Theatre in a Media Culture: Production, Performance and Perception Since 1970

Amy Petersen Jensen

227 pages $39.95 softcover
Appendices, notes, bibliography, index
ISBN 978-0-7864-2877-9 2007

As the media have increasingly become the lens through which we see the world, media styles have shaped even the fine arts, and contemporary theatre is particularly indebted to mass media's dramatic influence. In order to stay culturally and financially viable, theatre producers have associated theatrical productions and their promotion with film, television, and the Internet by adopting new theatrical practices that mirror the form and content of mass communication. This work demonstrates how *mediatization* , or the adoption of the semantics and the contexts of mass media, has changed the way American theatre is produced, performed, and perceived.

Early chapters use works like Robert Wilson's 3D digital opera *Monsters of Grace* and Thecla Schophorst's digitally animated *Bodymaps* to demonstrate the shifting nature of live performance. Critical analysis of the interaction between the live performer and digital technology demonstrates that the use of media technology has challenged and changed traditional notions of dramatic performance. Subsequent discussion sustains the argument that theatre has reconfigured itself to access the economic and cultural power of the media. Final chapters consider the extent to which mediatization undermines theatrical authorship and creativity.

Amy Petersen Jensen is an assistant professor in the Department of Theatre and Media Arts at Brigham Young University in Provo, Utah.

McFarland

Enclosed please find:
Jensen.

Theatre in a Media Culture

Publication date: Available Now
Price: $39.95

This book is sent to you:

__X__ with the compliments of the author/publisher.

____ for examination.

____ as your desk copy, with our compliments.

____ for review. We ask that you include our website
address (**www.mcfarlandpub.com**) and our order
line (**800-253-2187**) in any review. **Send one copy**
of your published review, preferably via e-mail as
a PDF file (or a link for online reviews), to
bcox@mcfarlandpub.com. Alternately, publications
and tear sheets can be mailed to Beth Cox,
McFarland, Box 611, Jefferson NC 28640.

www.mcfarlandpub.com
orders 800-253-2187

ican stage. These are purposeful omissions because I recognize the tension between my own nostalgia for a pure theatre, which embraces its own medium-specific qualities, and the reality that theatre has always communicated within the language and context of the culture that produces it. This conflict between a nostalgic ideal and reality exists in all studies of historical artifacts but is usually unstated because of the distance between the historian and the reality of her or his subject. In this manner, historians have always described theatre from diverse periods for the most part as being different, but not better or worse. What I want to demonstrate is that theatre in an age of technology has changed (not necessarily for the better or worse) because of the mediated environment in which it has come to exist. I approach my subject then as a theatre historian, hoping to describe contemporary American theatre at the beginning of the twenty-first century.

Daryl Chin, associate editor of *PAJ: A Journal of Performance and Art*, uses an analogy to describe how technology alters art:

> [D]uring the 1950s, when acrylic paints became widely available as a medium for painting, the differences between acrylic paints and oil-based paints were widely known. Acrylic paints were designed to dry faster, because they were water-based; this also meant that acrylic paints were not as dense as oil paints. Because of the faster drying rate, which was due to the differing oxidizing speed of the lighter material, the hue, shade and color of acrylics were not the same as oils upon drying. "Burnt sienna" was slightly more orange, less earthy, more metallic in acrylic than in its oil counterpart. Also: because acrylics dried faster, the colors changed more than oils. The rate of oxidation with which acrylics dried could not be controlled as with oil paints, so that the (slight) variations in appearance ("burnt sienna" could be more orange, or more brown, or more beige) could not be predicted.... But acrylics were easier to use, and, by the end of the 1960s, had become the medium of choice for many painters. Few (if any) commentaries were written detailing the changes in painting occasioned by the capitulation to acrylics over oils [Online].

In the theatre, there is the same sense of irrevocable change, because media technology is undeniably omnipresent. The hegemonic weight of the media has altered contemporary stagings of reality. The contemporary theatre audience's acceptance of staged reality is governed by the constructs that are learned by the general populace through the assimilation of media's forms into their collective consciousness. This is demonstrated in the work of two television creators of the 1950s, Worthington Miner and Fred Coe, who manipulated classic texts to purposefully direct television audiences to value televisual forms over traditional content. This is substantiated in the work of Anna Deavere Smith, whose documentary theatre is imbedded with a media presence despite her concerted efforts to reproduce "authentic" contemporary voices on stage.

In order to stay culturally and financially viable, theatre producers have purposefully associated theatrical productions and their promotion with film, television, and the Internet by adopting new theatrical practices that mirror media's form and content. While this is most evident in the current theatrical trend, the musical movie remake, overt references to media are abundant in the production choices of performance artists, playwrights, actors, designers, and directors. This trend towards the location of theatre within the media is clearly evident in the 2003 Broadway season, which featured, among others, theatre director-filmmaker Sam Mendes's production of *Gypsy*, a visual replica of the 1962 film of the same name, which in turn was based on the original Broadway play. The season also included *Nine*, a musical version of Federico Fellini's film *8 1/2* (1963), starring film actor Antonio Banderas and television actress Jane Krakowski.

The American consumers' collective interaction with media has created a "participatory spectator" who, influenced by interactions with media forms, has learned to advance theatrical narratives beyond the threshold of the theatre space into their own private space. In the case of the "participatory spectator" the body becomes the site of negotiation between the dominant media and the smaller but still relevant theatre. The spectator's body becomes an *interstitial space*, or a site in which the competing claims of both theatre and media reside, each contending for cultural power and prominence to maintain cultural efficacy.

Many scholars have explored interactions between theatre and media, each with a specific focus. Historical accounts about the interactions between theatre, film and television from the end of the nineteenth century to the present include: Robert C. Allen's *Vaudeville and Film: 1895–1915, A Study in Media Interaction* (1980) (which focuses on the shared space, talent and promotions of vaudeville and film through the early development of the cinema), and Robert Mc Laughlin's *Broadway and Hollywood: A History of Economic Interaction* (1974) (which focuses on theatre's economic interaction with both film and television and includes full discussions of exchanges between the mediums based on his review of historical finance journals and trade papers).

Nicolas Vardac articulates the transition from the melodramatic stage of the late nineteenth-century to the advent of film. His study identifies melodrama as proto-cinematic and he concentrates on the similarities between the two mediums in their presentation of spectacle. Ben Brewster and Lea Jacobs address the similarities in the delivery of the two mediums as well as the unique differences in the staging and presentation of theatre and film in *Theatre to Cinema: Stage Pictorialism and the Early Feature Film* (1997). *American Theatre from Pre-Columbian Times to the Present*, written by Felecia Hardison Londrè and Daniel J. Watermeier, provides a broad overview of theatre, and their book is a helpful resource that provides general connections between theatre and the media. While the connection between theatre and media is not the sole purpose of their work, it does include wide-ranging information about dates, people, places and events that connect each medium.

Theoretical and praxis texts have also been helpful in making connections between theatre and media practice. I was certainly influenced by the early work of Erwin Piscator and Bertolt Brecht in my initial investigation of the relations between theatre and media. John Willett's *The Theatre of Erwin Piscator: Half a Century of Politics in Theatre* (1979) and *Brecht on Theatre: The Development of an Aesthetic* (1964) each provide examples of the writings and work product of the two men. These books have been helpful in shaping questions that I had regarding the historical interactions between theatre and media.

Roselee Goldberg's *Performance Art: From Futurism to the Present* (1988) contains interesting observations about the evolution of the performance artist through the acquisition of media tools. Her book focuses on the work of individual artists from the early twentieth century through the 1980s. Gary Edgarton's *Film and the Arts in Symbiosis* (1988) examines associations between theatre and film in content, form and presentation. Brenda Laurel's *Computers as Theatre* (1993) and *The Domain Matrix* (1997) by Sue Ellen Case both explore the performative nature of the electronic screen culture and are helpful investigations of what performance might become in cyberspace.

The December 1999 issue of *Theatre Journal*, titled "Theatre and Technology," also makes a significant contribution to the investigation of contemporary performance and technology. This issue examines how technology is being used to enhance many aspects of the theatre field, including the discovery of individual performance bodies, dramaturgical studies and historical reconstructions of previous dramatic events.

Finally, Philip Auslander's *Liveness: Performance in a Mediatized Culture* has had the most influence on my study. While his book is not directly about theatre practice, his insights about popular media culture and performance have been very helpful. Auslander looks at specific examples of live performance such as concerts, sporting events, and courtroom testimony to investigate media's penetrating power in popular culture. Auslander demonstrates that media technology has influenced live events to the point that most are not live at all. Auslander's core question, "what is live performance and what can it mean to us now?" is one impetus for my study of theatre as it relates to media in the present day.

While the core of this project is to document the strong influence of media's form and content on the production and reception of contemporary theatre, it is also important to note that media, while clearly being omnipresent, is far from being omnipotent in contemporary theatrical practice. Media technology does not limit the creativity of theatre artists, nor will it determine of the course of theatre evolution. However, because of mass media's effect on the collective perceptions of contemporary theatre audiences, influencing both the production and reception of theatre, academics must recognize its operation in theory and practice. Additionally, we must acknowledge the power of hybridity, for it is only in a hybrid space of understanding theatre in a mediatized context — a space where producers and receivers recognize and explore the nature of the mediatized stage — that theatre can effectively claim humanity as it strongest element of distinction from other forms of communication and expression.

Chapter One of this work establishes a theoretical context for my argument that theatre has reconfigured itself in the late part of the twentieth century to access the economic power of the culturally hegemonic media. In this chapter, the ongoing discussion of presence as it relates to theatre in a mediatized society is documented. My argument is influenced by the practical application of theoretical constructs. Practical works like Robert Wilson's 3D digital opera *Monsters of Grace* and Thecla Schophorst's digitally animated installation *Bodymaps* are used to demonstrate the shifting nature of presence as it pertains to live performance. These interactions between live performer and digital technology demonstrate that the use of media technology challenges traditional notions of what a performer's body might be and what a theatre space might include. More important, they challenge what the notion of presence means in a contemporary theatrical space infused with media technology. The idea that theoretical scholarship and contemporary practice's use of media technology has created a new dynamic between the stage space, the performer, and the audience is introduced by drawing on the scholarship of Susan Bennett and Phillip Valle.

Chapter Two offers a historical context between theatre and media technologies — film, television, and the Internet. The connection between the various mediums, both practically (in space and time) and intellectually, is established. The key assertion is that the contemporary theatrical viewing experience grew out of nineteenth-century discussions of vision as they related to the spectator's perception of time and space. This nineteenth-century exploration of human vision, as it was affected by mechanical means, caused a dramatic shift in the presentation and reception of theatre. Theatre responded to the sense of immediacy created by the technological and mechanical features of film, leading first to naturalism and realism in the theatre and then to an assimilation of media's forms and content. This contemplation of media as it shapes the contemporary spectator's vision from the nineteenth century forward helps demonstrate theatre's own imperative need to compete with the popular and commercial success of these technological mediums. In this case theatre alters its own nature and is marked by its resistance to or assimilation of the boundaries established by media corporations and their technologies.

Chapter Three explicates how technology has influenced our physical reality. Through the application of technology, the virtual has become tangible — with perceptions being a crucial component to our physical reality. Reality, therefore, has been altered for us by technology. Correspondingly, the presentation of reality in the contemporary theatre has to be presented differently from how it was presented in the past, whether or not technology is employed in that presentation. This is necessary not because the process of theatrical communication has changed, but because our lexicon of associative perceptions has been exponentially enhanced through mediated messages. Reality (in its complete sense, and cultural reality in particular) must be achieved on the stage today through association, rather than through imitation, as it has been in the past.

Chapter Four scrutinizes theatrical distribution strategies, expressly investigating the ways in which nostalgia is used as a commodity to market theatre produced for mass consumption. The chapter goes on to explain how the audience's familiarity with media forms is used in marketing Broadway movie musical remakes. Two texts are used as models for discussion: Andrew Lloyd Webber's *Sunset Boulevard*, a remake of Billy Wilder's film of the same title, and Mel Brooks's theatrical adaptation of his film *The Producers*. Nostalgia is one of many distribution tools used in professional business models. It is investigated because of its widespread use in theatre as well as other cultural products that are currently marketed as consumable entities. To understand the relevance of investigating theatrical distribution in terms of nostalgia one must simply consider the number of revivals that have played on Broadway or toured the country during the 1990s. This discussion of nostalgia as a distribution tool is significant, especially as it allows for the consideration of presence as it fits in the re-creation of a mediatized performance in a live stage production.

Chapter Five investigates overt textual and staged representations of the media through an analysis of two texts and their premiere staged performances. The central discussion of Adrienne Kennedy's *A Movie Star Has to Star in Black and White* and David Mamet's *Speed the Plow* address media as an explicit presence in the written and staged versions of each play. However, media as a presence despite its purposeful absence in texts and on the stage is also considered. Two themes emerge in the discussion of these play texts: (1) Media technologies are identified as pervasive entities through which authentic communication is subverted and material capitalism reigns, and (2) media technologies are identified as the disseminator of cultural relevance for the disenfranchised.

Chapter Six considers contemporary theatre's intense focus on corporeal performance as an aspect of spectacle. The body has practically become a mechanized part of the performance; it is central yet interchangeable between various performers with virtuosity in execution being the only common element. The performance planning and execution forgoes individual emotive skills inherent in other performance styles. Individual human content is vetted from the presentations and the performing body becomes a controlled and integrated, even mechanized, tool of the director. Technology has made the performing body a component of the theatre much like the lighting, sound, or other mechanical elements of the production.

Chapter Seven is an examination of what theatrical authorship might mean in a mediatized culture. The work of Anna Deavere Smith serves as a case study of mediatized authorship. Smith's work as creator, writer, and performer of the documentary theatre series *On the Road: Search for American Character* allows for an examination of authorship from the plays' conception through all phases of rehearsal and presentation. Smith, who is most recognized for her verbal re-presentations of real people, is dependent on film and television theory and practice in her creation of the text. Smith's use of media technology in performance presentation and her creation of performance texts is compared with the Russian filmmaker Dziga Vertov and his formal style, cinéma vérité. Finally, Smith's authorial voice is established as being influenced by the televised media coverage of the historical events that she depicts.

Chapter Eight considers the performative nature of reception in a mediatized culture by examining the audience as performer in cult performances associated with the viewing of *The Rocky Horror Picture Show* and the international touring production of *Sing-a-long Sound of Music.* Each event allows audience members to assume physical characteristics of characters and props from each film and encourages verbal and physical interaction with the cinematic presentations. The ways that audiences can both resist and assimilate media culture through their own performative interaction with media technologies are considered using these mediated theatrical events as a template. This leads to a discussion of the lived experience as re-presentation of the mediatized. The theory that the lived experience can be described as a performance of the mediatized is supported with an analysis of performative qualities inherent in Disney's planned community, "Celebration." This planned community is designed to provide inhabitants with a live "Disney" experience in their dwelling space.

The recognition of the establishment of the participatory theatre spectator is key to this work, as is the recognition that theater producers in America increasingly access the semantics and practices of mass media to create meaning. These two changes in American theatre production and reception alter the very nature of performative, American theatre-communication. These new elements, brought on by new technology and mass-media communication, are key to understanding American theatre in the twenty-first century.

ONE

The Mediatized Stage:
Theatre, Visual Culture,
and Presence

*The very definition of the real has become: that of which it is
possible to give an equivalent reproduction.... The real is not
only what can be reproduced, but that which is always already
reproduced.*

— Jean Baudrillard, *Simulations*

Contemporary American theatre practice can be defined by its polemical response to the production and reception of reality. Propelled by the work of Russian realism and French naturalism, the twentieth-century American stage, with a few notable exceptions, continually tried to define and produce some version of reality on stage. This convention of theatre continues to this day to take on a variety of shapes and forms.

Although staged reality was often the goal of twentieth-century theatre artists, the attempt to achieve reality was approached in various ways at different historical moments. Reality on the stage was defined by the access to and presentation of factual information in the socially conscious Workers Theatre Movement of the 1930s, which attempted to represent the plight of the American working class through its presentation of legal documents, newspapers, and biographical statements. Alternatively, the psychoanalytical work of Lee Strasberg and the Actors' Studio of the 1950s

11

defined realism on stage by the ability of its actors to access personal experiences through sensory and emotional memory exercises that establish a unique artistic voice in each performer.

Other theatre practitioners explored the presentation of reality through its material constitution. In a play written in 1977, *Fefu and Her Friends*, playwright Maria Irene Fornes explores theatrical conventions of time and space. Fornes attempts to demonstrate a more realistic temporal and spatial reality by moving the play's audience to four locations so that they see four scenes, each occurring at the same time. The audience is split into four groups so each group sees the four contemporaneous scenes in a different order. Reality for each spectator shifts depending on the order each sees the scenes and on his or her ability to move from scene to scene.

The intermingling of performer and audience explores possibilities in the delineation between performance space and audience space. For example, interactivity guides the 1988 Broadway play *Tony and Tina's Wedding* in which the audience participates as guests at a wedding. Audience participation, and the individual spectator's ability to perform as part of the narrative, determines the success of the play. The reality of the play depends upon the spectator's full participation in the improvisational experience.

Reality for the audience in both *Tony and Tina's Wedding* and *Fefu and Her Friends* depends upon the social construction and emotional connection of the spectator to the staged work and not upon either of their disparate methods of presenting that reality. The spectator's acceptance of the staged experience as authentic determines the success of any theatrical production's approach to reality. The acceptance of a staged reality shifts and changes as individual audiences shift and change, and the constructs and conventions acceptable to the participant spectators govern their perception of reality. With this in mind, I propose that any contemporary analysis of theatre spectatorship must address the production and reception of that staged reality in relationship to media. For my purposes, media is defined as the means of communicating mechanically delivered messages of persuasion that bind large populations into communities. The examples I use draw from film, television, and the Internet.

Certainly the spectator who enjoyed the nineteenth-century staging of realism and naturalism was influenced by cultural attitudes towards Darwinism and the scientific method. Because of their cultural context, those spectators believed that truth was verified through detailed scientific observation. Similarly, the cultural context of today's audiences, and the proximity to the dominant media technology that delivers that context, influences contemporary theatrical reception. The spectators' acceptance of staged reality has always approximated what they know about the world around them.

Working as a graduate student in the Computational Vision Department at the Massachusetts Institute of Technology in 1997, Claudio Pinhanez developed a project that interjected computer technology into theatrical space. In his play *It/I,* Pinhanez used media technology to explore the possibilities of computer-actors, where the computer automatically controls a character. This technique establishes a true interplay between man and machine. Digital technology becomes a means of expanding the body of an actor on stage, enabling the actor in Pinhanez's plays to produce sound, images, or music as expansions of his voice and body. He describes this extension as a "hyper-actor."

Performed at the Philippe Villers Experimental Media Facility ("The Cube" of the MIT Media Laboratory) in November of 1997, the play included fully developed computer characters and animations that reacted to live stage actors. The play used a live actor and a computer actor and addressed life in a world increasingly populated by technology. Employing high-tech computer vision technology to follow the actor and different modules that controlled the physical devices, the characters communicated with each other using a new performance language that utilized both traditional theatre paradigms and computerized interval scripts to describe and control both the characters' behavior and the overall structure of the play. This allowed for a flexibility and interactivity between human and computer actors.*

Pinhanez's works, and others such as Robert Wilson's 3D digital opera, *Monsters of Grace,* and Thecla Schophorst's digitally animated installation, *Bodymaps,* demonstrate the shifting nature of presence as it pertains to live performance. The interaction between live performer and digital technology in *It/I* makes it clear that the use of media technology can challenge traditional notions of what a performer's body might be and what a theatre space might include. It might also challenge what presence means in a theatrical space infused with media technology.

As demonstrated by Claudio Pinhanez, media culture permeates

---

*Pinhanez's practical and theoretical observations about the computer play It/I are available online at http://web.media.mit.edu/~iti/.

much of the performance practice in the twenty-first century.* Many of the rituals and patterns associated with theatrical performance have been traded for a more accessible mediated stage, one that impersonates the business practice, forms, techniques, and performance ideologies of the recorded media. This conscious reproduction of media practice is theatre's response to the contemporary "culture industry."

Theodore Adorno and Max Horkheimer first coined the term *culture industry* in their essay "The Culture Industry: Enlightenment as Mass Deception," from *The Dialectic of Enlightenment.* In the essay Adorno describes the culture industry as "the false identity of the general and the particular." According to Adorno, a perceived but false unity between microcosm and macrocosm presented by industrial monopolies lures the masses into becoming identical to each other. Adorno says that the lines of the culture industry's artificial framework begin to show through in popular entertainment like movies and radio. For Adorno the purveyors of popular culture no longer need to pretend to make art. Instead they make business an ideology that justifies the material they deliberately produce:

> The whole world is made to pass through the filter of the culture industry. The old experience of the moviegoer, who sees the world outside as an extension of the film he has just left (because the latter is intent upon reproducing the world of everyday perceptions), is now the producer's guideline. The more intensely and flawlessly his techniques duplicate empirical objects, the easier it is today for the illusion to prevail that the outside world is the straightforward continuation of that presented on the screen [120–21].

Adorno's idea of a false unity of identity can easily be applied in interpreting the successes of Broadway shows such as *The Producers, Hairspray, The Lion King, Beauty and the Beast,* and others that feature an overt media connection. Certainly long-lived theatrical traditions of spectacle and celebrity play a part in drawing audiences to Broadway. However, I see a new influence that connects the audience to these productions — reality, specifically a new mediated reality that is part of the audience members' lived experience. The false unity of identity tells each audience

In this work I use the term media to describe organizations, mediums, and ideas associated with contemporary visual culture. The editors of October 77 describe the dual role of visual culture, saying: "[Visual culture] is both a partial description of a social world mediated by commodity images and visual technologies, and an academic rubric for interdisciplinary convergences among art history, film theory, media analysis and cultural studies" (Rosiland Krause and Hal Foster for the editors, "Introduction," October 77 [1996]: 3). I will use both definitions of visual culture in the body of this work, but my focus in this chapter is on the first meaning.

member that she or he has a special and unique connection to the performance: each has foreknowledge of the plot or perceived intimacy with the performers or special knowledge of the genesis of the work. All of these emotional responses to the theatrical production are enhanced by a media influence, be it the original film, or television shows that acquaint the audience with the performers, or information on the Internet that promotes, discusses, and contextualizes the play, the film, the performers, the creators, or anything else connected with the work.

Herbert Blau says media practice (specifically the cinema) shapes all current cultural discourse — including theatrical discourse. Blau describes film as more socially credible than theatre because it has "more credit (on the money market and in the libidinal economy)" (121), which makes it seem more authentic and relevant in a climate devoted to cultural and economic currency. Blau frames his argument with a statement from Karl Marx's *Grundrisse*, a treatise on industrial labor under bourgeois capitalism: "In all forms of society, there is one specific kind of production which predominates over the rest, whose relations thus assign rank and influence to the others. It is a general illumination, which bathes all the other colors and modifies their peculiarity. It is a particular ether which determines the specific gravity of every being which has materialized within it" (121).

Like Blau, I believe Marx's discussion can be applied to cinema but that it is even more relevant to the media conglomerates of the 1980s and 1990s that produce, distribute, and exhibit multiple mass media outlet forms. Through a groundswell of media mergers in the last two decades of the twentieth century, seven large corporations took business control of all mediated forms. These parent companies* now control the promotion and selling of most media talent and products disseminated in the United States and Europe. These corporate mergers allow associate organizations, working under the auspices of the parent company, to exchange information and cross-promote products under the guidance of the conglomerate.

As of 2005, five U.S.-based companies include: Rupert Murdoch's News Corporation Ltd., which has media holdings in the United States, Canada, Europe, Australia, etc.; AOL Time Warner, the largest corporation, a result of the largest media merger in history (the media powerhouse integrates communication, media, and entertainment across all platforms — computer, film, television, sports entertainment, and handheld wireless devices); Walt Disney Corporation, whose year 2000 revenues topped $25 billion, with 27 percent derived from parks and resorts, 24 percent from studio entertainment, and 17 percent from media networks; and Sony Pictures Entertainment, which has 180,000 employees worldwide and over $58 billion in sales for 2001 (its Sony Pictures Entertainment is one of the seven major movie houses in Hollywood); and Viacom, the second largest media conglomerate worldwide, after AOL Time Warner, with 1999 sales of over $12 billion (transcripts from the Frontline *series "Merchants of Cool,"* www.pbs.org).

For example, Disney, the third largest media corporation in the world, owns ABC, Walt Disney Pictures, Miramax Film, Disney Theatrical, Hyperion Books, ESPN, Walt Disney Theme Parks, Disney Cruise Lines, as well as several prominent radio stations and Internet companies. Through this network the Disney Corporation has the power to cross-promote the products and people it sells. One case in point is the success of Disney's product *Beauty and the Beast*. Disney Corporation's original product, an animated version of the classic fairy tale *Beauty and the Beast*, is now a Broadway musical, a children's book, and a primetime television special, all capitalizing on the vision that created the motion picture. Animated characters from the original film have spawned sequel videos, action figures, and costumed characters in theme parks and on cruise lines. The wealth, predominance, and interconnectedness of such corporations as Disney allow them to present ideological perspectives through media technology that affect all aspects of popular cultural thought.

Media's cultural and economic power makes it more than a competitive means of conveying expression. Media technology is a central and determining element of cultural development that influences the way foundations of culture, including theatre, are conceived and practiced. Media conglomerates and their technologies model the dominant mode of cultural production and commodification. They wield the power to shape and even alter the cultural economy of other commercial and artistic productions because of their dominant presence in the collective cultural mind. James Lull suggests that these corporate entities have the power to infiltrate and impose ideological patterns on the public consciousness: "Media technologies enter cultural settings in ways that extend the characteristic traditions, values, and styles that are already in place while at the same time they also challenge and transform the foundations of culture" (44).

My examination of media's redefinition of theatrical presence is shaped by post-modern thought, specifically the work of Jean Baudrillard. In his essay "Simulacra and Simulations," Baudrillard describes a "hyper-real" cultural mindset in which America's communal identity relies on the production of "imaginary" worlds, like Disneyland, an "other" which verifies its own reality. Bauldrillard's essay distinguishes between representation and simulation. Here representation starts from a point where the sign and the real are equivalent. In stark contrast, simulation starts from the point of equivalence but negates the sign as value. While representation tries to absorb simulation by construing it as counterfeit representation, simulation shrouds the whole edifice of representation as itself a simulacrum. Baudrillard sees the transition from representation to simulation as the decisive turning point in which there is no separation of the real from the artificial:

> When the real is no longer what it used to be, nostalgia assumes its full meaning. There is a proliferation of myths of origin and signs of reality; of second-hand truth, objectivity, and authenticity. There is an escalation of the true, of the lived experience; a resurrection of the figurative where the object and substance have disappeared. And there is a panic-stricken production of the real and the referential, above and parallel to the panic of material production. This is how simulation appears in the phase that concerns us: a strategy of the real, neo-real and hyperreal, whose universal double is a strategy of deterrence [Baudrillard 169].

Baudrillard describes Disneyland as a place in which the collective phenomenology of American citizens is embalmed and its values displayed in miniature form, a place in which the presentation of the imaginary is used to contrast and validate the reality outside of the theme park. For Baudrillard, reality no longer exists in the world, and venues like Disneyland are destructive masks of that lack reality. Baudrillard describes Disneyland as one of many imaginary stations "concealing the fact that the real is no longer real" (Baudrillard 171). For instance, California, the state that hosts Disneyland, also hosts Hollywood; Hollywood is an industrial city that benefits from the infantile artifice of Disneyland because it feeds "reality energy" to Hollywood by portraying itself as the site of the imaginary. In this manner Hollywood is made to seem more real in contrast to Disneyland. Relying on Disneyland's hyper-imaginary status to counter its own lack of reality, Hollywood is free to reproduce the essential features of a perceived reality in its products because its own lack of reality is deterred by the simulations in the amusement park. Baudrillard asserts that reality vanishes in this interplay between the established imaginary and what is perceived as real.

However, traditional art forms, attempting to remain commercially viable in today's environment, must also reproduce this model wherein reality is not the everyday world but rather the interpreted content of mass media outlets. And, in their attempts to reproduce the same balance between the established imaginary and a counterfeit reality, older art forms such as theatre must mimic mediatized circulation.*

Representations of perceived reality adopted from media and then

---

I am using Baudrillard's definition of the word mediatized. In For a Critique of the Political Economy of the Sign *(1981) he says, "What is mediatized is not what comes off the daily press, out of the tube, or on the radio: it is what is reinterpreted by the sign form, articulated into models, and administered by the code" (175–76).

performed by theatre and other art forms are valued and accepted culturally only because they assimilate the already accepted form and content of
media reproduction. It is in this mediatized context that I have come to
understand that a post-modern theatrical presence is more a practice of
marketing than an interaction between performer and audience member.
Frederic Jameson describes this adoption of form and content as a condition of late capitalism in which "traditional fine arts ... come to a consciousness of themselves as various media within a mediatic system" (162).

Roger Copeland's essay "The Presence of Mediation"* challenges
readers to think of presence as a conflict between theories. Antonin Artaud
and his practitioner successors of the 1960s (Judith Molina, Julian Beck,
and Joseph Chaiken, et al.) believed presence exists in stripping away
artifice. Theatrical presence takes its participants back to the original
moment of presentness, before even speech, to what Artaud describes as
a "frightful transfer of forces from body to body."† Materiality, even physical contact, is required in this definition. In contrast, Jacques Derrida,
following his theories of absence, suggests that living presence is not accessible or concrete and that any attempt to create or acknowledge presence
is derived and therefore not authentic. If presence can be defined, as
Copeland argues, within this conflict of physical presence and presence
deferred by absence, the simultaneous involvement of spectator and performer is always mediated (I mean this in the traditional sense of the
definition) by some entity whether physical or psychological. This argument opens the door to a definition of theatrical presence that does not
require a physical interaction between spectator and performer but instead
focuses on presence as a perception of the collective community, a constructed aura that is agreed upon by the mass public.

Chantal Pontbriand also draws a distinction between a "classical presence" and "post-modern presence." She describes "classical presence" as
temporality in which performance involves a physical proximity for the
performer and the audience. This form of presence unfolds in real time
and does not transcend imaginary time and space. Pontbriand depicts
"post-modern presence" as developing through an ideological interaction

---

*Copeland's essay addresses all sides of the theatrical presence polemic. It has theoretical insight
but is also a solid resource guide to productions that incorporate a mediated presence.

†In The Empty Space, Peter Brook describes Artaud's concept as achievable in process but not
product. For Brook and his company the search for authentic presence took shape as an acting
exercise in which the performer discovers what the very least he or she needs before understanding takes place. In their work it comprised barely audible utterances, sounds, movements, and
rhythms (50).

with the mechanically reproduced. In the post-modern, presence is no longer dependent on materiality but instead depends on the artwork's exhibition value, its multiplicity, and its accessibility (and therefore its proximity and immediacy to the audience) (155–56).

As I construe and extend it, Pontbriand's argument suggests that post-modern theatrical presence is no longer concerned with the temporal or spatial aspects of the stage or the location of its audience. She asserts that while modernism seeks out the unique theatrical essence that depends on temporal and spatial proximity, post-modern theatre producers and spectators in the age of media technology view presence in terms of exhibition value. In effect, presence then is really about reproduction. Producers and audience members influenced by media conglomerates and their technological infrastructures no longer desire the unique theatrical experience that includes proximity in time and space; instead they create or purchase a facsimile of the original — an advertised experience, the same experience that everyone else is getting. Being present is no longer about closeness — it is about accessibility, and therefore presence is a product of cultural hegemony.

A prime example of this is the press release for the national tour of Mel Brooks's musical *The Producers,* which states: "*The Producers* is the funniest, most fearlessly irreverent thing ever seen on stage! And now you can experience the Biggest Tony Award winner in Broadway history when it comes to your city" (*The Producers* online). This press release gives the reader the impression that he or she will be seeing the original Tony Award winning Broadway production starring Matthew Broderick and Nathan Lane. To a certain extent this is true: national tours for productions like *The Producers, Les Misérables, Chicago,* and *The Lion King* replicate costumes, settings, and staging to manufacture the original Broadway experience for people across the globe. In these examples exactness in reproduction of the original experience is more important than liveness, or even name recognition (especially when most touring companies employ lesser-known performers).

Because an association with the popular determines the relationship between commercial theatre and the culturally dominant media, theatrical material currently produced on the Broadway stage reflects the pervasive presence of media as a factor in determining what is marketable on the profit-driven stage. For example, the August 2002 Playbill Online lists six fully mounted theatrical productions that are remakes of well-liked films, including *The Graduate, The Full Monty, Beauty and the Beast, Hairspray,* and *Some Like It Hot.* Writing for the *New York Post,* Clive Barnes provides insight into the selection of the material. Speaking specifically about the theatrical remake of Mike Nichols's classic film *The Graduate* (1967), Barnes says: "Comparisons with the movie might be invidious, but the play wouldn't be on Broadway — or indeed, anywhere else — had not the fame of the film preceded it" (48). Although Barnes's statement reflects the contemporary trend of remaking film into theatre, his statement could also include television and the Internet media that have also become models of form and content for the contemporary commercial theatre.

Media's hegemonic power is equally acute when we examine its influence on contemporary thought and practice. Scholarly investigations of theatre practice as it relates to media technology are abundant. Recent theatre scholarship that examines the cultural, social, and economic interaction between theatrical performance and media technology documents the field's eagerness to embrace the way that media technology shapes contemporary theatrical boundaries.

Many theoretical investigations of theatre and media technology that were conscious of the cultural efficacy of media and contextualized their critical dialogue as simple calls for further exploration of the practical interactions between the two artistic mediums. From a perspective conscious of media influence, an "ideological imprint" (Schiller 9) or a "postmodern presence" (Pontbriand 155) of mediatized forms is clearly evident even in scholarly efforts specific to theatre.

Phillip Valle's "The Digital Frontier: On the Virtual and Material," published in a recent issue of *TYA Today,* provides an example of this. The article points out that the technology currently used by youth theatre is dated and argues for the integration of new media technology in the rehearsal and development of youth theatre productions. Valle's frustration over the lack of technology in plays for young audiences leads him to look to media for a new model. His call for media integration is his reaction to theatrical texts that are removed from reality because they lack a connection to technological environments.

Valle sees this as a necessary condition for the continuation of youth theatre because, according to him, theatre removed from mediated forms is theatre removed from the reality of young people. Digital media technology, for Valle, provides an opportunity to remake youth theatre as a more palpable and immediate entity: "New works call for new methods of creation. The integration of new technologies in performance calls for a fresh and innovative rehearsal and development techniques" (12).

Valle's description suggests that, in its embrace of media technology, theatre can reinvent itself by affiliating itself with the digital medium and therefore increase its cultural, emotional, and economic power with its target demographic. Youth theatre's presentation of self would then reproduce the form and content of the more prominent and emotionally realistic digital medium. Although Valle no doubt believes that new digital media offers artistic opportunities for stage presentation, his call can easily be viewed as an attempt to associate theatre for youth with the current cultural language of media in order to communicate in a more viable fashion.

Valle's perspectives are not unique to youth theatre. Other scholarly works address theatre's historical mediatization and the acknowledgment of the pervasive power of media technology to affect the field. Much of this work describes theatre as a medium that must view itself within the dominant system of media technology. Conceding that a relationship with the prevailing media is a crucial and determining element of cultural survival for theatre practitioners, the December 1999 issue of *Theatre Journal* published by the Association for Theatre in Higher Education devoted an entire issue to the examination of theatre and media technology. In the introduction to the "Theatre and Technology" issue, Susan Bennett says, "The impact of new technologies extends far beyond its role as a performance tool or subject and affects the very way we, as theatre scholars, do our business" (Bennett i).

Bennett's appreciation of theatre's relationship to media technology is just one of many recognitions that theatre scholars and practitioners are making. Other examples include Internet access to *Theatre Survey*, the journal published by the American Society for Theatre Research, and the recent publication of "The Drama of Everyday Life: One Nation under Television," written by Sarah Domet for *American Drama*. Examining, in 2002, the influence of television news coverage surrounding the September 11th crisis in 2001, the article, which is placed prominently in the journal's "Spotlight on American Drama" segment, asserts that American fine art takes too long to serve the populace in times of crisis. She also asserts that popular art — in this case, television's forms — should be adopted by theatre practitioners (Domet online).

In addition to these scholarly acknowledgments of media's pervasive influence on theatre practice, many new productions exhibit a high level of media saturation in theatre performance. Commercial theatre appropriates the form and content of media technology to vie for economic stability. Contemporary performance artists explore media technology and its interaction with the live body of the performer in events that address issues of media technology and presence. Both of these efforts often use performance as a means of expressing human reactions to a larger system of control.

Johannes Birranger suggests that contemporary performance artists have mastered media technology because they were born surrounded by it and are continually exposed to it through popular cultural means. According to him: "The notion of composition [for performance artists] has undergone significant changes since current generations of young artists grow up with video and electronic media that imply and facilitate the convenient sampling, mixing and remaking of the products of consumer culture. Most of the reference points of contemporary media are indeed the experiences of the media culture itself" (Birranger 367).

This description of the confluence between live performance art and media technology suggests that the boundaries between each form have blurred to the point that many artistic performances are significantly dependent on media technology to deliver their content. The artists engage in technology because it is the language that they understand and know how to manipulate for their own uses.

Based on the interactions between theatre and media technology, it is clear to me that purveyors of media technology have attempted to colonize contemporary America. Given its efforts to compete with the dominant form and content of the media, theatre has apparently agreed to this colonization. It is also clear that this colonization has infused theatre practice and scholarship with the need to investigate its own place and shape as it relates to the dominant medium. The very nature of this investigation opens a door to the consideration that theatrical presence can be a perception, a constructed aura agreed upon by a public and used by theatre to compete in a mediatized world.

Two

Theatre's New Visual Literacy: Production and Reception in a Mediatized Culture

The contemporary concept of reality increasingly centers on the use and understanding of technology. Film, television, and other electronic technologies have shaped the mental and physical identities of individuals. These technologies have even offered alternative methods of bodily representation. People do not need to be in corresponding time, locations, or settings to communicate directly. Encounters with media technology have also transformed communities through the manipulation of time and space. Devices of immediacy, such as the Internet and international news broadcasting via satellite, now allow people to have intimate knowledge of global, political, economic, and social forces. Many view this immediate, technologically constructed reality as having a hegemonic influence over a new global community/audience.

Cultural hegemony is a concept first recognized by Italian Marxist Antonio Gramsci. Gramsci replaces earlier notions of a dominant ideology with the idea of many dominant discourses, which are each unstable and temporarily powerful. Gramsci sees a dominant class who seeks to contain and incorporate all thought and behavior within the terms and limits of their own interests. On the other hand there are subordinate classes who attempt to maintain and further the validity of their own realities. This creates a continuing struggle for dominance among the definitions of reality, or ideologies, which serve the interests of the ruling classes with those other social groups hold. Institutional devices like the media become a site in which these forces compete for attention from the masses, each retaining power for a period of time.

In February 2003, cultural organization representatives from thirty-five different nations met at the Louvre in Paris to discuss the ongoing negotiations of the World Trade Organization. The issue at hand was the so-called "cultural exception" that a group of French movie producers, directors, and actors had successfully lobbied for in 1994 to exclude cinema and other forms of audiovisual entertainment from international trade agreements. According to the *New York Times*, what this meant was "that France — and any other country that opted for the cultural exception — could favor its movie, television, and radio industries with subsidies and minimize foreign competition through quotas" (Riding 5). The purpose of the meeting in 2003 was to preserve this "cultural exception" in the face of a strong lobbying effort from Hollywood that hoped to reopen the cultural exception debate. Thirty-four other countries now bolstered the French delegation's belief that "such protectionism was necessary ... to prevent Hollywood and a handful of international media giants from imposing their will on the global entertainment market and wiping out all expressions of local culture" (Riding 5).

This same type of argument had been advanced in 1994 by then Culture Minister Jacques Toubon, speaking in favor of the French language law that would eventually take on his name. At the time, Toubon argued that France was being "menaced by a new form of colonialism." Said Toubon, "The United States is in the process of taking the dominant position. If we do nothing, it will be too late. We will be colonized" (quoted in Swardson 1996). French President Jacques Chirac also expressed a parallel contention, saying, "If, in the new media, our language, our programs, our creations are not strongly presented, the young generation of our country will be economically and culturally marginalized" (quoted in Swardson 1996).

Positions criticizing U.S.-based cultural hegemony first developed in the late 1960s. Members of a broad international community worried that inordinate amounts of cultural products created in the U.S. and then disseminated through telecommunications networks would eliminate the need for native materials and content, destroying the culture of individual communities. Herbert Schiller, one of many academics who scrutinized the United States' exploitation of its own material dominance, described its effect, saying:

The concept of cultural imperialism today best describes the sum of the process by which society is brought into the modern world system and how its dominating stratum is attracted, pressured, forced, and sometimes bribed into shaping social institutions to correspond to, or even promote, the values and structures of the dominating center of the system.... The public media are the foremost example of operating enterprises that are used in the penetrative process.... Directly or indirectly, the outcome is the same. The content and style of programming, however adapted to local conditions, bear the ideological imprint of the main centers of the capitalist world economy [9–10].

It is this "ideological imprint" as it applies to contemporary American theatre that interests me. While the penetrative or invasive power of the mass media is the fodder for continued debate, I seek to document the presence of that "ideological imprint" on American stages in the late twentieth and early twenty-first centuries. My study specifically applies to the manner in which American theatre is "attracted, pressured, forced, and sometimes bribed" (Schiller 9) into shaping its conventions to correspond to the conventions of the mass media in order to approximate a conversant and emotional reality for the theatrical audience. For the purpose of this work, then, cultural hegemony is not a matter of France or any other country being inundated with Disney movies and Big Macs. Cultural hegemony for me refers to the penetrative powers of electronic forms to create a new grammar of images, iconography, celebrity, marketability, and altered immediacy for the American stage.

Cultural reinterpretations and appropriations may be observed in the exchange of meaning within American theatrical culture. Meaning, or ritual, or even simple spectacle is projected by the producers of theatre, and the reception of that message, or rite, or image is governed by cultural orientations and norms. The culture into which theatre is projected in America is a technology-accelerated, mediated culture. The implications of this are that theatre means something when it is produced — it means something else when it is seen — and continues to change in identity and structure when it is produced by a mediated culture and received by a mediated audience.

HISTORICAL INTERACTIONS BETWEEN THEATRE AND MEDIA

From the inception of film in 1895, the intermingling of theatre and media technologies has been well documented by historians in both fields.

The history of the production, distribution, exhibition, and reception of both mediums demonstrates that this interaction between theatre and each new media technology (film, television, and other electronic technologies) is both competitive and cooperative. At times in history, theatre and media technologies each appropriate the other's narrative content and formal elements as well as the other's marketing and economic structures. Theatre and media corporations regularly work to control, manipulate, and even reinvent the techniques of the other medium to benefit the unique strengths of their own medium. Any theatrical study focused on the interaction between these fields must recognize that theatre, in order to maintain its own cultural efficacy, has allowed and even fostered each new medium's appropriation of its own forms and content, but was in turn influenced by the ideological shifts in the collective cultural perception as each new medium gained popularity, and therefore cultural power. This chapter documents three historical moments that show the interaction between the stage and media technology: the inception of film, the development of television production, and the arrival of the Internet.

The first ten years of film history are replete with interactions between theatre and film. Popular theatre was often viewed as a resource for early filmmakers who borrowed content material for stories that were developed on film. Fully developed theatrical performances were also recorded on film. The Edison Company's *The Kiss* (1896) and Edwin S. Porter's film of *Uncle Tom's Cabin* are both examples of the newly formed film industry's adaptation of theatrical material. But film historian George Hendricks describes an atmosphere of filmed material that also included vaudeville acts, scenes from staged burlesque, and dance routines from Broadway musicals.*

Film's unique features became evident as the two performance mediums shared venues.† This occurred during the height of variety performance from 1880 to 1920. In the last decade of the nineteenth century, theatre entrepreneurs B.F. Keith and Edward F. Albee partnered to produce a vaudeville, or variety show, circuit. The vaudeville circuit capitalized on tested conceptual and business methods of the legitimate theatre syndicate run by the Shubert Brothers to form a variety show booking

---

George Hendricks provides a complete discussion of early film's use of theatrical material in "New York: The Beginnings of American Film" from The Kinetoscope, *1966.*

†*Douglas Gomery makes it clear that the success of film in vaudeville houses was short lived and that film distributors soon moved on to amusement parks and nickelodeons, eventually giving birth to the "movie only theatre."*

syndicate that held monopolistic control over American touring venues as well as theatrical venues in New York and other theatres along the eastern seaboard. While vaudeville was an alternative to the legitimate theatre, it also distinguished itself from burlesque and saloon entertainment by reaching out to the working middle class with wholesome entertainment that included song and dance artists, comic sketches, impersonations, and animal acts.* As developed by Keith and Albee, the vaudeville model had nine to ten different acts that included headline performers alongside less-familiar acts. New York vaudeville theatres regularly incorporated films in the lineup of vaudeville acts by 1897.

Robert C. Allen asserts that in the shared venue of the vaudeville circuits the film industry learned to model theatre's successful distribution structure that included wide dissemination and a constant experimentation based on an audience's attraction to the material: "[Vaudeville circuits] affected the rapid national diffusion of the motion picture and gave it a huge national audience ... [and] encouraged cinematic experimentation" (144).

Unlike vaudeville performances, which were booked to travel from venue to venue for days or weeks, many moving pictures eventually became stable fixtures in vaudeville houses (Musser 273–76). This permanence is important to note because patrons constantly reviewed the same set of films each time they went to a vaudeville house to see a new headline performer. Because of this, vaudeville theatres became the first place that the American middle class was regularly introduced to the distinctive language of film. By revisiting the films with each new performance, audience members had time to embrace the nuances of the new medium even before they realized that the mechanism for delivery might be a significant new way of viewing narratives or documenting history.

While films were never featured as headlining acts at vaudeville houses, they regularly appeared as one of eight or more fifteen-minute acts on a program. Drawing on popular theatrical forms of the late nineteenth-century that depicted "live" portraits of the newly established immigrant working class (Londré 209–28), films could present portraits of local communities in such images as hometown sporting teams performing athletic feats, local laborers constructing buildings, or volunteer fire departments saving neighborhood homes. Film could provide detailed visual information about family and friends in faraway places. One

*It is important to note that like African American counterparts to the legitimate stage, vaudeville also had a segregated black syndicate that functioned from 1910 to 1920. Functioning under the Theatre Owners Booking Association, black entertainers also utilized the vaudeville model that was developed by Keith and Albee.

particular example of this is the documented success of films that provided realistic footage of battles that had been staged as popular acts in vaudeville houses during the Spanish-American War (Gomery 15–17).

The popular images taught middle-class patrons to admire a new intimacy produced by the pictorial close-up, and in many ways endorsed a singular mind-set about what was important at home and abroad based on the visual images presented in these venues. The American public now had a forum for examining themselves close up and collectively, but the point of view or perspective was distinctly homogenous.

The burgeoning film industry's short stay in vaudeville houses is also noteworthy if we consider how the physical partnership between the two mediums provided a forum in which filmmakers could learn from the successes and failures of vaudeville's form and content while developing a rapport with vaudeville's specific audience base, eventually leaving the venue and then seizing the audience in the next decade. Felicia Hardison Londré and Daniel Watermeier document a noteworthy example of this transition from vaudeville to other forms of entertainment.

> In the late 1920s vaudeville's popularity was eroded by the rise of musical comedy and revues, radio and especially the motion pictures.... Entrepreneur Marcus Loew built a large circuit of cheap-priced vaudeville theatres in which live entertainment was presented between film showings. In 1930, the Keith-Albee Orpheum circuit was combined with the Radio Corporation of American (RCA) to create the Radio-Keith-Orpheum circuit (RKO) corporation, a major radio, movie and later television company [225].

Most vaudeville theatres, including the prominent New York City vaudeville house, the Palace Theatre, were quickly converted to movie theatres during this transition and performers were taken in to other performance mediums and venues. As vaudeville died out and film came to the fore, vaudeville stages became the physical site for discussion of both, film and the altered position in which it placed its older counterpart, vaudeville.

One primary source leads us to believe that as early as 1915 working-class theatre professionals were aware of the film industry's potential to usurp the cultural and financial appreciation of their paying audiences. An examination of a vaudeville script from 1915 helps us understand the dialogue between performers and patrons. Junie McCree's script "A Vaudeville Luncheon: In Three Courses" examines this decline of theatre in the face of film popularity in the guise of an old theatre performer:*

---

*McCree's text was originally published 28 April 1915 and is currently held at the Library of Congress and can be accessed at http://memory.loc.gov/ammem/varstgquery.html.

From the stage to the screen is the way of old actors.
The road has been paved and the going is good.
The bad ones the fair ones the good one and rare ones,
They'd all love to pose if they could.
When the footlights no longer demand their appearance,
and the color of youth starts to fade.
Outcasts from the stage door, as types they're engaged
for the ranks of the movie parade.

Chorus:
When you miss a favorite star from the stage.
You'll very often find him on the screen,
as an actor he may have been in most every scene.
But the actor is forgotten when he's seared with yellow age.
While the picture actor he is evergreen.
Although he's aged and broken hearted.
Even life may have departed.
But his shadow still cavorts upon the screen [1].

McCree's focus on the significant changes in the staged performance industry are important because her words imply that the move from vaudeville to film forms and personas was both an emotional and a financial choice based on a consumer-audience engaged in a new form — the stage is depicted as "seared with yellow age," while film is described as "evergreen." McCree's material also asserts that the vaudeville writers and performers who were leaving the stage left because of the popularity of the new medium and suggests that they (the writers and performers) would reassemble themselves in the new medium to "cavort upon the screen" (1).

Key theatre historians also recognize theatre's plight because of the popularity of the nickelodeon and other film venues. In this case Robert McLaughlin describes the popularity of film as the major reason for the decline of a national theatre:

Between 1910 and 1920 ... the entire economic structure of the theatre reversed itself, with New York production becoming the main concern and the road shrinking in economic importance.... No single factor could be said to have more powerful influence on the commercial operations of the theatre during the first quarter of the century than movies. The unleashing of this immense economic force in the show business world ... had a direct role in the organizational, and economic restructuring of the American stage.... [T]he fall of theatre activity outside of New York and the advent of movies as an industry parallel each other so closely that it is difficult not to conclude that the movies were primarily responsible for the sweeping economic changes that took place in theatre [2–4].

The anecdotes described by both McCree and McLaughlin each demonstrate that the economic and emotional attraction of the general populace to film made it more financially and culturally accepted than traditional theatre during this period. They also reveal the need for theatre to accommodate the growing mass media audience with systems of mediatized production, promotion, and distribution techniques and practices to remain culturally and financially viable. It is therefore only through technical means that theatre could access the irresistible economics of the mass audience. From its earliest performances and venues, the American theatre related its own success to its profit margin, but the shift of the American theatrical syndicates away from vaudeville venues (and even from the legitimate stage) to film venues, and the accompanying shift from the purely present to the technologically mediated, could be seen as a purely commercial transaction on the part of theatre organizations based on the reality of its audience. Prior to this point theatre was driven by profit but also by the desire to create a national theatre. Syndicate owners like the Shubert Syndicate or the Keith-Albee vaudeville enterprise were concerned with economic success, but they were also eager like predecessors Laura Keene and Harry Jarrett (developers of the combination touring system) to establish a national legitimate theatre where patrons across the United States could be exposed to great artists in traditional theatre spaces unique to the theatrical medium. Instead, with investment dependent upon predictability, theatre's economic engine was now driven solely by profit, leaving behind the goal of a national theatre. Theodore Adorno would describe this change of focus as part of the "circle of manipulation" (119). Adorno argues that capitalism feeds people and organizations with accessible, consumable products designed by a "culture industry" to keep them passively satisfied, politically apathetic, and economically profitable for the producers who benefit from the status quo (119). Adorno would view this transition in the American theatre, which McCree and McLaughlin describe, as a nearly perfect example of how aspects of theatre's liveness are reduced in a process of comodification to match new technology. Because technology was identified as the reason for people's satisfaction with film and lack of interest in the animate stage, theatre began to affiliate itself with the new medium.

Prior to the transition from vaudeville houses to movie theatres, American theatre remained culturally and financially relevant by relying on its own unique liveness. The transition forced theatre to advertise itself as a part of the new media. Today theatre is easily seen as similar to other popular media products in terms of standardization (they are basically formulaic and similar) and pseudo-individualization (incidental differences make them seem distinctive, but they're not). Products of the culture industry may be emotional or apparently moving and the purpose of such products may at times enlighten, or educate, but their main purpose today and in history is to solidify profits as the unifying system of media technology grows stronger.

It was very nearly this same set of historical circumstances that repeated themselves in the next decade when the predominant production form would again shift — this time from film to television. The cumbersome nature of television production and broadcast equipment dictated that the production elements of early television were more akin to the theatre than to the world of film production. The effective transition was an intermingling of theatre techniques with those of the new medium rather than a direct transition from the cinema screen to the new boxes in American living rooms.

Television's first experimentation with theatrical forms occurred in June 1938 when producer John Golden welcomed television audiences to a "new and glorious era in the world of theatre" (Dunlap 94). The brief telecast was a stilted rendering of several scenes from Rachel Crother's Broadway hit *Susan and God,* restaged exactly as it had appeared on Broadway. Combining scripted storyboards with the brief live performance of Gertrude Lawrence, the production played to a small studio audience and to several hundred viewers who watched the production on their 7-by-10-inch screens. According to an account by Orrin E. Dunlap, the twenty-two-minute production made no concessions for television: "[the actors] went through their roles as if on a stage — there was nothing in the acting to indicate that they had adopted a new technique for television, or that they were conscious of the camera's presence" (97).

To some extent, the arrival of televised theatre was an answer to the critical financial situation the New York theatre community faced. Despite producing a watershed of critically important American playwrights, including Arthur Miller, Tennessee Williams, and William Inge, and reproducing the works of other critically acclaimed pre–World War II playwrights like Eugene O'Neill and Maxwell Anderson, the years following the war were meager for theatre box offices. Broadway faced financial difficulties deriving from the increasing cost of materials after the war and the new demands of an aggressive workforce that produced powerful unions.

Government regulation of theatre monopolies also causes significant changes in the economic realities of theatre. For example, the monopolistic Shubert organization was subjected to a federal investigation in 1949, and the government brought an antitrust suit against it. The organization was eventually forced to disband its empire, which in turn dismantled the lucrative prewar financial-production model. This gave way to individual producers who sought financial backing from various sources outside the industry.

These changes in business practice led to inflated ticket prices that were well above the average consumer's means. In his introduction to *The Encyclopedia of the New York Stage*, Samuel L. Leiter provides examples of these changes and dramatic repercussions:

> A major part of Broadway's problem stemmed from skyrocketing production costs and a consequent rise in ticket prices that made theatre going too costly for the average consumer. One significant reason for the higher costs was the prices paid during the war for hard-to-get materials and labor. Another was the inflated salaries of stars, presumably emulating the demands of their Hollywood and broadcasting brethren. Playwrights were also seeking a larger cut, including a share in the subsidiary rights of their plays. Still another cause was rampant unionism and its featherbedding requirements [xix].

The impact on theatres because of these changes in the labor market was significant. When Margaret Webster staged the *Tempest* in 1945, her use of incidental music led the American Federation of Musicians to deem the show a musical; although only twelve musicians were used, the union demanded that sixteen be hired, each earning $92 a week. Several subsequent revivals ran into similar obstacles. The stagehands and designers unions could be equally troublesome, especially when it came to transferring a noncommercial production's sets to a commercial engagement. No longer could one produce a modest play for $15,000 or $20,000. Prices were now three or more times as high as in the previous decade. The Kaufman and Hart hit *You Can't Take It with You* cost $16,000 in 1936, while Hart's *Christopher Blake* tallied up a sum of $180,000 a decade later. *Life with Father* had cost $23,000 at the Empire Theatre in 1939. A similarly sized cast appeared in the same theatre with *Life with Mother* in 1948; the original scenic design was supplemented by only one additional setting but the new show cost over $85,000. And according to Leiter, "No small number of these shows lost every penny" (xix).

Beginning in the early 1940s, the relationship between television and the theatre became intermingled. Initially, the theatrical community welcomed the infusion of new jobs and the sudden demand for the skills necessary to produce dramatic resources. When television began co-opting the content and form of theatre to give structure, substance, and significance to this neoteric medium, there was an early assumption by theatre practitioners that together television and theatre would create a new theatrical form; others worried that the combined efforts would be no more than a technological amplification of previous theatrical patterns. Instead, purveyors of television used theatre content as a tool to demonstrate technical acumen and as a bridge that linked an elite cultural venue with the incremental development of a new cultural space.

At the dawn of the television era audience participants in the new television experience hoped to tune into high culture. This perceived mandate to use the medium for educational purposes is so strong that even today laws are passed to reclaim a focus on the educational value of the medium. For example, with the passage of the Children's Television Act of 1990 the FCC released the following statement:

> The CTA requires the Commission, in its review of each television broadcast license renewal application, to "consider the extent to which the licensee ... has served the educational and informational needs of children through the licensee's overall programming, including programming specifically designed to serve such needs." In enacting the CTA in 1990, Congress found that television has the power to teach children by assisting them to "learn important information, skills, values, and behavior, while entertaining them and exciting their curiosity to learn about the world around them" [Federal Communications Commission Online].

The tacit understanding of the public from the beginning was that viewing television was both an entertainment and educational opportunity. By taking part in this new television experience, communication barriers would be broken down, and each viewer could be initiated into a new technological community that shared in the highest ideals of art, culture, and social interaction. Despite some early successes, television did not deliver on its promises.

In the early years of its history, television counted on the cultural qualities of the theatre to attract early viewers because the initial appeal of the technology was that by participating in the television ritual, the audience could become metropolitan, even cultured patrons of traditional art forms. This shared experience was never realized, not because the audience was insincere or unprepared in their efforts to join the community of the cultural elite, but because television was not initiating the masses into high culture. Instead, television was simply introducing the masses into the practice, or habit, of watching television. Art, culture, and theatre were merely the attractions and the tools whereby the promise of equality in cultural education could be cleverly capitalized on by the industry that was really trying to sell soap.

The early history of television is sated with examples in programming that promised high art and classic theatre, but showcased technology. In many ways, the relationship between television and theatre could be characterized as a marriage of convenience with theatre being drawn to the economic capital of television, and television being seduced by the perceived virtues of live theatre. From 1938 until 1948, television was portrayed roughly as a supplementary advertisement for theatrical performance in New York. It was widely believed that "properly and deftly handled, television may prove to be a good trailer or bait for the theatre by just tossing out morsels of the show. That television can do this has been demonstrated" (Dunlap 94).

Although the televised production of *Susan and God* was seen as successful, the onset of World War II brought a ten-year interval between the experimental use of theatre on television and recurrent programming of dramatic theatre. Dramatic scripts on television appeared and gained prominence at the close of the war, but it was not until the very end of the 1940s that the intense growth in the television industry created a demand for material that necessitated the use of dramatic texts. Specifically, by the fall of 1948, television networks were experiencing a tremendous growth in dissemination. The televised World Series of 1947 established a mass audience in New York, Philadelphia, and Washington, D.C. According to Tim Brooks and Earl Marsh's *The Complete Directory to Prime Time Network and Cable TV Shows,* the 1947 World Series was seen by an estimated 3.9 million people with 3.5 million of the people viewing the series from local bars (xiii). This introduction to the medium led to a contagious desire for television ownership. These new television owners began demonstrating their desire for quality television programming. Network programmers also had to comply with the FCC's "28-hour rule," which required twenty-eight hours of programming a week (*Broadcasting* 28). These demands for both quality and quantity forced the new networks to move from an uneven fare of wrestling matches and dog shows to more structured programs that would build an audience base and help them acquire sponsors to buy commercial time.

Initially, vaudeville-like programs such as Milton Berle's *Texaco Star Theatre* and the *All-Star Revue* with Jimmy Durante successfully provided the first theatrical solution to the networks' programming problems. However, it was the dramatic anthology programs that eventually wed live theatre and television in order to attract audiences that sought a civilizing experience. The NBC New York affiliate WNBT pioneered a monthly Sunday evening drama series entitled *Television Theatre* in 1947. That was mimicked in 1948–49 by the *Philco Television Playhouse*, and later was imitated and improved upon by *The Ford Theatre, Kraft Television Theatre*, and *Studio One*.

These popular programs soon proved profitable for the television stations that played host to the new national theatrical audience and for the companies that provided financial sponsorship. In November of 1948, both the *Philco Playhouse* and *Kraft Television Theatre* and one other "unspecified" play program were voted among the top ten programs by readers of *Television: The Business Magazine of the Industry* (4). The popularity of the programs among both audiences and sponsors created a heightened demand for theatrically trained writers, producers, directors, etc., and the New York theatre community was quick to rush in and fill the vacuum.

Television's use of dramatic material supplied by popular Broadway playwrights was a quick fix for the infant networks' programming problems, and in turn the nation's new taste for televised theatre was met with wild enthusiasm from the New York theatre scene's critics and financial managers. In 1949 *Curtain Call's* Jack Gaver announced his support by citing the possibility of a new employment source for theatre professionals and insisting that television might even provide a remedy for the ills inflicted upon theatre by film:

> Broadway anticipates that television will have no great effect on it and may even prove a friend. The feeling is that mechanical entertainment already has done about all the harm it can to "live" entertainment. Broadway producers and actors have been among the first in the television field, and the best of television's dramatic material has come out of Broadway hits. The argument is that once the novelty and convenience have worn off ... people will realize that, after all, they are merely looking at pictures ... if they want to see actors in the flesh they will still have to patronize theatres [310].

In his essay on the culture industry in *The Dialectic of Enlightenment*, Adorno describes cultural settings like these in which elite art forms are brought up to date by their electronic counterparts but do not extend upon or improve the more excellent original form. Instead these capitalist-driven forms only improve on the traditional form's commercial accessibility: "The culture industry can pride itself on having energetically executed the previously clumsy transposition of art into the sphere of consumption, on making this a principle, on divesting amusements of its obtrusive naivetés and improving the type of commodities" (135).

While Adorno's statement is based on a modernist perspective that delimits art to elite spheres, it does make a clear point about accessibility. While theatre practice has always been commercially driven it had never to this point reached mass audiences in the same way that television could. In its beginning moments television accomplishes this accessibility, quickly replacing the more difficult and critical art forms, like theatre, and instead re-packages them as newly shaped products, which barely resemble the traditional form and are reproduced and disseminated throughout the populace. False needs are cultivated among that same populace by television, and these needs can be both created and satisfied by the capitalist system imbedded in television. Media technology becomes so popular that all artistic forms must be seen through its pervasive lens.

CREATING A NEW VISUAL LITERACY

The introduction of the new media grammar into the language of theatre affected two appreciable changes to the theatrical viewing experience: the forced gaze and a new asynchronous presence. The forced gaze originates in the mechanized conventions of framing a scene, or of directing the perspective of the viewer. The specific change that media influence made on the gaze of theatrical audiences was to create new intimacy: the audience's visual experience via the close-ups, slow motion, multiple angles, etc., of various media forms gave them the expectation of a theatrical equivalent. Personality, contextualization, and perceived intimacy became more important. For example, facial expression has risen in importance to the audience while the importance of gesture has declined.

Asynchronous presence, or the ability to create the perception of presence without the constraints of physical proximity within time and space, is achieved by drawing on the cognitive constructs of the mediatized audience to produce theatrical elements or impressions that do not exist physically on the stage. To this end, touring companies of many commercial theatre-producing entities go to great lengths to precisely replicate performances, as well as settings and costumes, in order to capitalize on a performance of a well-known actor who might have had the role on Broadway. Because theater plays in a mediated environment, audiences come with sweeping foreknowledge of an event, and come to the theater expecting to see not just a character, but also a specific interpretation of that character. In a way, audiences mask the performance that they witness with an imagined performance that is constructed from their mediated experience with the text.

These changes in the theatrical viewing experience which introduce audiences to the forced gaze and asynchronous presence grew out of nineteenth-century considerations of vision as it relates to the way a spectator thinks about time and space. The exploration of human vision that took place in the nineteenth century explored sight as a means of understanding the phenomenology of the spectator, or the perspective of spectator's perception as it was affected by mechanical means. Many philosophers suggested that visual knowledge was based on the audience assimilation of competing ways of seeing in a new visual culture influenced by new technologies Writing about techniques of observation and thought, the nineteenth-century philosopher F.W.J Schelling says:

> We do not live in vision; our knowledge is piecework, that is, it must be produced piece by piece in a fragmentary way, with divisions and gradation.... In the external world everyone sees more or less the same thing, and yet not everyone can express it. In order to complete itself, each thing runs through certain moments — a series of processes following one another, in which the later always involves the earlier, brings each to maturity [88–9].

Schelling's statement, made in 1815, reflects common contemplations on vision in the early part of that century. The statement also reflects a shift in the cognitive mind set of the culture that led to the assimilation of media's grammar into the language of nineteenth-century world and therefore into the language of theatre. Schelling's description of vision as a series of overlapping moments is clearly demonstrated in the relationship between theatre and media during this period in which both explore the idea of vision as it relates to their medium, each compete for and share cultural power, and each aid the other to some degree of maturity. For example, theatrical studies of the relationship between nineteenth-century theatre and early film position the theatrical mise en scène as the predecessor of early film technique.

Nicholas Vardac's early research in *Stage to Screen: Theatrical Origins of Early Film: From Garrick to Griffith* connects visual techniques used in the staging of English and American theatrical melodrama to cinematic staging and suggests that the combination of melodrama and theatrical realism in the later part of the nineteenth century paved the way for the advent of film. Vardac specifically addresses the concept of spectacle as it relates one important claim — that theatre audiences had knowledge of, and interest in, film-like techniques that had already surfaced in the theatrical mise en scène of the late nineteenth century:

For Vardac, film solved problems that the melodramatic stage of Dion Boucicoult could not solve in the theatrical space. Vardac sees filmed actualities that depict real fires, train wrecks, and volcanic eruptions as the poultice to the audience's dissatisfaction with similar events staged before live audiences that lacked the same ability to effectively transport audiences in time and space. Vardac describes tensions between the capabilities of the melodramatic form, saying:

> Melodrama relied upon a large variety of settings and upon speed in their change, since both of these qualities depended upon the conventional methods of existing staging facilities, melodrama and pictorial realism were incompatible and actually impossible upon the stage.... In an effort to combat the waning popularity [of melodrama] and the breakdown of these traditional techniques, individual realistic properties were introduced. Water tanks, buzz saws, carriages, dead cats, live pigs, horses, dogs, chickens were all employed, but while conventionalism governed the overall production, such realistic items usually destroyed the illusion of a stock stage picture. In the face of the breakdown of the traditional methods these compromises were rarely successful ... with the breakdown of the conventional came the gradual withdrawal of the stage melodrama. The film, boundless in its capacity for both spectacular and realistic pictures, naturally fell heir to the cinematic objectives, which had been the principal appeal of this form on the stage [66].

While Vardac's understanding of cinema is limited by his knowledge of film's visual predecessors, he does document an important progression in the gaze of the theatrical audience — the creation of the forced gaze in theatrical production. His notion of a proto-cinematic theatre demonstrates that theatre practitioners, like the architects of other developing visual mediums such as photography or the camera obscura, were exploring the power of the mechanized or mediated perspective in much the same way. Theatre, in essence, was making the same cognitive shift in theatrical reception that was reinforced in other explorations of a new visual grammar — that the spectator's body, specifically their vision, was becoming a part of the mechanical apparatus. Nineteenth-century artists and inventors immersed themselves in experimenting with the spectator's focus, arguing that the spectator's own subjectivity was linked to his or her assimilation of the mechanical. Drawing on the Renaissance paradigm of perspective in which the single eye of the spectator becomes the center of their world,* the nineteenth-century filmmaker and theatre practitioner each

---

*See John Berger's Ways of Seeing (1972, Viking Press), which discusses the visual perspective based on European paintings from the Renaissance.

experimented with the conventions and limitations of their medium establishing varying visual vocabularies that the audience learned and used to engage with and used to evaluate the aesthetic status of the other.

Ben Brewster and Lea Jacobs demonstrate visual considerations that theatre and film artists and technicians made as they worked to achieve realism on stage and in film during the late nineteenth century and early part of the twentieth century. Brewster and Jacobs establish that both mediums sought complicity between the staged picture that is presented and the audience, who participates in the event by admiring the picture. Both theatre and film achieve this purpose in distinctive ways that suit the medium.

Brewster and Jacobs present realism in this case as it relates to the perspective of the audience that is freer in theatre than the guided perspective of the camera. This distinction between each medium is instructive in its demonstration of the development of a new visual language that is established for the viewer, through the directive of the camera lens. Brewster and Jacobs articulate the traditional approach to the visual image in their discussion of theatre when they describe the pictorialism presented on stage in the following manner:

> Nineteenth-century [theatrical] staging is characterized by a stage picture of a relatively fixed and large size with often great perspective-rendered depth. These perspective affects enforced a planar organization of the space, with little movement in depth and action distributed across the stage; the demand for visibility of the action to a widely distributed audience, and for a large proportion of the audience to see a relatively similar pictorial composition drove the principle action to the front of the stage [159–60].

From this account of theatrically staged pictorialism we can see that the human body is in full view of the audience and is presented in its entirety in space and time. The distance of the audience to the stage is the only deterrent to experiencing the body in its full and realistic form. Theatrical staging in this case attempts to provide each audience member with a similar view but is affected by the differing distance between audience and performer and the vantage points from which spectators could see the stage.

In contrast, film technicians (who are seeking the same authentic visual connection between audience and performer) direct the audiences' attention much more specifically to particular parts of the mise en scène or even to parts of the body and exploit the conventions of the new medium to provide each audience member with the same specific and intimate experience. According to Brewster and Jacobs, even filmmakers who attempted to achieve the same pictorial aesthetic on film as their stage counterparts were forced to rework and eventually re-create the theatrical pictorial stage space through new filmic techniques. Filmmakers found that the visual space could be manipulated during the filming by bringing the actor to a position near the camera so that they appeared very close, even lifelike, to the viewer. The close proximity of the camera lens also allowed audience members to visualize details of the human body close up, fulfilling the same aesthetic pictorial need that theatre practitioners did on stage. However, these filmmakers presented the picture from a position that theatre could not. Audience members experience the picture from a monocular perspective — that of the camera lens.

It is important to note that the final product of film limited the contextual choices of the viewing audience. The camera lens, providing this singular vantage point for all audience members, guided the viewer to privileged visual images, determining what the collective audience saw and completely controlling when they saw it.

Asynchronous presence became a vital part of the new pictorialism on the stage in a new media-saturated environment. Settings were increasingly designed to frame performers rather than the scene. Audiences were relied upon to bring a specific visual history to bear in order to fill in the empty spaces or to create meaning of the physical attributes of the stage. Also, the new projected intimacy with the performer was often created in the imagination of the individual audience members because of the mediated familiarity with the performer or, more frequently, with the dramatic situation, if not the text itself. In effect, the close-up began to be approximated from the last row of the theater because the audience could easily approximate it in their mind.

This new visual grammar is reflected in theatres across Europe and the Americas in the gradual acceptance of both naturalism and realism. Emile Zola's naturalism, which focused on the intense visual details of the human experience, and theatrical realism of Ibsen and Strindberg, which projected characters as intimate beings, each depended on a new visual mindset that can be connected to the new mechanically driven and focused spectator discussed in the nineteenth century. By the beginning of the twentieth century the spectacle-driven, sensational melodrama of Augustin Daly and David Belasco was replaced by material that required sparse settings, small spaces, and a focus on the intimate nuances of performance.

ACQUAINTING THE AUDIENCE WITH THE LANGUAGE OF MEDIA TECHNOLOGY

In 1949–50, New York theatre owners struggled to fill their houses. The number of productions dwindled to a half-century low of fifty-seven new productions in the season. Because of sparse attendance, several theatres closed. Theatre producers, directors, and actors looked towards employment possibilities in the television industry, which was a burgeoning industry that could utilize skilled writers and directors in need of work. By 1947 stations were hiring directors and producers who had previously worked in the theatre. The Pulitzer Prize winning director Worthington Miner, who was hired by CBS, produced televised dramatic anthologies. Yale-trained Fred Coe, who left his job running a little theatre in South Carolina to work in television, was hired by WNBT to direct *Television Theatre.*

While some theatre professionals working in the television industry promoted the connection between traditional theatre and televised theatre, Worthington Miner and Fred Coe were immediately interested in defining dramatic television outside the perimeters of traditional theatre. For tele-drama production teams at both CBS and WNBT, the traditional theatre context was only a basis from which they developed their television projects. Required texts and spaces of traditional theatre presentation were systematically altered and reshaped into new theatrical models that worked for television.

Initially, conventional play texts drawn from the theatre seemed a ready-made form of entertainment that could easily fill the programming void. However, problems of translation from the stage to the small screen forced television programmers to rethink scripts used for the new medium. As early as 1946, television professionals began to consider altering the text for the purposes of television programming. At first the biggest concern was meeting the time constraints. John Reich of the *Televiser,* an early television industry magazine, reports that by late 1946 the half-hour and one-hour program slots were the industry standard. This resulted in an industry-wide discussion about the adaptation of play texts. Because of the discussion Reich and others addressed the need for programming that would meet television time constraints and exploit the multiple uses of the television camera. Reich's particular advice to television writers and producers suggested a move from traditional dramatic texts to altered texts with a visual emphasis. Reich wrote: "In selecting his material from the vast storehouse of the dramatic stage, the program director may well follow his instinct for the video art rather than an artificial set of rules. He should be guided, however, by three characteristics of television, namely: immediacy, fluidity, and emphasis on objects" (11).

Reich's emphasis on video art rather than on the text is key to understanding the transfer of play texts to television at both CBS and WNBT during this historical moment. Essentially the adaptations of play scripts became translations that exploited the advantages and concerns of the medium rather than televised attempts to reproduce the original play text. An example of NBC's interest in the translation techniques specific to television is provided by Coe's description in *Theatre Arts* of the process of adapting *Othello* for a television audience:

> In our television planning on "Othello" we were forced by the lack of precedent to be daring. We had a story that in the theatre usually takes at least two hours to perform.... This meant that great slices must be made in the text. We cut the play to the basic scenes of the story; we re-arranged them to suit our studio and equipment, and then we composed enough dialogue and action to unite the scenes we wished to retain. We also knew that we had little time to set the background of action and characters, so instead of using Shakespeare's expository scenes we wrote a complete narrative in Elizabethan style dialogue to introduce the characters and the situation confronting them [96].

What is interesting about Coe's description of this process is not the liberties taken with the text — certainly liberties have been taken with Shakespeare's texts for centuries — but that the text was arranged to suit the studio and the equipment. The production, therefore, was not only about presenting a given text for audience consumption. It was about demonstrating the powerful ways in which the text could be manipulated and played with given the new qualifying factors of the medium.

This interest in connecting the audience with the instrument of communication rather than the text is evident in several discussions concerning tele-plays from 1948 through the mid–1950s. One discussion in *Theatre Arts* makes the priorities of the television industry clear. The December 1955 issue describes a televised production of *Macbeth* in which high school students were encouraged to write in and give their impressions of the play. Both the students' responses to the play and the author's response to students demonstrate a strong interest in the technology rather than the play text. The students' replies typically dismiss the play and address the work of the camera. "That scene would have been better if you'd used a medium shot over Lady Macbeth's shoulder," one student writes (Bentley 96). The author of the article ignores the fact that the narrative was not addressed and responds enthusiastically to the comment saying, "Their letters were both flattering and caustic but the most impressive thing to me was their awareness of camera technique on TV" (96).

The exploration of television techniques also leads to other manipulations of traditional theatre practice and alterations of theatre texts to benefit the television medium. Eventually the conventional theatre space was altered to meet the needs of television staging and programming. Writing for the *New York Times* in October 1948, Jack Gould makes a clear distinction between the theatrical stage and the television stage. He directs the notice of the readers to television's elimination of the proscenium arch. For Gould, this elimination of the demarcated audience and stage space is television's significant contribution as an art form. He says:

> Television's claim as a new art form rests essentially on a factor which is not noticeable — and should not be noticeable — on the professional video production.... This factor is the almost magical elimination of the proscenium arch, the structural arc in the theatre which traditionally has marked the dividing line between the "live" player and the audience. The camera lifts the television viewer out of the usual balcony seat and takes him directly into the group upon the stage.... What television has done is introduce the elements of intimacy and immediacy to a degree scarcely imaginable before the advent of home theatre. For the writer, the actor, and most importantly the director this entails a whole new concept of compact craftsmanship, wasteful motion or wasteful thinking standout like the proverbial sore thumb [11].

As Gould suggests, the elimination of the proscenium arch was the impetus for television producers and directors to reconsider what the theatre audience sees. Whereas the proscenium stage separated the audience from the performers, television encouraged an intimacy between the performers and the viewers. Additionally, television directors privileged the vantage point of individual viewers. Each audience member saw the actors and the space from the same perspective. Good seats and bad seats, which are often determined by one's rank or station in a community theatre, had no place in television. Instead, the audience was accorded a locality from which they could participate in the experience with an equal vantage point.

By adopting film-like photographic techniques to live theatrical programs, television directors aggressively replaced the classic perspective of theatre with new mechanisms that privileged and enhanced their unique medium. Early television production manuals encourage directors to make lavish use of this intimacy in their story-telling. John Reich's programming and production note for television directors encourages the use of "video's trick devices" (11). For Reich the story is only well told when it uses camera techniques like fades, dissolves, and wipes to draw in the viewer.

Reich's suggestions to producers were not uncommon. Television producers were interested in showing the audience how television worked, and soon the traditional stage was reshaped to educate the audience in television techniques. The tool in this reformation of the conventional stage was the camera. The camera's movement took the audience from balcony seats and placed them at the center of the televised action. Close-ups invited the audience to experience intimate details of production that no theatre performance could provide. Television theatre viewers, guided by the eye of the camera, saw the intimate details of the performance. In this manner, television audiences participated in the action: they saw close-ups of the actors' faces, were directed to examine symbolic inanimate objects that revealed plot points, and moved fluidly from scene to scene with the camera.

This interest in camera techniques as the focus of staging was most evident in the work of Worthington Miner's dramatic anthology, *Studio One*. Evaluating the impact of the CBS program, Tim Brooks and Earle Marsh conclude that it was Worthington Miner's interest in the camera that made the plays produced in the CBS studio unique:

> Miner's approach to television was somewhat different from many of the other producers of early dramatic shows. His concern was with the visual impact of the stories, for television was a visual medium, and he placed a greater emphasis on that than on the literary merit of the story. It was not that he produced second-rate plays, ... but Miner's major contribution to television drama was more in his experimentation with camera techniques and other innovations in what the viewer saw [990].

Studio One's production of *Julius Caesar* in March of 1949 was the first play to demonstrate the new technical abilities of the television stage. Confined to a 46' by 28' space, Miner produced a one-hour version of *Julius Caesar* in the 7:30–8:30 p.m. time slot for CBS-TV. Richard Rychtarik's set was described by viewers as bound by colonnades, with seven archways — each separately lighted. Gould commented that "there was no conventional thinking in terms of theatre's proscenium arch and walls: the emphasis was on movement in which the audience participated" (11).

Following the camera's lead, the television viewing audience moved like a participant in the crowd. With the camera, the audience was asked to share in the flux of the staged movement. The camera moved through lit arches and kept time with marching soldiers who paraded by in modern dress uniforms. Throngs of people dressed as if they lived in the present day crowded in front of the lens to catch a glimpse of Caesar as he entered. Close-up shots of an assassin's knife and a guard's gun foreshadowed the imminent death of Caesar. Depth of field shots compensated for the camera's difficulty in showing the whole stage and also captured the intimate details and the fashionable simplicity of the contemporary setting. According to Gould, this technique was illustrated best in Brutus's oration over Caesar's body: "On the left-hand side of the screen only the head of Brutus was visible as he spoke in the distance, the foreground being filled by the shoulders and backs of the crowd arranged in graduated perspective. On the right hand side of the screen there was a pillar against which Anthony stood in close-up, a cigarette hanging from his mouth as he smiled derisively and waited his turn to alter the course of events" (11).

Through television techniques, Miner allowed the audience a new intimacy into the characters' minds. After the death of Caesar, as Antony delivers his famous lines that call Caesar "the noblest Roman of them all," the camera picks up Antony's foot rolling Caesar's lifeless body into the street. At one point, the camera zooms in on Cassius in deep contemplation while a prerecorded voice-over plays his thoughts, and the viewer seems to hear what he is thinking. In the final moment of the televised production, the audience is left with the image of Cassius's scheming eyes as the camera moves to an extreme close-up.

The critical response toward the production focused on the technical manipulation of the story. *Variety* gave high praise to the production, particularly noting the technical achievement: "The fine integration of movement, lighting, camera, and staging ... gave breadth and intensity to an exciting version of Shakespeare" (*Variety* 33). Jack Gould touted the televised production as "a magnificently bold, imaginative, and independent achievement" (11). Comparing the televised work to Orson Welles's 1937 modernized stage play, Gould noted that the existence of the Welles precedent did not detract from Miner's triumph in television. For Gould, Miner's production was a model for the future of televised theatre: "In his production he went to the heart of video's needs, which is to make a picture and not take one.... What Mr. Miner did for sixty minutes was to truly think with his eyes. With inspired disregard for the supposed limitations of video he imbued the Shakespearean tragedy with a visual power and vitality that lifted television to the status of a glorious art" (11).

Like any new artistic or commercial form, television instructed its audience about the structures and conventions and intended uses of the programs they created. Televised dramas were tools used by the purveyors of television to instruct the audience in the vocabulary and practice of the new television ritual. These tools, whether they were used intentionally or not, reshaped the audience perspective through the visual images produced for both narrative programming and the advertisements that were interspersed between those programs. It is generally held today that watching television, even the best television, doesn't make you cultured or educated or even informed. This reaction comes from our repeated participation in the television ritual that tells us again and again that the means has more effect than content. Our education has been so comprehensive that it is possible for the great dramatic works of our culture to become the consumable elements of a diversionary activity.

The Internet has added to that atmosphere of leisure and diversion an element of participatory immediacy. Howard Rheingold, who wrote the book *The Virtual Community*, says, "If you have a computer, you have the power to broadcast. It gives the power to individuals that used to be only that of the privileged few" (Cooke and Lehrer 38). This power to broadcast over the Internet is central to the interactive nature of modern communication. This broadcasting element makes events in New York, Chicago, or Los Angeles immediately accessible to a participatory mass audience. Through Internet access productions can be commented on, and casts can be critiqued. The immediacy, and its presence, is no longer limited to the walls of a theatre or the boundaries of the city where an event is produced.

For example "Playbill Digital" allows online fans of Broadway plays to interface with other audience members in chat rooms. An online spectator can digitally view scenes from the revival of the musical *Gypsy*, as well as scenes from the pre- and post-show experiences of the cast and audience. They can also watch an online lecture about the director, Sam Mendes, and his directorial style and the choices that were made in the pre-production staging of his version of the famous musical. This mass, interactive communication environment means that theatre productions of national standing are present to a mass audience, and in turn the mass audience is present at theatre events.

The irony of this new broadcasting capability is that it solidifies the standing of the few theatre production centers of national importance. This happens as the mass audience chooses the venues and locations that it deems the most prestigious or legitimate purveyors of the product because today's audience can engage with a theatre event anywhere in the world.

Even live theatre events in physical proximity to individual audience members are sifted through this filter of national prominence by a process of labeling theatre works in terms of where they came from (Los Angeles, Chicago, New York), or where they are going ("good enough for Broadway"). This process of legitimizing is taken even further as theatre is disseminated from these production centers in a nearly identical manner to the national distribution of a film, where a show is judged as to its approximation to the original. It appears that what the audience is really looking for is a precise duplication of the audience's experience at the original event.

At the contemporary inception of the Internet, media's overarching power over theatre's access to the American population still exists. While the relationship between theatre and the Internet is more symbiotic than theatre's early relationship with film and television, theatre must still conduct its business and present its art form through the material and phenomenological contexts of the popular media technology. Educated by their relationship with the other electronic mediums, theatre practitioners have established a beneficial relationship with Internet technology. At one high culture center, the John F. Kennedy Center for the Performing Arts, the performance facility showcases its creative use of this technology. The center's Internet homepage is described by the facilities' directors as the "seventh stage," or an online counterpart to the six actual stages that exist at the performance compound. While the site was primarily established to attract a new, younger audience base to the performance facility, it also provides a communication hub for arts practitioners, education components for young artists, and live cybercasting of performances, such as the center's annual "Messiah Sing-Along." Leigh Buchanan describes the cooperative relationship between theatre and the Internet:

> Popular appeal is especially important at a time when studies show that young adults are turning away from "high culture" performances, such as classical music-concerts, theatre and ballet. Those are the people whose hearts and entertainment dollars the center must win as its established audience grays; they're also among the most avid Internet users. In addition, the organization wants to heighten its visibility outside the Washington Metropolitan area so that taking in a play at the Kennedy Center ... becomes as established a part of the visitor's agenda as climbing to the top of the Washington Monument [2].

With the Kennedy Center's "Seventh Stage" as evidence, it can be projected that the homogenizing affect of technology will be increasingly manifest as we progress in the age of the Internet. Theatrical centers of standing, such as Broadway or the Kennedy Center in Washington, D.C., will monopolize interest because of patrons' access to the Internet. To a mass audience, given the choice between local voices and the voices of reputation, the draw of established, media-reinforced, corporate producers of theatre will be irresistible. The interconnected nature of their promotion will ensure dominance, and dissemination of theatrical art from those centers looks increasingly like cinematic or electronic distributions rather than restagings.

THREE

Theatrical Space in Mass-Media Culture

In Steven Daniels and Denis Cosgrove's introduction to their book *The Iconography of Landscape,* they describe the value of identifying space as an iconographic site that reflects the ever-changing nature of any given culture that exists in, presents, or represents a given site. Speaking of landscape particularly, they say: "A landscape is a cultural image, a pictorial way of representing, structuring or symbolizing surroundings.... The meanings of verbal and visual and built landscapes have a complex and interwoven history, ... [and] every study of a landscape further transforms its meaning, depositing another layer of cultural representation" (1).

Their discussion of landscape is helpful as we consider the verbal, visual, and built representations of theatrical space in the twenty years before and after the millennium. Like landscapes, theatrical space is transformational. The language of theatrical space changes as the world changes. As society, theory, or praxis alter in a given period of time, the language that defines theatrical space is reformed or re-envisioned to meet the confines of each new style or genre.

Theatrical perception of meaning-bearing spaces and meaning-bearing images also changes throughout time. Visual identification with the culture at large is important to theatrical space. Throughout history theatre spaces are sometimes stripped bare, and at other times are ornate or filled to capacity with costumes, properties, and set dressings. Each of these represents physical choices that reflect the period in which they were made.

Actual, built theatre spaces are also converted regularly as form, function, and technology demand changes that enhance the theatre. The function of repertory theatre space clearly demonstrates this point. In a repertory space, sets are recombined or changed every night to meet the needs of the theatre's rotating schedule of plays. Such flexibility in the programming of stage events has become expected because technology has acclimated audiences to anticipate and even require constant change as a sign of vitality and of contemporaneous consequence. Technology is, therefore, employed through innovative materials and equipment to make that flexibility in programming possible.

Technology has always served two roles in theatre. First, it has been, and is, an enabler or facilitator of theatrical innovation (which is the case in the repertory theatre example mentioned above); and second, it has been, and is, a cultural signifier. After all, it was the technology of the day that was used to construct ancient stages, but the fact that such construction technology was employed for amphitheatres is a cultural signifier of the importance of theatre to the ancient city-states. It was the technology of the day that lit the grand theatres and opera house of Europe in the eighteenth century with candles; but it is also a culture signifier of the wealth and resources of a community that so many expensive and consumable candles could be used for diversion and cultural high-mindedness.

Each of technology's roles contributes to our understanding of theatre through history as a demonstrator of the cultural reality. The concept of cultural reality is important in relation to theatrical technology because it was, and is, the goal of most theatre to demonstrate cultural reality. After all, even the best materials and technology for the stage still require the willing suspension of disbelief. Theatre has not survived through history because of its virtuosity in recreating physical realities; rather, it has thrived because of its ability to accurately communicate cultural realities. In the end, the approximation or imitation of physical reality serves the goal of bringing cultural reality to the stage.

Historical Theatre and Physical Reality

Stages throughout theatre history were filled with evidence of cultural reality. The Greeks depicted contemporary social problems and represented their historical and mythical past in their presentation of public plays. Medieval liturgical drama staged biblical events for the common people of their communities in which priests used symbolic objects and actions to represent Christian rituals and dogma. French theatre of the 1700s was governed by rules set forth by Cardinal Richelieu's French Academy, which served as an organized cultural and political body that studied and codified the language and style of French theatre. In the English stage of the 1830s, managers William Charles Macready and Lucia Elizabetta Bartolozzi (Madame Vestri) equipped rooms as if they were true to life — they laid flooring, attached knobs to cabinets and doors, and put books on bookcases (Brockett, 362).

Certainly the theatre of the late nineteenth century was marked by an intense focus on staging reality, as directors and theorists began to consider and dialogue the importance of bringing actual objects from the real world into theatrical space. As the turn of the century approached and beyond, the staged expression of cultural and social realities was reinforced by the physical depiction of reality. From the birth of realism and naturalism in Europe of 1875, to contemporary stage projections, the physically and tangibly real aided in the assertion of emotional and psychological realities of the characters on stage. It also became an important factor in the audience believing in the realities portrayed. Several theatrical examples demonstrated the advent of this new focus — this spatial, even physical reality on theatrical stages in the service of the cultural reality of the production as a whole.

In 1866 Georg, the German Duke of Saxe-Meiningen, assumed control over the Meiningen Court Theatre. He had extensively studied the work of prominent directors from Paris and London and was intent on improving his little theatre's repertory and the quality of its productions. Working with the director Ludwig Chronegk he developed a new system of theatre that included an intense focus on the authenticity of materials used to design his theatrical productions. Meiningen's productions utilized bona fide weapons. Both chain mail and armor were imported to meet his demand for accuracy. Meiningen also manufactured furniture and properties at the theatre so that he could ensure the proper dimensions.

The influence of the Meiningen troupe was so significant that an increased number of builders and theatrical supply houses were established in Germany to meet the desire for authenticity (Brockett, 33). Meiningen's intentional focus on staged reality is evident in the notes of his essay "Pictorial Motion:"

> When both painted and sculptured pieces are used on the stage the director
> should see to it that the different materials employed do not achieve two

different effects which are disturbing to the audience. Transitions from natural or artificial flowers to painted ones for example, must be made with unusual smoothness, so that the one can hardly be distinguished from the other. It is complexly inartistic, even absurd, when for example, the one rose that has to be plucked from a rosebush is a palpable flower whereas the rest are painted rose [Cole, 83].

Cultural reality through physical approximation was also a primary concern for the French scenic designer Andre Antoine. His sets, properties, and lighting were drawn from real world objects. Antoine experimented on stage with genuine objects — replacing painting with real wallpaper, leather, and woodwork paneling. He also designed ceilings in relief, with visible beams, as well as complete door and window frames. Real beef carcasses lined the walls of Antoine's production of the Fernando Core play *The Butchers* (1988), and the furniture and décor from a small student living room were the stage set for the play *Old Heidelberg*.

In their book *Century of Innovation*, Oscar Brockett and Robert Findlay describe a war council lit entirely by on-stage lanterns in the Theatre Libre production of Henrique's *Death of the Duc d'Enghein*. Organic natural elements like the sun and moon were often used as lighting sources through open windows and doors. Antoine states his concerns for reality in the essay *Behind the Fourth Wall*: "For a stage set to be original, striking, and authentic, it should first be built in accordance with something seen — whether a landscape or an interior. If it is an interior, it should be built with its four sides, its four walls.... Logical exits should be taken care of, with due regard for architectural accuracy; and outside the set proper, the halls and rooms connecting with these exits should be plainly indicated" (Cole, 95).

Antoine fought for correct proportions on the stage. He also articulated reasons for reality on stage as a necessity of the independent theatre movement, which was influenced by naturalism. The theoretical movement worked to manifest the psychological and social realities of the day, and Antoine perpetuated those realities in his portrayal of space through scenery, properties, and other design elements. For Antoine, the reality of space determined the success of the performance: "[I]n modern life our living rooms, bedrooms, and studies, the floor plan ... causes us unconsciously to live and work in certain places rather than others.... [The Director] must furnish [the set] sensibly and logically decorating it with all the familiar objects which the inhabitants of the place use, even outside the action of the play itself, in time lapses between acts. This operation, conducted painstakingly, ... gives life to the set" (Cole, 96). Antoine believed that the director's careful attention to the setting and properties of the play would aid the performance of the actors, increasing his or her ability to portray a real emotional sensitivity on stage.

While Andre Antoine provided real life objects on the stage to benefit and augment the preparation of the actors, the originators of the American Melodrama sought reality on stage as a form of spectacle that would draw audiences. In the late 1800s the power of the visual image was of foremost importance to writers and producers of theatre. Powerful images that seemed to be real to an audience resonated in the culture of the day. The famous abolitionist Harriet Beecher Stowe called her own writing "pictorial" and wrote: "My vocation is simply that of a painter.... There is no arguing with pictures, and everybody is impressed by them, whether they mean to be or not" (Wilson, 260).

Stage melodrama was also concerned with reproducing vivid, spectacular pictures for its audience. Theatre historian Daniel C. Gerould describes the intense desire to project an emotionally believable physical picture for American audiences:

> Whatever melodrama lacked in psychological insight and artistic depth, it made up for by sheer technological skill. If its style and thought were primitive, the special effects of melodrama were sophisticated products of the latest advances in applied science. American materialism and entrepreneurial capitalism found in melodrama a congenial art. Intensely competitive and responsive to market conditions, theatre deployed battalions of stage hands to reproduce ever more faithfully train wrecks, fires, snow storms, steamship explosions, and avalanches [9].

George Aiken's stage adaptation of *Uncle Tom's Cabin* provides us with a vision of this commitment to emotionally real representation of space. In scene six of act one, the heroine (Eliza) runs to escape the predators Haley, Marks, and Loker. The scene consists only of a stage action with no dialogue. The descriptive notes for the scene from the Samuel French publication, first published in 1858, are as follows: "SCENE VI — The entire depth of stage, representing the Ohio River filled with Floating Ice.— Set bank on R. H. and in front. ELIZA appears, with HARRY, R. H., on a cake of ice, and floats slowly across to L. H.— HALEY, LOKER, and MARKS, on bank R. H., observing.— PHINEAS on opposite shore. END OF ACT I" (Ai[AU1]ken p.).

This scene and others demonstrate the power of visual and spatial images in American melodrama. The audience sees the river, watches the ice move, and then sees Eliza traverse the space on a piece of the ice.

Gerould describes Aiken's play as expertly highlighting the visual dynamic of the pictorial novel: "He does this through a spatial unfolding of the action — continuous physical movement in scenically differentiated place — that anticipates the techniques of film.... A camera seems to track Eliza; the dynamic spatial progression of a film scenario has replaced the fixed perspective of old fashioned verbal dramaturgy" (16).

While theatre spaces change because of politics, social circumstance, and functionality, nevertheless the creation of those spaces is consistently driven by a desire to make a communal connection through the demonstration and identification of cultural realities. To create that communal connection, theatre must always attach itself to the symbolic images that resonate in the community at large. Performative space is always imbedded with symbolic power. In *Media and Modernity*, John B. Thompson describes this power as: "the capacity to use symbolic forms to intervene in the course of events, to influence the actions of others and indeed to create events, by means of the production and transmission of symbolic forms" (17).

This reliance on symbolic power to connect with communities is obvious in many twenty-first century performance spaces. For example, the intent of rock musician Gwen Stefani's 2005 live stage show, "The Harajuku Lovers Tour," was to expose audiences to a variety of iconic symbols that aided them in making a connection to Stefani. The production team accomplished these audience "connections" to Stefani through a video rich environment in which audience members viewed a variety of images that were culled from Stefani's own music videos as well as additional animation sequences and cartoon bubbles. In addition to the prepared video material, live content was produced that depicted audience members as central to the show. Images were projected of screaming fans in the audience, as well as fans posing with Stefani and members of her crew. All of these images were input and projected by the tour video director during the course of the show to give the concert a feeling of immediacy and direct connection with the audience.

The visual experience of the concert was key to the audience's understanding of Stefani's message. Through the visual design the audience grasps the meaning of songs, recalls Stefani's past video performance personas, and sees related and referential visual metaphors — all of which provide an efficacy to the experience. They also engage in the new footage being created as part of the show. In Stefani's concert, visual representation is the source of symbolic power. Ray Woodbury, creative tour director, describes the experience, saying:

For this show, I really wanted new information and new concepts for people to see.... The creative goal was to make every song appear ... with a clearly defined look.... The appearance of a one-dimensional show is really not there, but the flow is there, catching the meaning of songs through digital images, while not over-stimulating the audience. You watch the screens and the entire show instead of just Gwen.... It's an overwhelming visual and musical experience, and that was the goal [Sandburg, 38].

James Lull points out that "all sources of symbolic influence depend on symbolic forms to leverage their power in today's mass mediated world" (161). This suggests that the production of symbolic forms cannot be created randomly or in isolation, but must convey meaning through codes and conventions that community members understand. Functional, successful, symbolic forms require a literate audience. Certainly symbolic forms are choreographed to serve the purposes of the organization using them. It is widely acknowledged that companies and organizations shape their narratives with the discourse and the actions that follow in mind. Therefore they carefully craft their visual and verbal symbols. Lull reminds us that "symbolism ... functions in the boundless and vital realm of the human imagination. Symbolic forms can never be used up. They are inherently open to an infinite, diverse progression of possible interpretations, a condition which encourages people to use [and understand] symbolic forms creatively" (162).

Lull describes symbolic forms as *polysemic*, or meaning different things to different people, or as *multisemic*, because they can mean different things to the same people depending on the moment or space they encounter them in. Lull also says that symbolic forms can be *combinatory*, because they can be synthesized, altered, recontextualized, or added to other forms for the purpose of creating new meaning and symbolic power.

Combinatory power has been an effective means of conveying theatrical messages from the earliest forms of theatre. For example, medieval liturgies that employed theatrical techniques often used relics, or symbolic images, that belonged to the Catholic Church. The icons were imbued with emblematic religious power to project visual themes and messages of spiritual salvation to common parishioners who could not read. The creators of liturgical theatre purposely made connections to religious icons in an effort to create a communal experience. The priests' presentation of religious symbols through theatrical means provided a common language and understanding of sensibility between the audience and the creator.

This communal understanding and connection remains central to theatrical productions today. Theatre practitioners depend on symbolic forms to communicate with their audience. Symbolic forms are intentional interactions designed by a theatrical team to specifically convey meaning in order to create a community that experiences an event together. Whether the symbolic form is a performative gesture, a verbal utterance made by a performer, a physical property, or a set dressing, the symbols are intended to communicate a clear message to establish symbolic power.

Because symbolic power is only powerful when the intended audience understands and accepts the symbolic form, combinatory symbols must be created from entities that have more cultural power than the organization that is borrowing them. Synthesis, alteration, and recontextualization of symbols are only effective in the postmodern world when the symbols already have global power. In the twenty-first century this explains the theatrical co-opting of media's own symbolic forms and therefore their employment of media's combinatory power.

THEATRE AT THE MARGINS AND COMBINATORY POWER

The use of media in theatrical production became important to the avant-garde in the 1950s. Practitioners and theorists at the margins of the theatrical community began to experiment with the combination and intersection of the two art forms. The most influential exploration of media as an integral scenographic tool began with the work of the Czechoslovakian artist Josef Svoboda. Svoboda, a Czech stage designer who was working with the stage director Alfred Radock, brought his vision of a multimedia theatre to the 1958 Worlds Fair in Brussels. The scenographer and the director who had spent years together considering the use of media projections in live production brought two multimedia exhibits to Brussels — *Polyekran* and *Laterna Magika*. The two productions were both rich in media content. *Polyekran* was a solely mediated experience and explored both the simultaneous and synchronous projection of slides and film on a variety of static screens suggesting interplay between each screen image. Svoboda describes the effect and purpose of the dramatic presentation, saying: "*Polyekran* offers the possibility of free composition, a free shaping and creation on several screens. Real objects and people are projected, but the relationships among them are not realistic, but rather supra realistic.... [This] contrast of varied things on stage is basic to theatre: the objects thereby acquire new relationships and significance, a new and different reality" (Burian, 81).

Svoboda did not see *Polyekran* as a simple demonstration of media projection. Instead he used the images and light of the projection as poetic sculptors of other scenic elements. For example, audience members describe a wall of cubes, which shifted position, moving first forwards and then backwards. Inside each individual cube a projector threw images onto the surface of the cube facing the audience. According to one observer, "Light, photographic image, object, and object manipulation combined to create a living, moving work of performance art" (Hope, online).

In the setting of the Brussels Worlds Fair Svoboda further explored the interaction between the actor and the physical presence of media forms. The second, more theatrical piece, *Laterna Magika*, was devoted to the theatrical synthesis of media and the human body. To demonstrate this concept the theatrical event featured a pastiche of performers and projections incorporated into live action and scenic elements.

In the *Scenography of Josef Svoboda,* Jakara Burian describes the staged production as utilizing three film projectors and two slide projectors that were synchronized to project simultaneously. The portable theatre space also included eight mobile screens, which could rise and fall as well as rotate or disappear. Human voices and media projections were all enhanced by stereophonic sound. The stage itself rotated on a moving belt to aid in the necessary, immediate response of the actors to the film and other images (83–87). Jan Grossman, a theatre director who witnessed the work, describes *Laterna Magika* in the following way: "[It] offered the dramatist, film scenarist, poet, composer a new language; a language that is more intense, sharply contrasting, and rhythmic. One which can captivatingly project statistics as well as ballet, documents as well as lyric verse, and is therefore capable of absorbing and artistically working together the density and dynamics, the multiplicity and contrariety of the world in which we live" (Grosman, 76).

Svoboda's design for *Lanterna Magika* is a progression away from the ideas about media use set forth by earlier Eastern European practitioners. For example, Svoboda moves far beyond the purposes prescribed by practitioners like Bertolt Brecht and Erwin Piscator, who saw media as an aid to help explain or document ideological production and meaning. While these German theatre practitioners were mainly interested in using media forms to instruct or document, Svoboda saw the complex and integrated use of film and other images as a means to project emotive and lyrical atmospheres to audiences. Svoboda's work in this lyrical atmosphere was focused on the amalgamation of art forms to create a new art form, which synthesized the elements and conventions of both theatre and media.

This new approach considered synthesis an art form, which presented theatre with new combinatory possibilities. Svoboda's work was an advent for scenic design and conception. Randall A. Enlow, a professor of lighting at the University of the Pacific, describes Svoboda's work as the centripetal force that propelled designers to consider the unique possibilities of media as an integral part of theatrical design: "Beginning with the ground-breaking design work of Josef Svoboda, projected images have opened vast new panoramas of visual art to enhance the energy onstage.... With both static and moving images, now a viable alternative to manufactured realism, expressionism etc., the time tested requirements of the performance space [and] architecture and "scenes and machines" have relaxed" (Jensen, Survey Question 2).

Other significant contributions to a mediated stage space were made throughout the last half of the twentieth century. Svoboda's work influenced other avant-garde theatre practitioners in America throughout the seventies, eighties, and nineties. Drawing on the work of Svoboda, directors and designers immersed themselves in the incorporation of media into theatrical spaces. The work of performance artists Laurie Anderson, Robert Wilson, and Ping Chong reflects Svoboda's influence in their desire to utilize media as a cultural signifier. Laurie Anderson's performance art often portrayed the visual landscape of a technology-driven society and the people who live, work, and love in that society. In Anderson's early work, *United States I–IV* (1983), she utilized media projections (hundreds of slides and filmic images, which included diverse subjects such as maps, nature, space, animals, and electronic materials) to depict the connection between America's visual and verbal landscape. Anderson's projections combined familiar world images, objects, and situations to produce this intersection of the geographical and emotional. In more recent work, Anderson collaborated with the National Aeronautic Space Agency (NASA) to create the multimedia documentary piece, *The End of the Moon*. Serving as artist-in-residence at NASA in 2003–04, Anderson produced a mediated performance filled with philosophical observations about culture, people, and technology. Anderson's approach to media in *The End of the Moon* included video-projected visions of the moon's surface.

Like Laurie Anderson's, Robert Wilson's career has focused on experimentation of images, sounds, and lights to convey a message or a story. Best know for his avant-garde work *Einstein on the Beach* (1976) and the multicultural narrative *CIVIL warS: a tree is best measured when it is down* (1980), Wilson has consistently experimented with light and media in his productions. Theatre critics have described Robert Wilson as "a towering figure in the world of experimental theater and an explorer in the uses of time and space on stage. Transcending theatrical convention, he draws in other performance and graphic arts, which coalesce into an integrated tapestry of images and sounds" (*New [AU2]York Times*).

In Wilson's 1998 original creation, *Monsters of Grace*, he combined opera, poetry, and film in performance. Created in conjunction with Philip Glass (music) and Jelaludin Rumi (lyrics), the production emphasized the possibilities of using mediated forms in performance spaces. In this case the media included a computer-animated stereoscopic film produced for the performance by Diana Walczak and Jeff Kleiser. Wilson worked to reinvent the traditional stage using projected, three-dimensional landscapes, still images, and other visual portraits that he imagined for the stage. Technology writer Wendy Jackson described the efficacy of these visuals for theatrical performance, saying: "The animation itself is in extreme slow motion, so slow that one wonders if it is really moving at all. It's more like 24 frames per minute than the film speed of 24 frames per second. But as time progresses, scenes change and new views become apparent. The imagery is abstract in meaning, seemingly random in placement, yet hyper-realistic in its portrayal of real objects" (Jackson, online).

Monsters of Grace was first performed at the University of California Los Angeles' Royce Hall. The project included seventy-three minutes of animation that were designed, animated, lit, and rendered for seventy-millimeter film. The projected visual materials, combined with live staging, emphasized Wilson's signature experimentation with the theatrical presentation of elements — lights, sounds, and objects. The show's producer, Jedediah Wheeler, describes the powerful connection between Wilson's work and contemporary media technology: "We are using the same technology used currently in feature films and in theme park rides to create the visual aspects of this opera.... I consider *Monsters of Grace* to be 21st Century Theater.... [It] will appeal to a new generation of theater audiences who may not be familiar with the work of Glass or Wilson, but who will be excited by the digital process" (Jackson, online).

A contemporary of Anderson and Wilson, Ping Chong's work is dedicated to the synthesis of live performance and media texts. Chong, a theatre director and video installation artist, began using media as a component of production in the early 1970s. Working in conjunction with video projection artist Jan Hartley, Chong designed slides and media projections that are central to his experimentation with new narrative ideas and storytelling forms. Projected images in Chong's work include visual stills, moving film images, and slides of colors and words. Many of the slides that Chong and his company create state facts so that the audience can make connections.

For example, the play *Nuit Blanch: A Select View of Earthlings* employs a number of video projections. The play examines the nature of humanity in the contemporary world. Sequences take place in South America, Cambodia, the United States, and other locations. Audience members are also exposed to projections that depict, among other things, a prehistoric cave and its environs and the earth as it looks from space. This broad range of images seems to indicate the vastness of humanity, which serves as a theme of the show. It also provides historical and cultural connections among nations and people.

Throughout the production, slides function both as information bearers and as plot connectors. Slides inform the live performance and also stand alone as key components of the performance. The varied use and strategies behind the media suggest that media is used to evoke the emotional content of the play. The initial stage directions give the reader an indication of how these projections are integrated into the performance as emotional content:

> Bare stage backed by a large rear-projection screen, lit with soft blue light from above.... The lights dim and a small, filmed image is projected onto the center of the screen. What the image depicts is not immediately recognizable; it seems to be a picture of clouds, or maybe water, a horse's ear, or perhaps two figures on a country road. These separate images seem to emerge, disappear and reappear the longer one looks at the film. Accompanying the projection is a narrative sound progression: cold autumnal wind, a baby's squall, a horse and carriage approaching and then stopping, the tolling of bells and a preacher intoning the words of a burial service. Underneath the small image another projected image appears, a name: Abigail Smith — a name that does not recur at any time during the play. Below the name, a birth date dissolves into place followed by the death date, and finally, the cause of death: Smallpox [Berson, 7].

In addition to suggesting the emotional location of the play as depicted in the first stage direction, other directions make it clear that mediated slides are used to inform the audience about place and time and connections between people. In one slide/live performance sequence the audience is introduced to "Miss B," a mulatto woman who is running a private laundry business somewhere in the rural south. At the same time the audience encounters Miss B, they are also introduced to a black-and-white slide sequence of "a handsome mulatto man walking through a poor part of town." According to the stage directions, there are seventy slides that allow the audience to see the man as he moves along, "smiling, put–

ting his fingers through his hair, looking off, tilting his head and then finally moving out of frame, leaving only a desolate, burnt out road and the hungry bark of a stray dog" (13–14). The sequence of the man plays over in different variations throughout Miss B's long day. During the course of the scene the audience learns that the man being projected has left Miss B. In other words, the audience sees over and over again what Miss B is feeling.

Instances of experimental, mediated theatre, such as the work of Chong, Anderson, and Wilson, are often produced at the margins of most public spaces and theatrical communities. Early explorations into the process and power of combining the two art forms to depict their small community had little initial impact on the art form. However, as the century moved on, and technology improved, theatre designers and directors began to notice the cultural significance of that combination.

CONTEMPORARY SPATIAL REALITY, TECHNOLOGY, AND PUBLIC SPACE

Many scholars have written about technology tools and applications as extensions of the human mind and the new global mindset. They have also considered the importance of the virtual space, architecture, and occupation of virtual communities in the post-modern world. The French urban theorist Paul Virillio has compared contemporary space with Gothic space, specifically comparing technology spaces with Gothic cathedrals, which were built to transcend the confines of the real world. He suggests that architectural design is currently in a similar intellectual and emotional moment to that of the designers who built the luminous edifices. He uses the Chartres Cathedral as an example:

> The cathedral is really a virtual work, and executed at such a scale. It is a phenomenon of special effects and lighting as one moves from one space to another. We may be entering an electronic Gothic era, because the Gothic style is really a matter of moving from the real to the virtual.... Architecture and monuments are created over long periods of time and are long lasting. The primacy of local time, which influenced history will from now on yield to global time; the time of immediacy, of ubiquity in real time [61].

In like mind, the architect and designer Ammar Eloueini says that technology changes the way that contemporary space is recognized by both the designers of present-day space and those who occupy the spaces they design. Writing about up-to-date architectural design, he states: "We do not operate any longer in a system that is limited to three dimensions, but in a hyper-space we are used to perceiving and imagining…. New technologies we currently have at our disposal enable us to explore and exploit dimensions that were previously vacant. An architectural, conceptual, and projectual [sic], non-linear approach based on dynamic and evolutionary systems, responding to an architectural and urban complexity can be both developed and applied" (64).

While both architects' focus on the virtual nature of creation, building, and living is intriguing, it is equally important to consider the ways that virtual space and technology influence performance spaces and the perception of those spaces. Theatre at its heart is communication, and communication technologies have clearly had an effect on the cultural dialogue of our society. It is vital that we consider the ways in which high-tech tools influence the way that individuals live, work, and play in the real world spaces in order for us to determine how theatrical messages are perceived in performance spaces.

Technological tools are the language of the day. In essence, they are the tools that create contemporary public space. As they influence and drive the creation of public space, they also create a civic narrative that is present in public space and shapes the way that the architecture of public space evolves. In turn, that civic narrative serves as the framework for our public experience.

TECHNOLOGY AND THE CREATION OF PUBLIC SPACE

As thinking beings we are shaped by our experiences. The late twentieth century and early twenty-first century cultural and spatial landscape is a complex mix of media, commerce, and information gathering. The proportion of mediated experiences to tangible experiences is heavily weighted toward the mediated. By virtue of the accelerating technologies of media delivery, a person with ten minutes of time has the ability to sample the music of a different continent, see the streets of a distant city, participate in an armed revolution in an imaginary galaxy, or play a virtual soccer game alongside the greatest athletes in history. In this way, media messages dominate the way that individual people shape and contextualize their world. This particularly applies to the way that contemporary communities construct public space.

Collective virtual communities created in the early 1990s were propelled by complex message and information systems that valued and explored the interconnectedness of media images, retail consumerism, and information production in those communities. What is interesting about the use of these technologies today is their application in the real world, in tangible communities. In the real world, high tech tools allow for extended communication and connection to other human beings. For example:

- Cellular phone users employ technology and are connected to other members of a wireless community through phones with the capability to take and send images, retrieve email, and download and play music videos.
- Bloggers can write and post political, social, and personal information on the web, and other like-minded individuals can instantaneously read and respond.
- Through video gaming clubs and consortiums, individuals connect across states and nations to compete in fictional games.

Each of these experiential activities involves interaction with other human beings and extends the capacity for human interaction. These activities, and hundreds like them, imbed habits of performance and associative perception into the lexicon of our social communication.

Analysis of the use and display of technology in public settings offers many examples of the ways that technology tools work to make performance and associative perception the language of the day. These tools influence our intellectual and physical comprehension of contemporary urban landscapes. For example, individuals are monitored in ways they were not previously monitored prior to the communication technology boom. Video monitors act as surveillance devices in grocery, convenience, and department stores — capturing each individual that enters the space to shop. There is an expectation that if you walk into a bank, a casino, or an electronics store, you are being observed. Similarly, web-cams have been trained onto the most mundane of domestic existences for the sole purpose of providing others with an opportunity to watch. Technology has created an atmosphere where being watched or viewed is a part of the cultural landscape.

Consumers are also used to being encountered and questioned electronically in ways that they were not encountered prior to the invention of interactive technology. In contemporary screen culture, automatic teller machines talk to patrons — directly asking them specific information about the dispensing of cash and the balance of accounts. Individuals in a grocery store can scan and pay for grocery items by solely communicating with a machine. With the advent of smaller, multidimensional technology interfaces, computers can be imbedded in clothing, accessories, and intelligent workspaces where "smart objects" can sense an individual's need and then adjust the workspace accordingly.

While the many theatre companies are still trying to grasp the complexities of a technology-infused theatre, the Blue Man Group not only embraces the possibilities of a media messages in live theatric events, but also comfortably identifies and comments on the ubiquitous nature of technology and its accompanying cultural conventions. They regularly point out and simultaneously savage the notion that even the simplest forms of mediation equates to disproportionate cultural influence.

In one of their productions, this fact is demonstrated through a bit based on the traffic wands that airport ground crews use to guide aircraft as they taxi. In the bit, a Blue Man simply walks onstage with the familiar illuminated wands in both hands. He gestures in the expected way and directs and another Blue Man forward, then backward, and forward again, as if experimenting with the magical power of the wands. Next, he directs his gesture towards an audience member whom he has stand, turn around, and finally trade seats with another audience member in the balcony. Next he commands the entire audience to perform various synchronized movements. By the time the bit ends with the Blue Man "accidentally" summoning the life-sized nose of a jet aircraft out of the wings of the theatre, it is clear that the intent was to comment on the utter ridiculousness of the perceived power in the wands. When pointed out in this way, it seems incredible that by simply mediating gestures with light sticks, they somehow command the instant respect of the masses.

It is the subconscious impact that the presence of technology and mediated messages has on us that must be accounted for in the production of theatrical events — just as it must be accounted for in all exchanges of information. Technology hasn't just changed the physical attributes or appearance of theatrical events; technology has changed the nature of space itself.

AUGMENTED SPACE

Lev Manovich, professor of visual arts at the University of California, San Diego, describes this extension of technology tools into real locations as "augmented space." Manovich says the difference between the last decade of the twentieth century and contemporary space is that our vision of space in the 1990s was immersed in virtual reality. He recognizes the role of associative perception, and asserts that today's reality is more about the corporeal use of that technology:

> It is quite possible that this decade of the 2000s will turn out to be about the physical — that is, physical space filled with electronic and visual information. While enabling further development of virtual spaces — from more realistic computer games to new 3D technologies and standards for World Wide Web such as Director 3D to wider employment of compositing in cinema — computer and network technologies more and more actively enter our real physical spaces. The previous image of a computer era — VR user traveling in a virtual space — has become replaced by a new image: a person checking her email or making a phone call using her PDA/cell phone combo while at the airport, on the street, in a car, or in any other actually existing space [online].

This concept of "augmented space" emphasizes a cultural need to network or connect that is already present in virtual communities but is now extended and exploited in temporal venues as well. We see this extension in all aspects of life. Contemporary private life is filled with electronic transactions from email to instant messaging to computerized information processing through the Internet. Following suit, public spaces are now filled with technology. Further, technology seems to define commercial space as well as social, entertainment, and artistic space.

Individuals encounter technology interfaces in almost every aspect of their lives. This is important to remember when we consider how media technologies shape public spaces and public interactions in those spaces. Public spaces are filled with technology interfaces because they are an extension of the materials we value in our private space. Public space is also created by technology. Consider, for example, how MySpace.com is shaped by performance and new definitions of public space.

Every day, we engage in a personal performance of persona by how we present ourselves through our dress, vocabulary, and other outward expressions. We are consciously trying to communicate something about ourselves through these performances, such as what our interests are, what we do for living, our socio-economic status, and the like.

We constantly observe our environment for cues about how to act and what to wear. We are all concerned with resolving how we perceive ourselves with how we are perceived. We learn this by trying out different performances, receiving feedback from others, and figuring out how to modify the performance to better give off the intended impression. These performance practices make up more and more of our social interactions.

In essence, we have all learned to constantly be on stage, performing our persona.

The nature of the personal performance of persona plays out visibly on MySpace.com. Users of MySpace.com participate in new, virtual communities by creating and posting public profiles of themselves. Profiles are digital representations of themselves, public displays of identity where people can interact in a virtual space. Because the digital world requires people to write themselves into being, profiles provide an opportunity to perform the intended expression through language, imagery, and media. Responses and comments to these digital representations offer valuable feedback. Of course, because imagery can be staged, the entire environment is infused with performative characteristics.

MySpace.com, instant messaging, and similar technologies have become tools for people to maintain virtual communities. Such a shared cultural context allows people to solidify their social groups through performative practices and theatrical conventions. Thus, Internet technologies have allowed people to create a new public space. Online, people can build the environments that support new forms of socialization, and therefore new forms of performance. In fact, with each post being carefully staged to communicate a precise message, the forms and conventions of performance are required in these new public spaces.

TECHNOLOGY, SPACE, AND CIVIC DIALOGUE

Technology has the capacity to transform any space into public space through the requirement of performance. Videophones, for instance, clearly have the effect of transforming carefree personal communication into a personal performance of persona. Perhaps someday we will be as comfortable conversing with a video and audio connection as we currently are with an audio connection alone, but for now the evidence seems to suggest that an "always on stage" posture is beginning to be the social norm in our public spaces. People in our culture expect to be observed in public space, and they expect to perform. People have this expectation because of their relationship to technology as both a transmitter and observer of personal performance.

Technology, therefore, influences the creation of public space. It is a part of the dialogue that leads to construction of physical public spaces in contemporary culture, such as community centers and performing arts venues. Technology also influences the civic narrative that takes place within those public spaces. Mirjam Struppek, organizer of the Urban Screens 2005 Conference on "Discovering the Potential of Outdoor Screens for Urban Society," reminds us that the public spaces where human interaction takes place can be seen as a "stage" for those interactions. She asserts: "Public space has always been a place for human interaction, a unique arena for exchange of rituals and communication in a constant process of renewal, challenging the development of society. Its architectural dimension, being a storytelling medium itself, has played a changing role of importance in providing a stage for this interaction. The way space is inhabited can be read as a participatory process of its audience" (Struppek, online).

Struppek's vision of architectural space as the stage for community interaction and dialogue is an important basis to start from as we consider the ways that technology influences the intellectual and emotional exchange of ideas that are shared in public spaces. Her vision of architectural space as the arena of public discussion and participation is a valuable model to consider as we examine the way that civic narrative is influenced by technology.

Certainly, high-tech visual displays have predecessors. Electronic signage and billboards have communicated commercial messages with individual consumers and large population bases throughout the twentieth century. However, it is interesting to note that the improvement of technology and the more pervasive placement of larger than life urban screens within key commercial, art, and entertainment venues create a new collective visualization of what contemporary American space looks like. This collective visualization influences how members of a community speak to each other as they function within the new communal space.

It is important to note that visual displays embedded into urban landscapes (be they statuary, billboards, or large-scale video displays) have always reflected a multiplicity of visual messages back to the community that surrounds them. They can represent what is socially, politically, and aesthetically acceptable to a given community, but they can also encourage the community to embrace ideals or values that it has not considered before. This is all done through the practical use of images in physical environments and provides a means whereby reinforcing or revolutionary ideas can be simultaneously present.

Physical displays allow for specific messages, intended for specific audiences, to be observed by broad audiences. Therefore, reinforcing messages for the majority have the potential to become revolutionizing messages for the minority, and reinforcing messages for the minority can be revolutionizing messages for the majority. This idea is particularly important to consider when investigating technology-driven venues because of their ability to quickly change from one message to another, thus multiplying the potential for reinforcing-revolutionizing messages in the community dialogue. In this context, civic conversation extends between the broadcasting of the messages and the public stage where participatory personal performances are reflective of the nature of the community dialogue that is created.

Three prominent examples demonstrate how technology implementation in public spaces creates a community dialogue and shifts physical landscape towards venues of personal and public performance: Chicago's Millennium Park Crown Fountain, the Las Vegas Fashion Show Mall LED and Plasma Screen implementation, and the Las Vegas Freemont Street Experience. Each of these examples are representative of, or similar to, other large technology displays that are now regularly placed in commercial and communal venues, like community parks, pedestrian walks, and shopping malls.

Each of the three examples also demonstrates that technology has in some way altered the way that communities think and feel about each space. By implementing technology, the creators of each space use technology tools to create unique, new contemporary public spaces. Technology influences and drives the creation of these public spaces, but it also creates the civic narrative that surrounds the public space, thus infusing them with a theatricality through their display of performance and the encouragement of associative perception. In each case, it also shapes the emotional, intellectual, and physical evolution of the public space.

TECHNOLOGY, SPACE, AND PLAY

The Crown Fountain, which opened in the summer of 2004, is located in the southwest corner of the Millennium Park on Michigan Avenue in Chicago. The fountain is one of the anchoring art exhibits in the 24.5-acre park, which also includes other art, music, architecture, and landscape design venues. Designed by Spanish sculptor Jaume Plensa, the Crown Fountain consists of two 50-foot high glass block towers placed at either end of a shallow reflecting pool, which is 232 feet long. Each tower is animated with changing video images and lights. Water pours from the top and spurts from the center of each tower. The video projection panels display faces of Chicago citizens from every demographic in the city through constantly changing video images. Each tower's projected video images are considered a direct reference to the traditional use of gargoyles in fountains, where faces of mythological beings were sculpted with open mouths to allow water, a symbol of life, to flow out.

According to promotional material developed by the city, Plensa developed the concept by having water flow from the projected images of Chicago faces through a water outlet in the screen to give the illusion of water spouting from their mouths. The collection of faces that are projected in the permanent art object were reportedly taken from a cross-section of 1,000 Chicago residents. Owned by the City of Chicago, the Millennium Park, which houses the fountain, replaced a blighted rail yard. In its place the Millennium Park is the home of many works of art and culture, such as the Frank Gehry-designed Jay Pritzker Pavilion (a state of the art outdoor concert venue), and the Cloud Gate (British artist Anish Kapoor's 110-ton elliptical sculpture that reflects the city skyline and the clouds). All of the installations provide the Chicago community with a unique center for art, music, architecture, landscape design, and technology.

The Crown Fountain is an active site of play for Chicago's citizens. The projected images seem to have achieved event status. Adults line the reflecting pool to watch the images change from one face to another, commenting on the diversity of images that play out before them. Children play in the shallow pool, engaging with the larger than life faces. The children often return the images' digital gaze with looks of serious contemplation or boisterous responses of glee followed by a physical mimic of the image they have just encountered. The children also wait with anticipation as the projected faces cue a gush of water by making an O shape with their mouths. Wet from the fountain, children begin to engage with each other, splashing water and hurling challenges at the next child who waits on the spurt of the fountain.

A popular destination for tourists and the Chicago community, the Millennium Park marries technology and green-space for city residents. The once dangerous train yard gives way to spaces where young people can encounter and interact with technology. Technology adds a new dimension to the park's green space. It provides material for conversation, interaction, and observation. In this space the community acts out a dialogue where each member of the city's large demographic is represented through projection. What is most powerful about this fountain space is that situated between the two fountains, children are able to see themselves at the center of this diversity. This allows for interaction with individuals whom they would normally not encounter, individuals from every walk of life.

The Crown Fountain is a pure example of a visual display creating community dialogue through personal and public performance. Certainly the work can be seen as a type of municipal performance, where the city administrators of Chicago have staged their message of "Chicago: a place of art, culture, and life." The promotional materials for the park go so far as to say that the city has fulfilled the ambitions of its forefathers by asserting that the park "has become the crowning achievement for Chicago in the tradition of its original founders" (MillenniumPark.org, online). In other words, the city "performs" a reinforcing-revolutionizing message of cultural sophistication, diversity, and ambition for equality and civic mindedness.

The participant-performers engage in the community dialogue first through their presence: they assert that they belong at the heart of the city's aspirations through the simple act of placing themselves on the prepared stage at the Crown Fountain. They demonstrate their claim as heirs to the city's aspirations by both contributing to and absorbing the atmosphere of innocence and child-play that prevails around the fountain. They perform their reinforcing-revolutionizing message concerning the city's claims of social justice and artistic aspirations through their manner and conversation while at the site — theatricality being the energizing element of the entire scene.

The Crown Fountain demonstrates how public and personal performance can join in an expression of civic mythology and aspiration. The artist creates a mythology; the city performs its aspirations through installation; the citizens perform their aspirations through participation. Technology in this case gives license to the performances because it invites participation through the projection of visible cues of engagement, demonstrations of acceptance, and celebrations of individuality.

Technology is also the ticket for this new theatre of community dialogue because it has instructed all of the citizens on how to participate. There is no explanation needed, no printed directions are distributed. There is no need, because experience with technology has provided the grammar and lexicon for interaction. It is universally understood that large projections are intended for everyone. Their presence removes the exclusivity of a high-concept art work. The cues are understood, and the message is explicit because it is projected, not sculpted or constructed. It is a moving image of self-identification, where the audience sees themselves and their neighbors. They feel comfortable in its presence because of their intimate experience with it in their own homes. They each have a personal relationship to the message, not because of its content, but because of its medium.

TECHNOLOGY, COMMERCE, AND EVENT STATUS

The Fashion Show Mall, a high-end shopping center located on the Las Vegas Strip, employs LED and plasma technology to alter its visual presence. The Fashion Show Mall competes in Las Vegas with a multitude of electronic displays developed for the garish casinos that surround it. It recently completed a one billion dollar expansion that has enhanced the shopping space with large LED and plasma panels that are located both inside and outside the building. The space features the "Great Hall," a multimillion-dollar event area that features an 80-foot retractable runway — making it possible to naturally have fashion shows at Fashion Show Mall. In fact, house fashion shows are presented and projected several days a week.

The great hall houses three large LED displays that are suspended from motorized hoists in the ceiling to create a backdrop for a continuous stream of fashion shows and other special events, such as product introductions, that are presented in the large, open-air atrium at the center of the commercial space.

Phase two of the expansion project features a 480-foot-long steel structure called the "Cloud." The Cloud hovers 128 feet above a 72,000-square-foot plaza on the Las Vegas Strip and is an image projection surface. Four LED screens are situated just below the Cloud and are used to broadcast video, sponsored advertising, and synchronized live Las Vegas events. Phase two also includes four large LED screens that interface with the large electronic displays at the center of the shopping mall as well as a plethora of multi-use, flat, 61-inch plasma screens that broadcast commercials and live fashion shows both in and outside of the space.

According to designers, the screens serve the space as directories, advertising venues, and interactive, live simulcasts. Randy Byrd, the senior project manager for the Fashion Show installation, explains, "The [plasma] screens serve as high-tech bread crumbs, leading shoppers to the center of the live action" (Darek Johnson, online). But the ever-present nature of the screens seems to be more than just a trail that leads towards commerce. In many ways the screens place a new value on the shoppers' experience. Rather than a simple economic transaction between consumer and proprietor, the revised space takes on an event status.

Going to the shopping mall is now equated with televisual images of haute couture fashion shows projected from Paris and Milan. Average shoppers are guided to connect their own experiences with that of famous celebrities and models who attend the televised fashion events and sophisticated parties. Lev Manovich speaks of a similar technology space located in a New York City Prada Clothing location:

> The special status of ... clothing is further enhanced by the placement of small flat electronic screens throughout the store on horizontal shelves right alongside the merchandize. The clothes are equated with the ephemeral images playing on the screens, and, vice versa. The images acquire a certain materiality, as though they are themselves objects. By positioning screens showing moving images right next to the clothes, the designers ironically refer to what everybody today already knows: we buy objects not for themselves but in order to emulate the specific images and narratives that are presented by the advertisements of these objects [25].

The Fashion Show Mall competes with many commercial entities for its consumer. Surrounding casinos are filled with large gambling spaces, sporting and performance venues, art galleries, and buffets all vying for the consumer. The Fashion Show Mall competes successfully because it has mastered the idea of event status. In other words, the mall has been cast by its directors as something beyond its natural composition: it is performing a role. The electronic images presented on the ubiquitous screens transform the shopping space into a place where patrons are able to emulate the images that are projected around them, and they perform the roles that are demonstrated to them. The addition of technology to the expansion allows for this event status because it provides the electronic narrative that we already equate with purchase. The commercial enterprise generates enthusiasm and energy through performance and associative perception in a space designed with inherent theatricality.

POST-NOSTALGIA, TECHNOLOGY, AND TRANSITION

A few miles from the Las Vegas Strip and the Fashion Show Mall, the Las Vegas landmark Freemont Street has been a consistent center of commerce since the city's initial incorporation in 1905. The famous avenue was the first Las Vegas street to be paved, the first to house a hotel elevator, and one of the street's tenants (the Northern Club) was the first to receive a gaming license when the state legalized gaming in 1931. The Golden Nugget, which still stands, was the first casino built on Freemont Street. Freemont Street gained its most familiar representative trait — excessive neon lights — in the 1940s when hotel and casino owners filled the street with neon signs. Larger than life neon signs that included the Pioneer Club's Vegas Vic and his female counterpart, Sassy Sally, demarcated the Las Vegas downtown skyline, thereafter called "Glitter Gulch."

The iconic status of Glitter Gulch was propagated by its central position in films and television programming made from the 1960s through the mid–1990s. The film and television programs glamorized the downtown area of Las Vegas by encouraging viewers to see it as mythically dangerous and alive. Some key examples include *Viva Las Vegas* (1964), *Diamonds Are Forever* (1971), *Vega$* (television, 1978), *Casino* (1995), and *Con Air* (1997). This broad exposure made the downtown area a popular destination for Las Vegas visitors who wanted to experience what they had seen on the screen.

Technologically transferred emotional ideas about Las Vegas made a visit to Freemont Street a nostalgic event. Through the 1990s people were most notably drawn to the space by the U2 music video, "I Still Haven't Found What I'm Looking For," which features the band wandering the streets of Las Vegas, and finally ending the spectacle on a rooftop in Glitter Gulch. Individuals came to Freemont Street to experience the atmosphere of the music video for themselves. It became a part of their cultural memory of the space. This is evidenced in a posting to a "Rate Las Vegas" blog written on December 12, 2005. The posting by "Charlie" at 6:41 p.m. says: "My memory of Fremont Street is nearly identical to the great U2 video — glittering lights, the Vegas sky, and swarms friendly of people. The way it should be" (RateVegas.com, online).

Today the five blocks that make up Freemont Street are closed to through traffic, and an umbrella of LED space frames called the Freemont Street Experience encompasses the length of the historic street. The seventy million-dollar mediated space was designed by architect Jon Jerde, who also designed the media displays "Metropolis" in New York's Times Square and "City Walk" at Universal Studios in Southern California. The project was collectively funded by a coalition of downtown casino owners and the city of Las Vegas in an attempt to bring patrons back to the downtown area from the Las Vegas Strip. The Strip features not just casinos, but new gambling resorts with more services and more eye-catching lights and events. The downtown consortium's solution to the problem presented by a depressed and declining commercial area was to build a fully realized, gigantic media screen that projects hourly light shows from 6 p.m. until midnight each night.

According to the design specifications for the Freemont Street Experience, the project includes a visual display with a depth of 5 feet, and a curved radius of 44 feet, and a length of 1500 feet, all suspended 90 feet above its audience. Its inner-space frame is composed of 2.1 million computer-controlled lights. Steve Weeks, the assistant division manager with Young Electric Sign Company in Las Vegas and one of the contractors for the project, says: "Not only is the number of bulbs impressive, but their power potential is incredible. If all the lights were turned on at full power simultaneously, the output would equal 7.8 megawatts, or millions of watts, of energy. Each bulb is equal to a single pixel in a television picture tube, and like an LCD pixel, each bulb contains red, blue, green and clear lamps. Combined with 8 shades of dimming, the entire display is capable of producing 65,536 color combinations" (a2zlasvegas. com, online).

In addition to the powerful wattage, the space design specifications also point out the unique scale of the electronic sign by indicating that one-fiftieth of the total space frame is equal to the size of the world's current largest electronic sign. The space needs are so large that projected, animated images are controlled by thirty computers that are stored within the space frame and built into the sixteen 26,000-pound columns that support the vast frame as well as a master computer center that coordinates projected images.

The Freemont Street Experience is clearly a post-nostalgia happening. As individuals walk the street during pre-show hours, the space frame blocks any clear view of Vegas Vic and Sassy Sally. The familiar downtown Las Vegas skyline, which originally signaled a unique openness, is obfuscated. During show hours, the lights of old downtown are shut off so that passers-by can fully experience the new technology. The light shows last ten minutes and project animated caricatures of Vegas Vic and Sassy Sally, as well as other cartoonish images drawn from early eighties music video programming. This is clearly a space in transition. There is no nostalgic demarcation of downtown, no evidence that Freemont Street is alive and vital. Small crowds gather to see the light show and then quickly move through the space to other destinations in Las Vegas. The technological implementation of the Freemont Street Experience acts as a tomb, encasing old Las Vegas with less than familiar lights.

The current effect of this ambitious multimedia installation is to cast the downtown area of Las Vegas as a museum piece. Visitors to the area quickly pick up the cues to that effect and perform the appropriate response — the area is strangely quiet and the spectators quickly and respectfully move through this little interactivity. Attempts to bring interactivity into the equation are made through the actual presence on the street of performers from the video. These entertainers perform before the light show begins, and introduce the video, but they too seem caught in the installation, almost as if behind glass. The scale of the video seems to overwhelm their contribution to the event.

The Freemont Street Experience currently fails to provide its audiences with visual handles for cultural connection. Nevertheless, it is enticing to contemplate the potential for mediated public theatricality in this unique place. It is, after a mediated forum, capable of delivering multiple messages and amenable to constant change.

It would be interesting to see the effect that a truly interactive, cultural, or theatrical message would have. The possibility of live video or the continuous presentation of images or information to engage viewers in the civic dialogue of a mediated culture are things that would be worthy of consideration. No doubt the complexity and expense of producing new video sequences or implementing live video are prohibitive for the stake holders of the attraction, but the possibilities seem tantalizingly close at hand. Rather than settling for a spectacle of lights, those who decide the future of the Freemont Street Experience would do well to look to the theatrical applications of multimedia in an effort to better understand how mediated images and messages can engage audiences in dialogues of interactivity, associative connections, emotional projection, and personal performance.

MEDIA TECHNOLOGY AS AN EXTENSION OF SPACE

Multi-media design is now a prominent part of commercial theatre design strategies. Designs that implement media models into theatrical settings can range from the slide projections like those used in the early work of Ping Chong and Laurie Anderson to the LED screen technology being used by Elaine McCarthy, Jan Hartley, and other projection designers currently working in professional theatres across the United States. When asked about the viability of multi-media projection as a design element for theatrical settings, the Washington, D.C.-based projection designer Michael Clark (*The Elephant Man* and *Hedwig and the Angry Inch*) reminds us that the impetus for projection in the theatre is related to what designers and audiences have become accustomed to: "We receive media in so many different ways: television, the Internet, etc. We are used to multiple screens" (Eddy, Online).

Contemporary technology changes rapidly. Projection technology manufacturers are working steadily to increase their capacity to enhance live entertainment venues. The capacity to enhance production design in live performance is re-envisioned through the growing capacity of technology. Video projections used in contemporary theatre are now a method of communicating messages about character and space to an audience accustomed to media messages.

The visual nature of projected images allows for new explorations of characters within theatrical space and time. For example, Leonard Foglia directed the opera *Dead Man Walking* at the New York City Opera and described one use of projection in his production as an "extension" of what the character sees. Projection designer Elaine McCarthy designed a 13-minute sequence of video photography to accompany an aria sung by the lead character, Sister Mary Prejan. In the sequence, Sister Mary Prejan is preparing to meet death row inmate Mathew Poncelet for the first time. The images convenes the drive of Sister Mary Prejan from her home to the prison in Louisiana where Mathew Poncelet is incarcerated. Leonard Foglia asked the question of the projection designer, "How can I integrate the drive so that we see what she's seeing?" (Johnson, 2).

Elaine McCarthy responded by going to Louisiana and photographing the drive. The black-and-white video images she captured on the trip were then mixed with religious imagery that was interspersed throughout the images of the drive. Through the projected images, the audience was exposed to the character's complete journey — both the physical drive and the emotional passage. They experienced her deep conviction, as it is associated with the religious iconography and contexualized by the reality of the approach to the Louisiana prison.

The source of emotions is transferred, in this case, from the performance of the actor to the technology space. The actor becomes the screen, not for the projected image, but for the projected emotions that are elicited by the images. These emotions are, in effect, performed by the audience and projected onto the actor. This new type of technology-enhanced audience performance through associative perceptions is taught to the audience by everyday interaction with mass media technologies that bring us those constructed narratives of commerce and entertainment. The audience is cued to use those associative perceptions and begins its own performance, again through the medium employed rather than the message itself. It is the medium that gives the audience members license to feel for themselves and project those emotions onto the actor, rather than experiencing the actor's emotions through observation only.

Andrew Lloyd Webber's musical *The Woman in White* employs some of those same techniques but on a much grander scale. All of the physical settings are created through three-dimensional, computer-generated images to create the play's environment. The entire setting consists of one expansive curved white wall and a second smaller white wall on which video projections appear that guide the audience through the environment of the play.

A key to these projections is that the design allows the audience to move through the play's Victorian setting along with the characters. The audience progresses through a multitude of settings, including the English countryside, mansions, casinos, bars, and insane asylums. The production designer, William Dudley, describes the digital experience as "navigable space" in which technology is integral to the audience's investigation of the space and the characters in the space. As the designer and modeler of the three-dimensional space, Andrew Dudley describes a process in which he and his team would compose the high-resolution data: "[The team] would render all the frames, edit the frames to the music, and select a section of each image for each of the projectors" (Lampert-Greaux, online).

Their custom system, the Mesmerist, included twelve media servers, and allowed production designer William Dudley to produce a letterbox image that he split up into four sections. The sections were divided among four projectors and then put together to form one seamless image. This process allowed Dudley to utilize the curved canvases that he projected the images onto, thus creating the "sweeping panoramas" and "sculptural set" (Lampert-Greaux, online) envisioned by the director, Trevor Nunn.

This process of designing a space that can be navigated by an audience is the signature of William Dudley designs. Prior to his work on *The Woman in White*, Dudley had also engineered other three-dimensional computer-aided designs in productions like the 2002 staging of Tom Stoppard's play *The Coast of Utopia*, the Terry Johnson play *Hitchcock Blonde* (2003), and the David Hare play that depicts calamity on the British railways entitled *Permanent Way* (2003). Each used three-dimensional animations mixed with video, and all employed curved screens.

Critics have described the final moment of *The Woman in White* as Dudley's piece de résistance (Lampert-Greaux, online), in which a train crashes out towards the audience. In an interview with Lyndsey Winship, Dudley connects the theatre audience's experience in *The Woman in White* to a famous audience reaction in film history. He says that the three-dimensional designs were so convincing that audience members ducked as a train appeared to be bursting from the stage into the audience:

"[That's] exactly what happened when the Lumiere brothers did their first documentary which showed a train coming out of the cinema.... The audience ran out of the cinema. So I thought to get an audience to duck from a train was very satisfying" (Winship 26).

Dudley's aspirations for his design are clearly rooted in the cinematic traditions of a period drama, with its sweeping exteriors, epic scale, and kaleidoscoping transitions from baronial interiors to sunlit cornfields. Michael Billington's review in the *Guardian* describes the effect of the projections as reminiscent of early cinerama. Ben Brantley's review of the production for the *New York Times* hits precisely on where Dudley has misunderstood how audiences read cinematic images in a theatrical production: "The show is all big generic set pieces — of discovery and catastrophe and confrontation — that fail to stir because they seem only to further the plot, not define the characters" (online).

What was missing in the production for *The Woman in White* was an interactive transaction of meaning from the audience to the performances. There was no opportunity for the audience members to gather emotional or cultural information from the projected images, which left them with no opportunity to "perform" their own emotions. This deprived the performers of a true connection to the audience, because the audience-performer relationship was rooted in observation rather than experience. In essence, the production lacked a connection to the audience because the audience wasn't given the cues to extract emotion from the images, and therefore the audience was incapable of projecting emotional or cultural reality back onto the performers. Brantley seems to recognize this as well when he states in his review: "It's not surprising that the performers have little chance of establishing personalities beyond that of decorative chess figurines" (online).

Those who staged *The Woman in White* enthusiastically embraced technology's role as a facilitator of quick and interesting transitions of place and time. However, their failure to use the signifying or communicative nature of technology alienated the audience because its effect was to exclude them. Technology in our culture means communication and interactivity. The danger of using mediated images in theatrical productions is that it cues the audience members of our culture to very specific reactions because of the habits of information gathering, processing, and projecting that are established through everyday interactions with technology. When cues for interactivity with mediated images are not followed with opportunities to make connections through associative perception, the audience is left strangely disconnected and uncomfortable.

MEDIA TECHNOLOGY AS DEFINER OF SPACE AND CHARACTER

In contrast to *The Woman in White*, the 1995 revival of the 1961 musical *How to Succeed in Business Without Really Trying* seemed to connect with its audiences without really trying. This was accomplished by providing the audience with numerous opportunities to make those connections through intellectual associations often cued through mediated images. Rather than reinventing or updating the concept of the play, the entire production seemed to be focused on making overt links to the original production, beginning with the venue; both the original run of the show and the revival were housed in the same New York theatre space on Forty-sixth Street.

The first run, which began in 1961, ran for 1415 performances. Frank Loesser's Pulitzer Prize winning show starred Robert Morse and Rudy Vallee, and was a huge commercial success, making a profit of $470,000 on the original investment of $400,000. It was also a critical success, winning both the Tony and the Outer Critic's Circle Awards in the Best Musical category. The successful 1995 revival of *How to Succeed in Business Without Really Trying* starred Mathew Broderick and ran for a year in the same theatre (the Richard Rogers Theatre, formerly the Forty-Sixth Street Theatre). That production was nominated for a Tony Award for Best Revival.

The play follows Pierpont Finch, a smart young window washer who buys the book *How To Succeed In Business*. Following the book's advice he begins work at the multinational "World Wide Wicket Company." Starting from the mailroom he rises to vice-president in charge of advertising using underhanded means; he makes sure that each person above him either gets fired or moved to another section of the company.

Comparing still photographs and written reviews of the original production with the 1995 revival, it is obvious that there has been one large change in the re-staging of the play — technology. While the script, props, and costumes are nearly the same in both productions, the setting is very different. The 1960s art deco set design, which provided a clever cartoonish atmosphere for the setting in the original production, has been re-envisioned as technological space. The emphasis on technology in design is evident from the first moments of the play when the audience is introduced to an enormous video backdrop.

The projection designers, Linda Batwing and Robin Silvestre, utilize LED video screens to animate the physical environment of the office space.

For example, as the play opens the LED screens aid the audience in transitioning from the outside of the large office building to the inside of the fast-paced World Wide Wicket building. The screens help us to understand the staged space.

Motion video on the LED screens help the audience to transition through various parts of the building. Video images serve as windows, elevators, and the company logo as well as a number of other shapes that help the audience understand the structure and make-up of the workspace the characters inhabit. The images alter the space so that audiences experience inherent differences in each unique space of the World Wide Wicket building. In one example the World Wide Wicket insignia appears on office tower windows. The logo looms high above the desks, defining the focus of the office setting. Minutes later a large animated airplane flies past the window, giving the space dimension and context. Then the World Wide Wicket sign is replaced by an abstract sign, which the audience can guess at and eventually learns is a piece of mail. That piece of mail further divides to become many pieces of mail in the mailroom.

Projections also present us with visual knowledge of the characters. Images present us with information about significant character stereotypes or personality traits. For example, when the chief executive officer's mistress, Heddy La Rue, enters the World Wide Wicket corporation building for the first time, animated flames consume the corporate insignia, letting the audience know what her presence could do to the company at large.

Characters' thoughts and feeling are also revealed through messages conveyed in the technology space. Animated and still images let us know what characters are thinking and feeling. In one example, J. Pierpont Finch's love interest, Rosemary Wells, sings "Happy to Keep His Dinner Warm." Animated images propel the audience from the city scene to a suburban house with a white picket fence. As the character sings about her dream of living in a small home in New Rochelle, the animations allow the audience to see the details of the fantasy home she imagines. As Rosemary ends the song, there is a close-up of the doorknocker, and then a cutaway to the original cityscape. This careful cut helps the audience realize the difference between Rosemary's imagination and the office space. The reprise of this song includes images that represent J. Pierpont Finch's ambition to progress through the company. The incongruity of the images is apparent, and the competing images indicate a conflict in the plot. They also help the audience to see the internal perspectives of each character as they fall in love, thus allowing the audiences to "perform" the internal conflict and project it on to actors.

This type of opportunity for interactivity with the audience demonstrates a savvy understanding of how messages in a mediated culture are delivered. While the artistic ambitions of *How to Succeed in Business Without Really Trying* were modest in comparison to other Broadway shows (considerably more modest than the ambitions of *The Women in White*), those who staged it clearly demonstrated a sophistication in their ability to communicate using multimedia messages and cues. Such sophistication is becoming increasingly commonplace in theatrical circles. Often that sophistication goes beyond demonstrating an understanding of the language of mass-media culture. The Blue Man Group, in particular, chooses to comment on mass-media culture.

MEDIA TECHNOLOGY AND THE EXPLORATION OF NEW THEATRICAL SPACE

The Blue Man Group is a team of creative artists who build and perform art installations which incorporate theatre, visual art, popular culture, and media. The group's originators (Chris Wink, Phil Stanton, and Matt Goldman) began performing in the streets and performance art venues in New York's East Village in the latter part of the 1980s. Working in combination with experimental video producer Caryl Glaab, they developed their first show, which was a combination of their street performances and instillations from other art venues at the small New York experimental space La MaMa. The show gained recognition and eventually moved on to other, larger New York City venues. They also began to attract widespread critical and popular acclaim. The show now performs in large, resident productions in New York, Boston, Chicago, Las Vegas, and Berlin.

The show combines sketch comedy, music, and video installations in a one hour and forty-five minute exploration of connection — between humans and other humans, between humans and their natural environment, and between humans and technology. The performance of each show features three bald blue men and a rock band and is designed to be interactive with the audience. In an interview with Dinah Toltan, Blue Man Group collaborator and video creator Caryl Glaab said the aim of the performance team is to create a collaborative, interactive relationship between the performers and the audience: "The fundamental goal of the performance is to create a tribal experience with the audience, asking the audience to take off their masks and revel in a world that's designed not to encourage that kind of thing.... [The show is] a clownish, comedic performance, with pop culture following the vaudeville tradition of letting the audience in on the joke before it happens" (Toltan, online).

The Blue Man Group accomplishes their intent through media-driven conversations with the audience. These conversations are designed to make each member of the audience think, feel, and respond verbally and physically throughout the show. Audiences fully participate in the antics of the performers, even acting alongside them throughout the performance experience. Audience members near the stage wear plastic ponchos that protect them from objects and substances that regularly fly from the stage. Individual audience members also work with the Blue Men, acting as performers through various aspects of the show. For instance, in some shows the audience chants the words to a rap written by the pop-rap artist Eminem, which are projected and scrolled in electronic super titles above the stage. In other portions of the show, the audience works together with each other and the stage performers to propel masses of white crepe paper towards the front of the stage.

Interactivity and connection are hallmarks of the Blue Man Group performance, but it is their use of media that solidifies these themes for the audience. Technology aids in establishing and sustaining these themes in every aspect of the production. From lobby displays to the performance inside the theatre, digital media is central to conveying the message intended by the group.

In the Toronto performance venue, for example, the lobby space acts as a mediated "portal" into the stage presentation that will come. The lobby introduces the audience to the theme of interactivity and connection even before the performance begins. The lobby is filled with a video art installation that includes thirty-eight plasma screens, each depicting the color, movement, and water imagery prominent in the show. Together the plasma screens create an interconnected movement. Thirty-two of the smaller screens are placed on the ceiling and six larger screens act as the base of the installation. Dinah Toltan describes purpose of these screens as introducing "information flow and interconnectedness" (online).

The combined placement of the screens and arrangement of the content projected on the screens — colorful abstract expressions interlaced with images of the Blue Man — create the familiar cause and effect theme that permeates every Blue Man Group performance. The content on one screen acts in a causal fashion, seeming to affect what happens on the next screen. This creates a visual display that prepares audience members for the coming show by asserting the importance of flow and action-reaction in art and nature.

Media is also a central component in the Blue Man Group's production staged in Las Vegas. This venue at the Venetian Casino Resort is the largest of the Blue Man Group endeavors, a house that seats 1760 patrons. The stage in this venue is filled with projection screens, including two full color ribbon board screens that engage the audience in a conversation at the beginning of the show. There is also a 15' by 8' LED screen that flies in and out above center stage.

Cameras also play a large role in the Blue Man Group's production. In the Las Vegas production, there are two cameras that function on stage and in the audience for portions of the show, as well as two smaller cameras, one of which is small enough to provide video during the course of the show of the plunge into an audience member's esophagus. Another remote-controlled camera provides a live feed of a variety of audience members from the balcony area. The camera records movements and reactions to the Blue Man Group. These are usually presented live on the screen above center stage. The screens also display animated sequences, words, and prepared video segments. Live video of audience reactions and interactions and off-stage activity are also presented on the screens throughout the show.

The use of cameras and video projections extends the theme of connectivity by allowing the audience to access the theatre space beyond the actual stage. The images produced by the live feeds from the cameras explore the audience space and the backstage space. The audience is aware of their whole environment, and the whole environment becomes a part of the performing space.

The cameras and the projections also seem to explore the nature of staged reality. Two of the show's sequences stand out in terms of the staged reality. In an initial sequence, latecomers are introduced to the entire audience through the camera. A member of the Blue Man team films them entering the auditorium using a camera. The camera follows the individuals to their seats as they are mocked by a member of the Blue Man Group for their tardiness in entering the theatre. Live-feed video images of these individuals are projected onto the large central screen so that we can see their embarrassment at being late. Close-ups are used so we can see the acute anxiety of the people being filmed. The audience member is left to wonder if this event is premeditated or staged in some way — are the latecomers performers, or are they drawn unaware into the action of the performance?

The ambiguity of what is staged versus what is real is enhanced and even extended through the use of the camera. The visual record of the experience is displayed live and provides the audience with an intimate connection to the two latecomers. If this is not staged but a real event, we feel embarrassed for them, even with them because they have been on public display. They are no longer audience members but have become participants. The visible use and placement of cameras is a good indication that any member of the audience could be forced to participate at any time.

In the second sequence, called "The Diner," four actors, including the Blue Men and one audience member, sit in a diner eating Captain Crunch cereal. The actors (including the audience member) perform a scenario in which they eat together. A camera is placed in front of the action and their images are simultaneously displayed on the large screen directly over the physical action. Audience members look back and forth between the video projection and the live action. The video camera works as an amplifier of the staged action. Each theatrical gesture performed for the audience becomes exaggerated by the proximity of the camera and the close-ups in the projected image.

The Blue Man Group also plays with the established centrality of on-stage theatre space. Traditionally theatre performance venues are driven by what happens on stage. In a key performance sequence the Blue Man Group contradicts the established use of theatrical space by leaving the large stage empty while they display video images of what is happening off stage. As part of the bit, the Blue Men take an audience member from the balcony. They dress him from head to toe in a protective plastic suit, and then whisk him through the audience into an off-stage area. All of the action is followed closely by a camera crew. Almost immediately the audience sees projected images of an individual whom we suppose to be the same man who was taken from the audience. He is being splashed with blue paint and hoisted onto a swinging rope. He is then propelled towards a canvas, leaving a large, blue streak on the canvas and creating an art object of sorts.

In this example, the off-stage projection becomes the focus of the audience's gaze, while the theatrical space remains empty. The displayed image replaces traditional space and takes the audience beyond the confines of the proscenium arch of the stage and into an alternate space where the performance continues. The camera and the screen produce, in a sense, a new theatrical space that was not available through traditional means of staging.

The stage show also introduces an ambiguity between what is real and what is projected. In a sequence entitled "The Wild West," the Blue

Man Group explores the indistinct physical boundaries between real, or live-space, and technology space. The scene begins with a fully lit stage space, which is filled with theatrical lighting and props. As the scene progresses, an electric billboard placed center stage becomes a video display space. At a certain point it becomes unclear whether the Blue Men are a video image or performing live. The ambiguity in this moment is one of many where the performance space seems to be simultaneously live and displayed through technology. This is reinforced in one instance by an animation of a bird that seems to be flying as part of a projected sequence, but then flies out of the display and is discovered to be quite present and tangible.

Such ambiguity is often the aim of many of the uses for technology in the theatre. The challenge continues to be to "make it real." The response to that challenge should be to recognize that the audience's vocabulary for reality has been expanded through intimate interaction and experience with technology. It must also be remembered that audiences are as likely to reject imitations of reality as they ever have been in history. Technology can truly aid the theatre in its quest "to make it real" by engaging audiences in a dialogue rooted in a cultural reality. Technology has the capacity to cue audiences to engage in personal performances of emotion. Technology can connect audiences to theatrical messages through their associative perceptions. More important, technology can be employed to invoke the necessary cultural signifiers to give theatrical works significance.

In an era of information overload, associations or intellectual connections increasingly shade theatre audiences' comprehension of theatrical messages. For example, the successful 1996 revival of the musical *Chicago*—and its subsequent distribution through mass media promotion, touring companies, film, Internet information, and a long presence on stages in New York and London—has created widespread familiarity with the style, choreography, and tone generated by director Walter Bobbie, choreographer Ann Reinking, and designers John Lee Beatty and William Ivey Long. Even people who have never seen the production on stage or the film come to the work with intellectual connections — they associate the play with black fishnet stockings; high heels; a shadowy, noir atmosphere; and a unique style of movement and dance. They also come prepared to compare live performances against their knowledge of celebrity performance clips that have circulated via mass media for nearly a decade.

It is not necessary for a show to have been in existence for ten years for an audience to generate such a laundry list of intellectual connections. In an atmosphere of twenty-four hour news, all on a one-hour news cycle, and instant access to information, it is the connections that we make between bits of information that drives our interest through repetitious news and entertainment. It is our associative perception that makes information new when we see something on the morning TV show, hear it again on the radio as we drive to work, read it again from a web page at work, and find it again in conversation with acquaintances at lunch.

To the mind of today's audiences, a lack of intellectual connections to a cultural or artistic work signifies triviality. In short, if it doesn't fit... it is inconsequential. Perhaps it is our collective unease with disconnectedness that dooms much of the truly original work of theatre to a struggle for existence in the margins. Conversely, perhaps it is our collectively learned dependence on connectedness that leads to the continued success of revivals (such as *Chicago*), stage adaptations of films (such as *Spamalot*), and works that are reinventions of other works (such as *Wicked*).

Connectedness is the handle that audiences use to grasp performative experiences in our culture. We experience our physical realities through our associative perceptions. The lexicon for those associations increasingly comes from virtual experiences mediated through technology rather than our physical experiences. This is the natural result of our increased interaction with technology, which accelerates our potential to gather information from those mediated sources. This information forms our lexicon of ideas, from which we form meaning through continuous association. Our perceptions then are built with those associations. Our sense of reality, in turn, stems from these associative perceptions.

In these circumstances, physical reality becomes more than the immediate measurement of our senses. The added dimensions to the physical come from our associative perceptions. In this way, the virtual becomes tangible — with perceptions being a crucial component to our physical reality. Reality, therefore, has been altered for us by technology. Correspondingly, the presentation of reality in the contemporary theatre has to be presented differently from how it was presented in the past, whether or not technology is employed in that presentation. This is necessary, not because the process of theatrical communication has changed but because our lexicon of associative perceptions has been exponentially enhanced through mediated messages. Reality (in its complete sense, and cultural reality in particular) must be achieved on the stage today through association, rather than through imitation, as it has been in the past.

FOUR

Nostalgia as Theatrical Presence and Commodity

The theatre that we are most familiar with is a commodified theatre where producers market a product to an audience that values the experience enough to make the effort to come and pay the price of admission. The question then is, what is it that the audience values? For Stephen Sondheim the answer is quite clear:

> You have two kinds of shows on Broadway — revivals and the same kind of musicals over and over again, all spectacles. You get your tickets for *The Lion King* a year in advance, and essentially a family comes as if to a picnic, and they pass on to their children the idea that that's what the theater is — a spectacular musical you see once a year, a stage version of a movie. It has nothing to do with theater at all. It has to do with seeing what is familiar. We live in a recycled culture.... I don't think the theatre will die per se, but it's never going to be what it was. You can't bring it back. It's gone. It's a tourist attraction [Rich 40].

Sondheim's reference to a "recycled culture" as a "tourist attraction" hints at nostalgia as an engine of commerce for theater producers. Sondheim himself seems to be a bit nostalgic for 1962 when he brought *A Funny Thing Happened on the Way to the Forum* to the Broadway stage for under $500,000. In today's market, even a show like *Rent*— which required virtually no set and featured costumes that could all be purchased at thrift stores — required a budget of $3,000,000 or more. For such budgets and payrolls to be met in theatre houses of 2000 seats, producers must utilize every available resource to draw an audience. More and more, the resource they rely upon — the commodity they chose to sell — is nostalgia.

EARLY PRODUCERS AS IMPRESARIOS

Until the 1880s American theatres were owned and operated by artists who formed their own companies and situated themselves and family members as the stars of the theatrical company they produced. In the last part of the nineteenth century the role of the American theatre manager was further developed in the careers of Augustin Daly, David Belasco, and Charles Frohman.

Charles Frohman in particular was less concerned about the emotional and aesthetic appeal of theatrical presentation than he was with the business aspects of running a financially solvent company. His success was built on long running theatrical shows and star-power. Frohman was known for his ability to understand and tap into plays that appealed to general American audiences. Because of his commercial accomplishments, Charles Frohman and his brother Daniel were able to build the Empire Theatre Company, which was widely regarded as the central model for theatre producing companies of the late nineteenth century. The company owned six legitimate theatres on Broadway and many more across the United States. According to the *History of North American Theatre,* the Frohmans influenced the tastes and theatrical practices of a generation. The company produced "as many as twelve productions annually and had thousands of employees, including several hundred actors" (Londrè, 182).

The outline of the impresario producer established by Frohman and his contemporaries has been a model used by theatrical producers throughout the twentieth century. The financial success of any entertainment entity such as this was in some ways tied to each company's history of prominent venues, productions, and stars, and their methods of business surrounding theatrical production were built on traditional strategies that relied primarily on one revenue stream — the box office. Three eminent, family owned organizations (the Shubert Organization [established in 1902], The Nederlander Corporation [established in 1922] and Jujamcyn Theaters [established 1960]) have thrived in this model. These three organizations controlled theatre spaces and theatre business on Broadway for most of the twentieth century, and remain a force today. The Shubert

Organization is still privately held and currently owns or manages seventeen venues on Broadway, one Off-Broadway, and one theater each in Washington, D.C., Boston, and Philadelphia. The Nederlander Corporation controls more that thirty live entertainment venues in the United States and the United Kingdom. Jujamcyn Theatres is the third largest organization with six theatre venues that include the historic venues of the Winter Garden Theatre and the Lyceum Theatre. Each company has operated privately throughout most of the twentieth century and each has a history of successful business practice.

MEDIA CONGLOMERATES AND CULTURAL SHIFT IN BROADWAY PRODUCTION

American theatre history will probably mark 1994 as a pivotal year for how Broadway theatre is produced and marketed. The show that made this lasting impact won no major awards that year, featured no significant star or celebrity, and was dismissed by most critics as fluff and of no consequence. The show was *Beauty and the Beast*, the first Broadway endeavor by Walt Disney Productions. Disney capitalized on a theatre environment that was more than a decade in the making — an environment of name-branding, mass-marketing, mass-audiences, and investment in the replicable rather than the unique.

The dawn of this environment can probably be traced to the early 1970s when Bob Fosse sought to jump start sagging ticket sales for *Pippin*. Fosse's solution was to use a previously untapped method of Broadway promotion — a television ad. Fosse's genius was his understanding of both the theatrical and broadcast notions of presentation, and he knew that the type of dancing that would look best on television didn't exist in the show. He remedied this by creating a new dance number specifically for the commercial. The commercial was successful enough to prolong the run of *Pippin* for several years. More than that, the ad created a type of *Pippin* brand name where the audiences' expectations for their theatrical experience were more connected to their experiences with the television ad than with the familiarity they might have of a star whose name appears above the title. Those expectations were so keyed to the television ad that the dance number initially created for the TV spot was eventually added to the stage production (Adler, 193). Similar television ad campaigns followed for *Grease, Shenandoah*, and *A Chorus Line*. The commercial used for *Shenandoah* featured footage that was shot in the countryside rather than the theater, and was a portent of the new expectations of mediated reality that theatre audiences would begin to bring to the Broadway venues.

The entire production of *A Chorus Line* was another indication of things to come. *A Chorus Line* celebrated "Broadway" as its own name-brand and questioned the very necessity of stars. It reveled in the idea that the every-man, the supporting player, was worthy of momentary celebration through association with the star, while the name-brand (in this case, "Broadway") was cast as that star, just as it is in any TV ad for Pillsbury, Budweiser, Pepsi, or any other product. This type of name-branding was later employed by Cameron Mackintosh in the promotion of *Cats, Le Misérables,* and *Phantom of the Opera.* All of these box office titans of the 1980s used branding as an effective marketing strategy, and all of them reached a status of international awareness. None of them promoted stars, rather they built their brand-name around things that the producers owned and could readily duplicate in multiple venues and touring productions; theatrical designs, orchestrations, and the characters created more through costumes than through the personality of the performer.

This was precisely the type of environment that the Disney Corporation had decades of experience with even before their venture onto Broadway in 1994. Disney theme parks had long benefited from entire armies of Cinderellas and Snow Whites as they delighted crowds by simply looking the part. When *Beauty and the Beast* opened on Broadway, critics were quick to recognize the theme-park-like presence of the new show with its mountains of merchandising and promotional tie-ins to travel packages and hotel stays. They universally decried the "new Disneyland" in mid-town Manhattan. The Disney corporation never shrank from proudly wearing its theme-park label, and by 2000 it was actively selling a three show package as "Disney on Broadway."

From the very beginning, Disney's financial strategy was not one of theatrical production — defined as a singular experience at a specific place and time. What Disney was interested in was mass-production of a referential event that could be replicated in multiple languages and multiple international venues. They also sought out multiple revenue streams with merchandising and cross promotion to its theme parks and other products. As part of the promotion of *Beauty and the Beast,* producer Robert McTyre said: "We are bringing a new way of thinking to the theatre, both creatively and business-wise. On the creative end, the show is a very collaborative effort, with many more people involved and contributing than usual. And, on the business side, we bring financial discipline" (Lassell 28).

This financial discipline in practice was not so much about holding down costs as it was about maximizing the return on their investment. This was demonstrated with Disney's second show to hit the Great White Way in 1997. *The Lion King* was another replicable, costume cavalcade, this time with puppets and elaborate head dresses. As of this writing, almost ten years later, there are fifteen active productions of *The Lion King* including Broadway and international productions in such countries as Germany, Japan, the Netherlands, and the United Kingdom. Writing for the *New York Times*, Jesse McKinley comments,

> With a mix of big-name talent, striking visuals and deep pockets, Disney was one of the most consistently winning producers on Broadway during the 1990's. It was also, not surprisingly, the prime target for traditionalists decrying corporatization. For them, the company is a force bent on turning the Great White Way into a slick, generic spectacle much like, well, Disneyland.... [B]eyond its knack for gobbling up audiences, Disney has presented many old-time Broadway producers with tough new competition for everything from press attention to Tony Awards to theaters themselves. The ability to develop many shows simultaneously is just one of the luxuries available to Disney, a company that also owns a stockpile of known material, large budgets, and ample cross-marketing opportunities — it owns, for example, ABC and Miramax, which have also invested in and produced Broadway shows [*Times*, online].

The new mediated theatre business caters to a tourist-consumer industry that has usurped the elite, literary-conscious theatre audiences of the mid-twentieth century. Profit from a corporately produced musical often follows the old axiom of spending money to make money. Not only did the Disney Corporation purchase and renovate the New Amsterdam Theatre (home of the *Ziegfeld Follies* until 1931), they also purchased the adjoining property in order to build a retail space to recoup much of that cost through merchandising. These venues sit alongside other Disney properties such as the ABC Times Square Studios and the ESPN store and restaurant, which are visible centers of commercial interaction.

This massive presence by Disney in New York's Times Square signals a clear investment strategy in nostalgia as a commodity. Steve Nelson describes this focus using the Disney Development of 42nd Street as an example. He says, "[The] shift from commercial development to street-level entertainment zone provides the perfect climate for Disney's version of 42nd Street: a formerly indigenous theatrical district transformed into a romantically idealized tourist version of its former self. The enterprise fit perfectly with Disney's usual practice of taking architecture, costumes, and other trappings of different eras and cultures and melding them into theme park and movie entertainments that are safe and accessible, yet still enticing to a mass audience" (83).

The Disney Corporation and other media conglomerates active in Broadway's Times Square emphasize a shift in promotion that highlights the interconnectedness between retail space, media spaces, and theatrical spaces in order to recoup their investment. With the average costs of mounting a Broadway musical having risen to eight million dollars, publicly traded corporations have a distinct advantage in scaling that initial economic mountain with ready capital at hand, access to multiple revenue streams, and risk spread broadly among shareholders.

Currently eight major Hollywood production companies, all of which are part of publicly traded and corporately managed entities, have attached themselves to the legitimate stage. Dreamworks, MGM, Universal, Warner Bros. among others (see Appendix A for more details) are producing Broadway musicals. Gordon Cox describes what brings Hollywood studios to Broadway:

> Studios are not enamored of the theatre because they want to secure film rights. And it is not because they're trying to develop scripts in front of an audience. And they're not expecting a Broadway windfall: A boffo week at a Broadway venue ($1 million) would be an embarrassment by Hollywood box office standards.... The studios are stage-struck for the same reason they are pushing for greater control of ancillary markets around the globe: They recognize that theatrical box office is no longer their primary engine of growth. For the [Hollywood] majors, Broadway represents opportunities similar to DVDs, remakes, sequels and videogames; Legit can extend a studio's brand and exploit its library [Cox, online].

The library of material that Cox refers to is yet another revenue stream that the Disney Corporation seeks to exploit through the eminent Music Theatre International catalog. MTI makes scripts available for community, regional, and educational theatre. New to their catalog is Disney's Musical Collections, a series of plays that are corporately crafted. The Disney film theatrical adaptations include: *Cinderella Kids, Jungle Book Kids, 101 Dalmatians Kids*, and *Aladdin Junior*. Each script is drawn from the corresponding Disney movie. They are shorter pieces for children's theatre, and they extend the Disney theatrical brand beyond New York. In this sense the media conglomerate is educating its future audience by expanding its brand name beyond entertainment venues and into schools and communities. Children no longer just watch *Cinderella* or *Aladdin*, they become the characters in these plays, a part of the narrative projected by the Disney Corporation that is sold to adults through DVDs, television programming, theme park admissions, and so on. In this manner Disney's corporate visibility and theatre name brand extends far beyond Broadway. Maurya Wickstrom depicts the cultural moment, saying:

> In a globalized market, characterized by transnational competition and potentially worldwide reach, the [theatre] industry can no longer rely on old techniques of displaying goods as objects for purchase. It is not enough to encourage consumers to have commodities; they must be compelled to become them. By creating environments and narratives through which spectators/consumers are interpellated into fictions produced by and marketed in both shows and stores, entertainment and retail based corporations allow bodies to inhabit commodities and so suggest that commodities, in turn, can be brought to life [287].

BORROWING FROM THE MEDIA CONGLOMERATES

The old guard of Broadway production and investment has taken note of these new juggernauts of corporate capitalization. The theatre impresario production model — in which one individual or one producing entity is responsible for business affairs, contracting artists, and commissioning new works — has limited access to ancillary revenue streams. Theatre producers of this ilk are therefore destined to struggle in an industry that has been invaded by media conglomerates like Clear Channel Communications, Disney Corporation, and others. Such producers are eagerly attaching themselves to these corporate deep pockets simply to remain in existence.

With the rising costs of theatre maintenance, promotion, labor, and other expenses associated with production, Broadway's private theatrical producers have begun to realize that it is vital to the health of their organizations to embody the messages, narratives, and business practices of media in order to compete with the corporations. Many producing organizations have joined forces with the American League of Theatres and Producers to investigate how they might embrace methods used by media corporations, and how they might consider business relationships with the conglomerates that could be a vital content resource and financial support for future productions. Jed Berstein of the League of American Theatres and Producers notes, "The days when you can say 'I'll never work with a corporation' are over" (Cox, online).

Both the Shubert Organization and the Nederlander Organization have co-produced with or rented theatrical spaces to Hollywood giants. The Shubert Organization experienced great success in 2005 by collaborating with MGM theatricals to produce the Broadway version of the film *Dirty Rotten Scoundrels*. They also produced the Tony-award winning *Spamalot* (another movie to musical example) with the media conglomerate Clear Channel Communications as well as *The Color Purple* with a host of media personalities led by Oprah Winfrey and including Quincy Jones and Bob and Harvey Weinstein. The Nederlander Organization has expanded their production offerings by co-producing, among many other examples, the critical and popular movie-to-musical subject *Hairspray* (2002) with Clear Channel Communications, and they are slated to co-produce and house Disney's *Tarzan* in one of their theatres despite the Disney Corporation's refusal to participate in the League of American Theatres and Producers, the entity that acts as the negotiator for most producing contracts on Broadway.

The new corporate visibility for theatrical producers also extends beyond theatre venues and productions to attention-getting promotional websites that link producers, potential producers, and consumer via the web. The American League of Theatres and Producers, the trade association for North American commercial theatre, hosts Live Broadway.com, a website that provides marketing information and statistical data related to New York theatre. The website presents a healthy picture of Broadway theatres through weekly box office grosses and season by season statistical information of playing weeks and productions. It also includes information about theatrical spaces, industry and theatre community news, and financial and research reports that explore topics such as the demographics of the Broadway audience, Broadway's economic contribution to New York City, and technical specifications for Broadway's major theatres. In addition to the economic reports, the league hosts a secondary fan website as well as connections to Telecharge, which is an Internet ticketing outlet that is owned by the Shubert Organization. According to the league, "the use of the Internet to purchase tickets has quadrupled in the last five years, from 7% to 29%" (Demographics, online).

Fully acknowledging the transition from the era of independent theatre producers to an era in which the financial resources of a corporate America is necessary to remain solvent, the league also seeks to copy the conglomerate model of business scaffolding. In an effort to spread financial burden and risk away from a small number of investors, the league trains a large population of financiers through a variety of yearly education programs. The league provides corporate training in the new methods of theatrical producing in its Commercial Theatre Institute. Through the institute the League of Theatres and Producers and the Theatre Development Fund provide yearly training and development of apprentice producers in intensive seminars held each spring that are open to the public; they also host a more comprehensive fourteen-week instructional seminar that is open to a small group of theatre professionals who are selected through application to the program.

In addition to the Commercial Theatre Institute, the league sponsors a Producer Development Program that encourages the expansion of profit-making industry professionals. According to the league's promotional materials:

> Though not a League membership category, [the program] offers many of the important networking and career development opportunities available to full voting and associate league members only. Participants in the Producer Development Program enjoy the following benefits:
>
> • The opportunity to attend selected sessions of the league's annual spring road conference at a discounted rate
> • The opportunity to attend marketing and group sales forums with professionals from venues around the country
> • Access to the league's research department data on the web
> • A special bulletin board on the league's website
> • The opportunity to tell other participants about readings and developmental productions via an e-mail distribution list
> • Invitations to the New Producers Alliance seminars and networking events
> • Evening seminars in labor and marketing designed specifically for this program
> • League membership contact information
> • NYC hotel discounts [League, online].

The last twenty years have demonstrated significant shifts in the demographics of the traditional Broadway audience away from the native New Yorkers and toward the out-of-towners. A new emphasis on capturing tourism dollars has led to higher attendance at Broadway theatres, larger grosses at the theatre box office, and an increased number of new productions and playing weeks per year. The following table extracted from the Season by Season Statistical Summary of Broadway Shows in New York (Broadway Season, online) demonstrates the growth in attendance and grosses over a twenty-year period:

Season	Gross (by millions)	Attendance (by millions)	Playing Weeks	New Productions
1984–1985	$209	7.34	1078	33
1994–1995	$406	9.04	1120	32
2004–2005	$769	11.53	1494	39

According to statistics form *Broadway's Economic Contribution to New York City 2004–2005* (a research report developed by the League of American Theatres and Producers), Broadway contributed 4.8 billion dollars to the New York economy in 2004–2005. Visitors' ancillary spending accounted for 3.06 billion dollars of revenue (online).

Nostalgia for an idealized New York City and an idealized theater experience continues to be a major draw for these visitors. Technology and the media companies who profit form mass communication have facilitated this nostalgia by creating a global familiarity and consciousness of Broadway. The Internet Broadway Database mirrors the structure and content of its media counterpart, the Internet Movie Database. The site allows visitors to make their own connections between producers, theatres, performers, and production teams. They can read information about Broadway theatre productions and performances from the past and the present and also get updates and previews on upcoming Broadway shows. This site allows visitors to connect with the theatre community even though they may be far distant from the New York City venues. The relationships of constructed familiarity that mass audiences have to Broadway shows are much the same as those they have with television programs and movies. What Broadway has that is distinct from broadcast media and film distribution is a connection to a single location. Purposeful recognition of this separation of Broadway and its primary audience fuels an evocative connection leading virtually all of the major producers to feature nostalgia as theatre's principal attraction.

THE PLACE OF NOSTALGIA IN OUR CULTURE

In a nostalgia-saturated world typified by blockbuster film sequels, the commercial theatre industry can apparently not sustain an audience large enough to pay its bills. It is no longer enough to present quality theatre in the traditional sense — theatre must compete as a mass-media form. A primary strategy is to present proven Hollywood narratives and re-create film environments on the stage. In doing so the theatre industry asserts itself as a new home of the Hollywood film remake. This attempt by corporate theatre to exchange traditional theatrical conventions for the visual content of film demonstrates the currency that mass media and marketing have in the contemporary economy. The re-shaping of theatrical texts, characters, and scenic environments to meet the expectations of that mediatized market demonstrates a new commercial theatrical practice, which breaks with theatre-specific traditions regularly associated with theatre's unique human presence. This practice replaces that original animate presence with images reproduced from the screen, or to paraphrase Guy Debord, an image that has become the final form of commodity reification (32). The result of this remaking of film into theatre is the re-shaping of traditional theatrical practice into a pastiche of the media culture.* This pastiche, or imitation, is generated through motives of profit and marketed through elements of nostalgia.

Certainly the overwhelming response to Mel Brooks's *The Producers* shows that the trend of big budget nostalgic promotion is now, and will continue to be, the staple of corporate theatre investment and marketing strategies: the value of nostalgia as a commodity has been firmly established. *The Producers'* use of the commercially successful and critically acclaimed original film text is noteworthy because of the show's purposeful use of nostalgic connections to create an aesthetic link between the Broadway production and the Mel Brooks 1968 film of the same name.

The Producers production team's specific connections to the film industry also contributed to the creative success of the musical's remake. Boasting $13 million in advance sales, *The Producers* was a financial success before it opened in April 2001. The symbiosis between the filmed version and the musical remake is consistently showcased in the production team's comments on *The Producers* and critical commentary surrounding the work. Richard Zoglin of *Time* magazine describes the pre-performance success of the show as a "kind of rapturous buzz" (*Time*, 16 April 2002), created by simple name recognition of the Mel Brooks's cult film, Hollywood star power (both stars, Nathan Lane and Matthew Broderick, have successful film, television, and theatre careers), and media savvy backers (David Geffen of the media conglomerate Dreamworks SKG initiated the project, and Bob and Harvey Weinstein of Miramax media distribution served as producers for the musical).

Nostalgic references to the film also abound in the production team's discussions of the musical. For example, in an interview with *Talk* magazine Matthew Broderick describes his desire to pay tribute to Gene Wilder's film performance of the character Leo Bloom in his own stage portrayal of that character. He says, "I just try to imitate Gene Wilder as closely as I possibly can, but it is more of a tribute than a thievery" (Brooks and Meehan 59). Robin Wagner, the show designer, also describes the impor-

*I am using Fredric Jameson's definition of pastiche: "Pastiche is ... the imitation of a peculiar or unique, idiosyncratic style, the wearing of a linguistic mask.... It is the neutral practice of mimicry" (17).

tance of the original filmed text to the production concept: "How do you live up to the movie has always been the question on this show" (Brooks and Meehan 59). But it is Tom Meehan's description of the development of the musical's book from the 1968 screenplay that sheds light on how nostalgia might work in both the aesthetic reinvention of the film text and eventually as a marketing strategy. He describes the translation of *The Producers* from screen to the stage as "disassembling the works of a finely crafted Swiss watch, and then putting it back together again, adding new pieces where necessary, taking out old pieces that no longer fit the new construction... ending up with it [the original screenplay] still ticking" (Brooks and Meehan, 22). Meehan's description of the adaptation facilitates our discussion of nostalgia as it relates to stage remakes of film texts.

Studies in popular culture such as Fred Davis's characterize nostalgia as the sense that "things were healthier, happier, or otherwise nicer in the old days" (75). Davis further defines the term by identifying three orders of nostalgia. The first is *simple nostalgia* that, according to Davis, is "the unquestioned conviction that the past was better" (64). Simple nostalgia manifests itself in the individual consumer's uninterrogated enthusiasm for representations of people, places, or things associated with the past. Simple nostalgia is displayed in the popularity of collectibles like baseball cards, dolls, and film memorabilia. The second order of nostalgia, or *reflexive nostalgia*, is empirically oriented and concerns the "truth, accuracy, completeness, or representatives of the nostalgic claim" (21). Reflexive nostalgia is most prominently displayed in the self-conscious distribution of the past in the fashion industry. Designers who market styles as "retro" or "reminiscent" create a reflexive worldview for their consumer, but they simultaneously scrutinize that past with a degree of distance or detachment as they present past designs as new, currently fashionable, or adapted. The third order, *interpreted nostalgia,* brackets portions of the lived experience. According to Davis, "[T]he actor seeks in some fashion to objectify the nostalgia he feels" through "analytically oriented questions concerning its sources, typical character, significance, and psychological purpose" (24). In other words, interpreted nostalgia shapes the nostalgic response. Interpreted nostalgia asks the consumer to step outside the nostalgic experience to identify its context, evaluate the authenticity of the original experience, and then connect that experience to the product currently being sold.

To achieve aesthetic and financial success in the stage production of *The Producers,* Brooks, Meehan, and other members of the production team utilized the aforementioned tenets of Davis's interpreted nostalgia to create their new musical text. In the creation of the new text, the production team stepped outside the nostalgic experience produced by the original film, identified that experience in its former context, then evaluated the authenticity of the original film experience, and connected that experience to the product they were creating and eventually selling. By framing a nostalgic response to the film for themselves in the creative process, they also provided a means to attract an audience later in the process. In this case, framed nostalgia is the bridge between the filmed antecedent and its musical counterpart, primarily used in the conceptualization of the new piece, but it is also latently used as a part of the musical's marketing strategy.

It is this same order of nostalgia that is used by the mass marketers to promote their products. One of the television commercials from a Gap Inc. ad campaign provides a prime example. In the commercial a Leonard Bernstein song and the choreography from the musical _West Side Story_ were employed to sell bright-colored chinos. The commercial implied foreknowledge of its source material and seemed to suggest that the consumer who purchases and wears the chinos will embody not only the attributes of the singers and dancers performing in the commercial, but also the experience projected in the recreated theatrical event. Thus, wearing Gap's chinos takes on a variety of meanings associated with the original popular film and the stage production.

Gap Inc. ran this ad campaign with the understanding that its customers would most likely understand it as an attempt to sell jeans. In fact, the company depends on the customer's ability to identify the commercial's intertextual markers and then enjoy locating themselves within the re-presentation of the musical — as part of the popular culture, as someone who wears jeans and remembers the pleasure of encountering _West Side Story_ on film, and, by extension, as someone who is nostalgic for the staged version of the musical. Even customers who are not familiar with the film or the musical and see the advertisement as new or unfamiliar can still locate the television commercial as a nostalgic product. Based on their understanding of the Gap's previous advertising promotions, which featured youthful performers clad in Gap clothing singing and dancing to popular music from the 1970s and 1980s, the viewer can determine that the specific references to the music and dance numbers from _West Side Story_ are yet another example of nostalgia as a commodity. By co-opting film and stage versions of the musical, the Gap becomes the purveyor of nostalgia for past cultural experience as well as the purveyor of the product.

This use of nostalgia to (re)frame the consumer's phenomenological experience is so common today that Anne Freidburg calls it a "postmodern nostomania" (188). Freidburg defines this "nostomania" as an excessive nostalgia in which there is an endless supply of sequels and remakes, each demanding a return to a past to sell the product. Freidburg specifically points out cinematic sequels of *Star Wars, The Godfather,* and *Die Hard* as examples of that nostomania.

Freidburg's assertion that sequels are not only manifestations of nostalgia for the original film but that they are manifestations of nostalgia for the original commodity experience has in recent years begun to be applicable to remakes of films as well as sequels to films. Traditional cinematic remakes were simply repackaged versions of previously filmed stories with no reference at all to any previous incarnation. Movies such as 1988s *Switching Channels* certainly make no blatant reference to the 1931 version, *His Girl Friday,* which, in turn, did not directly refer to the original movie, *The Front Page,* in its advertising campaign. However, marketing efforts such as those for *The Parent Trap* (1998*),* *Psycho* (1998), and *Shaft* (2000) blatantly referred to their original versions. In fact, the tagline "Remember Me?"—which was featured prominently in the advertising campaign for *Shaft* (2000)— speaks to an audience who is aware of the character of detective John Shaft and his exploits in films of the 1970s. It could also be asserted that Gus Van Sant's sole motivation for producing a shot-for-shot remake of Alfred Hitchcock's *Psycho* was to capitalize on the nostalgia for the original film. This is indicative of the way film sequels and some remakes deploy representations of the original film product to extend the consumer's desire for the first film. They also condition consumers to long for the promotion and publicity of the original film experience. The financial success of the film sequels that Freidburg lists and the recent success of many nostalgic film remakes prove the viability of this production and marketing strategy.

In the 1990s the commercial theatre industry also used this remake model. Throughout that decade and onward into the foreseeable future, critically acclaimed and blockbuster films were, and currently are, making money on Broadway in the form of theatrical remakes. For example, Blake Edwards' 1982 film *Victor/Victoria* was turned into a 1996 Broadway musical featuring the film's original star, Julie Andrews. Although the musical includes additional song-and-dance numbers written by Henry Mancini, the plot, characters, and settings remain close to the film. More recently an adaptation of the critically acclaimed John Travolta film *Saturday Night Fever* (1977) opened on Broadway in 1999. Promotional material for the musical advertised the Bee Gees' musical score for the staged version and linked the musical to nostalgic websites that focus on the 1970s.* Even the 1998 musical *Footloose*, which featured new music written for the spectacularly staged dance numbers, remains true to Kevin Bacon's popular 1984 film by the same name.

While *The Producers* and other nostalgic film-to-stage remakes incorporate nostalgia in their aesthetic, production and marketing strategies, and the evocative specifics of many of the film-to-stage productions are worthy of examination, it is the production of Andrew Lloyd Webber's *Sunset Boulevard* (a production, narrative, and event rife with nostalgia) that best illustrates the place that "nostomania" has assumed in American theatre. Everything about the production, from its staging and libretto to the circumstances of its American premiere, demonstrates how nostalgia was manipulated as a commodity and therefore as a vinculum to market viability and acceptance. The historical prominence of the production at the beginning of this trend (the play premiered in 1993) also helps illustrate how this commodification of nostalgia led to the cinematic approaches that are employed in theatrical practice today.

Drawing on the film industry's sequel/remake model, Andrew Lloyd Webber's production of *Sunset Boulevard* is not just a homage to the original film; it is instead a calculated embrace of the motion picture industry's financial formula of nostalgia. In this musical production, the Really Useful Theatre Company took full advantage of the film industry's durable formula to sell tickets to a new theatre audience — the filmgoer. Webber's stage production recounts Billy Wilder's acerbic critique of the Hollywood of the 1950s. Wilder's film exposed his own studio system's cold-blooded influence on the lives of fictional characters, the young screenwriter Joe Gillis (William Holden) and the faded film star Norma Desmond (Gloria Swanson). In the film, Norma Desmond desperately seeks a renewal of her long-gone silent film career. Joe Gillis becomes her lover and her link to Paramount Picture Studios. Their relationship plunges into a perverted illusory world where each character feeds off of the other's false hopes about their place in the film world. The film ends with Joe's death and Norma's descent into the delusional world of fantasy.

In an introductory scene of *Sunset Boulevard*, Webber's stage version of the original 1950 Billy Wilder film, Norma Desmond, the faded silent film star, utters: "I am big. It's the pictures that got small" (Perry 136).†

*See *www.feveronbroadway.com.*

†*George Perry's* Sunset Boulevard: From Movie to Musical. *The text includes a complete copy of the libretto for Andrew Lloyd Webber's musical. The libretto appears on pages 136–167 of the book.*

This line evokes multiple layers of nostalgia. Within the context of the show, Norma is longing for a return to the silent film era when she was star. The larger context of the spoken line recalls the film actress Gloria Swanson and her dramatic delivery of the line in the original film — which is so steeped in nostalgia that the emotions and attitudes of the character of Norma Desmond are now inextricably linked with the real and perceived emotions and attitudes of the real-life Gloria Swanson. Nostalgic dimensions are further multiplied when the line is delivered in the theatrical context because the line evokes nostalgia for a silent "picture" industry that few in the audience have little, if any, real knowledge of beyond pretended reminiscence. In essence, her words locate the audience inside the fictional world of the musical, but they also encourage the audience to relive a past cinematic encounter that appeals not only to the audience's sense of fantasy but also to their sense of a reality through a shared nostalgia for their past film viewing experiences.

This nostalgia is generated through more than superficial connections of the play to the movie in name, plot, and character. It was a carefully considered set of production choices that sought to cultivate and capitalize on this nostalgia for film. *Sunset Boulevard* and other productions that have followed the film-to-stage path — such as *The Producers, Some Like It Hot, The Sweet Smell of Success, Saturday Night Fever, Footloose,* and *Big* — are theatrical embodiments of film techniques, texts, and personalities created in an effort to reposition musical theatre into a prominent place in a mass-media/mass-marketing environment. To accomplish this goal, live performance corporations employ what Fredric Jameson would call a "nostalgic historicity" for the movies. For Jameson, nostalgia is one part of today's "image society" (xviii) in which history has become "a vast collection of images, a multitudinous photographic simulacrum" (18). To Jameson, the effect of nostalgia is a projection of this vast assortment of past images onto a "collective and social level where a missing past is now refracted through the iron law of fashion change and the emergent ideology of the generation" (19). Corporate theatrical productions like *Sunset Boulevard* are prime examples of how nostalgic representations can reflect and react to a dominant ideology — in this case, mass-media/mass-marketing capitalism and its reproduction of past images.

Webber's tale is a literal translation of this film narrative to the stage. Webber and his co-creator, Don Black, use visual motifs from the film, and even use dialogue from the film in the musical numbers, which are attempts to represent Wilder's film despite the fact that the musical numbers are not a part of the original film. However, unlike Wilder's original film, the musical is not an attempt to critique the Hollywood industry. Instead Webber's musical distinctly glamorizes the melodramatic film and the history which surrounds its making. The play's nostalgic focus and Webber's attempt to attract the filmgoer to the theatre through this nostalgic remake are most evident in the venue for the first U.S. production of Webber's adapted musical text.

Webber's stage production of *Sunset Boulevard* premiered in the United States on 9 December 1993, at the Shubert Theatre, located at 2020 Avenue of the Stars in Century City, California. The Shubert, once considered one of Los Angeles's finest legitimate theatres, traditionally mounted Broadway touring productions and was also equipped to support occasional movie premieres. One mile north of Rodeo Drive, the theatre is part of a complex that includes the former ABC Entertainment Center and also houses Twentieth Century–Fox Studios and the Century City Shopping Center. Built on the remains of the original Twentieth Century–Fox backlot, the complex is an interesting mix of modern commerce and nostalgic tribute to the film industry. This celebrated site, where William Fox's Movietone Newsreels originated and the Academy Award winning film *All About Eve* was filmed,* is currently the residence of the marketing and promotion teams for popular film sequels such as the *Alien* series and the *Star Wars* trilogy. Producers of *Sunset Boulevard* utilized this intermingled theatre-film-commercial space by treating the musical's premiere performance like a Hollywood film premiere. Advertising a "celebrity packed audience" for the opening night, guests included Kevin Costner, Kim Basinger, and Alec Baldwin, as well as Ronald and Nancy Reagan. Seeing-stars.com described the event like a film premiere:† "The stars arrived in limousines out front of the Shubert Theatre, and thousands showed up to watch them. Had you been willing to splurge on a ticket to the premiere, you could have rubbed elbows with many of those stars during intermission" (2).

The publicity machine designed to promote the musical never mentions the musical itself. Instead the promotion materials draw on *Sunset Boulevard*'s status as an event. The event in this case is a referent to the film world. This musical theatre premiere was staged as a Hollywood

*All About Eve *won best picture in 1950, beating out Billy Wilder's* Sunset Boulevard. *See Charles Albright's account of the awards in* Magill's American Film Guide, *Vol. 5. Ed. Frank N. Magill, et al. Newark: Salem Press).*

†*See http://seeing-stars.com/Meet/TheatreOpenings.shtml, a promotional website for the Century City complex.*

premiere. *Sunset Boulevard*'s cachet was not its live music or its live performance; instead it was the play's status as an event marked by its association with the film and the film industry that sells tickets. The performance then is the pre-show festivities, the intermingling of patrons between acts, even the site itself, which played into the marketing of *Sunset Boulevard* as a film event.

The text of the musical also attempted to connect the production to the film industry. The play's first image replicates Billy Wilder's original mise en scène in which the audience looks up from the bottom of a swimming pool were Joe Gillis has been discovered dead and floating face down.* The stage version uses theatrical gauze canted at a forty-five degree angle to the stage. The actor's body rests on the fabric while figures of the photographers and police can be made out from behind the gauze. The rippling water effect is a mirage manufactured by John Napier's lighting design. Although the effect is created by theatrical means, the attempt to duplicate on the stage John Seitz's original cinematic photography is evidence that a primary production goal is to reify the film experience.

While the opening moment hints at a significant resurrection of the film, other effects are even more obvious attempts to reconfigure traditional stage conventions of time and space to give the stage production a filmic time frame and spacing. This is most evident in the staging of key moments in the film — like the car chase through Hollywood that leads Joe to conceal his car in Norma Desmond's mansion on Sunset Boulevard. The chase scene, which requires two cars to move rapidly throughout a variety of outdoor settings, is achieved on film through rapid editing techniques and crosscutting. The staged version mimics these techniques by incorporating optically stretched film footage from Wilder's chase sequence with screened image insets that open like an advent calendar or a peek-a-boo window in a puzzle to reveal projections of each car's dashboard, a wheel, a speedometer, or a stoplight. The insets also allow live actors playing Joe Gillis and his pursuers to move into the film space and drive the filmed car. In effect, the stage becomes a movie screen capable of a film-like montage sequence.

There are two interesting questions that rise out of the scene. First, why did the *Sunset Boulevard* production team choose to solve a theatrical problem with film materials and techniques rather than through the

---

*In the film the camera seems to look at the dead man's face from the bottom of the pool. Technological constraints of the time prevented Seitz from getting a clear image while shooting through the water. He solved the problem by attaching a large mirror to the bottom of the pool and focusing the camera into its reflection (Crowe 240).

theatrical means, such as full-size cars displayed on stage or pantomimed actions depicting the driving of a car, options which were considered in the early stages of production? Second, why did they choose to insert live actors into the film sequence by placing their live bodies in the openings alongside the projected footage from the original film, which plays simultaneously with the actors' physical movements and gestures? The answer may be that the filmed material and the image of the stage actor, both of which move from the traditional stage into the screen image, are manifestations of the musical's larger ambitions to be more than a theatrical repackaging of the film. The inclusion of these elements makes it evident that the creators of the play are interested in replicating the film's most important filmic moments and maybe even producing a nostalgic remake of the film. These cinematic choices, like the selection of the performance venue and the promotional campaign, directly acknowledge and even celebrate the powerful societal functions of the original text and the institution that created it. Cinematic moments in the production embrace a dual context, as if to shout, "We are making a movie!"

This jubilant replication demonstrates an interesting shift in traditional theatre production and reception from that of live interaction between performer and audience to a larger theatrical matrix, which includes a mediatized replication within its boundaries. This choice could be viewed as a risk to theatre's unique potential when we recognize that, in its desire to replicate the film experience, the theatre production loses its capacity to maintain its own aura. In "The Work of Art in the Age of Mechanical Reproduction," Walter Benjamin describes aura as the "unique value of the 'authentic' work of art," which has its basis in ritual, the location of its original use value (736). Benjamin's term as it is applied in a theatrical context refers to the immediate presence of actor and audience acting together to produce a unique moment. As argued previously, commercial theatre's interest in a nonreproducible product is waning, while its emphasis on precise reproductions of performances within distributed productions is increasing.

Certainly the theatre is still a live experience, but it is a live experience no longer interested in its own capacity to produce a singular moment — a moment that cannot be repeated and is not disseminated by technological means. This loss of presence more commonly associated with the onset of mechanical reproduction signals an invasion of theatre's aura of proximity. As theatre embraces film's mechanisms, it also manifests its own loss of immediacy. This evolution of theatrical presence is evident throughout the production but is most obvious in the casting of

Glenn Close in the role of Norma Desmond and the circulation of her image as a film star rather than a stage star.

The withered character Norma Desmond fetishizes the power of personality. As she watches her own silent image move on a makeshift movie screen, she sings of her vanished stardom: "They took all the idols and smashed them.... They threw away the gold of silence when all they needed was this face of mine. With one look I put words to shame. Just one look sets the screen aflame" (Perry 142). On the surface, these lines serve as a theatrical demonstration of the character's melodramatic yearning for her past experience. However, Norma's focus on the silent film industry's circulation of her film persona and the power of that persona as a commodity is an appropriate image as we examine the dissemination of that persona in relation to the actresses who have played the Norma Desmond role on the screen and on the stage.

Director Billy Wilder drew on similarities between Swanson's silent film career and the character's fictional film career in the creation of the character of Norma Desmond for the screen. Wilder exploited that power of presence in the casting of Gloria Swanson as Norma Desmond. Like the character, Gloria Swanson reached the height of her career during the silent film era. Throughout the 1920s, she was the top star at Paramount pictures; for six of the ten years in that decade her films had the highest box office revenues of any actress. Billy Wilder used Swanson's personal association with Cecil B. DeMille and Erich von Stroheim, who played Norma Desmond's butler and sometimes husband Max von Mayerling, to inform the relationship between Norma Desmond and her male counterparts in the film. For example, DeMille's character addresses Norma Desmond as "young fellow," the director's pet name for Swanson. In addition, Stroheim's film *Queen Kelly,* in which Swanson starred, becomes Desmond's collaborative effort with Max von Mayerling. These allusions to Swanson's own faded career use the significant similarities between the actress and the characters to lend nostalgia and authenticity to the film's screenplay.

The publicity surrounding the opening of the film also marketed the picture as Swanson's return from the silent era. Magazines marketed the film as a retelling of her life experience, demonstrating comparisons between the film image and the actress-personality. Even Swanson herself sent personal letters to the Paramount distribution arm, addressing them as "dear colleagues" (Perry 76) and recalling the success they had had selling her movies in the 1920s. In this way Swanson's presumed past presence became a marketing tool for the film. In a sense Swanson's past image became nothing more than a product used by Wilder in his development of the screenplay and used by Paramount to sell the film to distributors, magazines, and the public.

Jameson would describe the circulation of Swanson's image as a "waning effect" — a post-modern condition in which famous human subjects are commodified and then transformed into their own images for profit just like any other object (11). For Jameson, the authentic person is valued only as a glossy advertised image of himself or herself. Although Jameson focuses on the dissemination of the human figure in his discussion of the waning effect, his model is nonetheless helpful as we examine the casting of the Norma Desmond role in the musical version of the film.

During the musical's London preview, stage star Patti LuPone was faulted for her inability to convey the celebrity status needed for the role. The theatre critic Frank Rich called for an actress who could "convey the heroine's legendary status in the show-biz firmament" (Rich 3). The casting of Glenn Close for the American production was in some ways a response to this plea. Like the re-use of Swanson's silent film career in the making and production of the film, the casting of Glenn Close was an attempt to use her successful film career as a catalyst between the theatre production and the film industry. While most reviews of the play modestly acknowledged Close as a two-time winner of the coveted Tony Award (a theatre prize), her work in films like *Dangerous Liaisons* (1988), *Reversal of Fortune* (1990), and *Fatal Attraction* (1987) were even more prominently displayed in Vincent Canby's analysis of her performance. He replaced the legitimate stage actress Glenn Close with her other more commercially productive cinematic image. Canby identifies her as a film personality who has "suddenly become a big, exciting new star of the American ... theatre" (209). He describes the transformation of Close and the character, saying: "As the show serves her with material that affects a career transformation, she serves the show.... [S]he takes the image of Norma Desmond, the demonic, reclusive silent film queen ... and fiercely shapes it into her own unexpected image (209).

Eventually the reshaping of the character to make it co-mingle with the image of the actress-personality was also used as a marketing tool. The intermingled image in which film actress Glenn Close and the character Norma Desmond became one was a tool first used as an advertising ploy by the newswriters promoting the stage musical. Inevitably the dual presence of the actress and the character becomes a commonly circulated image during the time period surrounding Close's performance in the stage role.

Two examples demonstrate this point: the first is an appearance of

Glenn Close as herself in the 1997 film *In and Out*. Close appears as a presenter on the Oscars. She is giving out the award for best actor, which would indicate that within the context of the film she had won best actress the year before. As Close enters to present the award, Norma Desmond's theme music from *Sunset Boulevard* plays, demonstrating her connection to the musical within the world of the film. The award for Best Actor presented by Close is also marked by a parodic transcontext. The actors and films nominated for the award parody previous film roles and character types presented by the actors in the real world. The film therefore demands that the viewing audience understand its parody of the real world actors and their performance types to fully enjoy the film. In this instance Close is represented as an icon of the film industry; the viewer can also link this performance to her performance as Norma Desmond and her connection to the character is marked when the music introduces her.

The second example of the dual presence of the actor and character is a photograph taken by Herb Ritts for his *Herb Ritts: Work* collection. The photograph, entitled "Glenn Close — Century City 1996,"* is a black-and-white still photograph depicting the actress partially made up for the Norma Desmond role. Though the face makeup and the high key light garishly recall the frenzied Desmond's line, "And now, Mr. DeMille, I'm ready for my close-up" (Perry 165), the presence of the actress herself is equally prominent. Her well-toned body is displayed in modern dress and the film actress's famed high cheekbones and Rooseveltian jaw peer out from behind the pale pancake makeup. The image first appeared in the Museum of Fine Art's Boston gallery and later appeared online alongside Jack Nicholson, who is made up for his role in *Batman* and Madonna dressed as Minnie Mouse. Each photograph suggests a trans-contextual appeal in which the role and the actor are given equal weight.

The image of Close/Desmond in the film and the photograph indicate that intermingling is marketable. Close the human subject and Close the character have been transformed into a glossy advertisement, a commodity for sale. The dual image sells films or at least a joke in a film, and the photograph sells an aesthetic. This aesthetic is the subject's transcontextual appeal. Close's own unique presence is less important in this case. It is the image of the actress/personality, Close, and its multiple contexts in the picture and within the transcontext of the gallery that make this picture interesting. In today's media-saturated world, the actress, like the musical in which she performs, is valuable to the extent that she connects

* *The* Herb Ritts: Work *photography collection can be viewed at http://www.boston.com/mfa/ritts/home.htm.*

herself to a performed experience in the media. The authentic presence that she may possess in private is negated and replaced by an image that sells the play, markets the movie, and merchandizes the photograph.

In his discussion of nostalgia and its present use, Jameson describes the need to reevaluate nostalgic films as representations of a historical past. For Jameson, nostalgic films (of which *Sunset Boulevard* could be an example) are the forerunners of a new nostalgic historicity, which is at work in contemporary marketing and consumption practice: "It is by way of ... nostalgia films that some properly allegorical processing of the past becomes possible: it is because the formal apparatus of nostalgia films has trained us to consume the past in the form of glossy images that new and more complex 'postnostalgia' statements become possible" (287). For Jameson this new practice of consumption associated with a nostalgic historicity for past time periods is really a longing to locate, evaluate, and understand our own present in the context of past images. Trained by the consumption of images from the past nostalgic films, new uses of nostalgic historicity become first and foremost allegories of their own development. Jameson's paradigm helps us to understand the commercial success of Webber's staged reproduction of the film's original images.

If we consider Jameson's description of nostalgic historicity accurate, we can identify Webber's use of glossy images of the past presented in the film as "postnostalgic" or newer more complex uses of historicity in which reality is secondary to the image presented. Webber's product, which relocates us both visually and aurally in the world of Hollywood in the 1950s, is simply a display of Wilder's past images of the 1950s on the stage. Webber is not concerned with representing the past or even remaining true to the film. Instead, he is concerned with maintaining the perceived nostalgic image that marks the film. His re-envisioned use of nostalgia both for nostalgia's own sake and as a selling point for the musical is simply a manifestation of the market's desire to situate itself in some kind of past memory image, which helps sell something in the present.

Staged versions of films are no longer in the minority in the corporate venues in New York, Los Angeles, and London. It could be argued that recent revivals on mass-marketed commercial stages of shows like *The Sound of Music, The King and I, The Music Man,* and others were more nostalgic theatrical remakes of the films than they were pure revivals of the original theatrical productions.

However, even without pushing the argument to that extreme, there are (and likely will continue to be) multiple examples of this commodification of cinematic/mass media/image nostalgia in the theatre. Mel

Brooks's unqualified success with *The Producers* has undoubtedly made a mark on the corporate entities that now dominate the larger venues in New York. The stage and screen actress Kathleen Turner reprised the role of Mrs. Robinson in the London stage production of Mike Nichols's film *The Graduate* (1967). As of the writing of this work, staged versions of several popular films continue to tour this country after successful Broadway runs. Theatre enterprises associated with the Disney Corporation and other media-based companies that produce theatrical translations of animated films like *The Lion King* or *Beauty and the Beast* are currently capitalizing on the revisited film experience in their replication of cartoons on the stage. These copied animated films, staged versions of nostalgic films, and cinematically informed revivals are all indicative of this process of making theatre a literal media machine.

Philip Auslander argues that theatre performance has become a mass medium because its generation stems not from interpretations but from performance templates. He explains:

> If we take the producer of [commercial theatre] at his word and assume that he does succeed in mounting numerous productions of a play that are functionally identical, would it not be fair to say that the interpretation used in all cases functions as a template? ... While the actors would have to possess a certain amount of craft and skill to replicate the performances established in the template (just as it takes a certain amount of craft and skill to be a good projectionist), individual artistry and imagination would be negative qualities in such a performance, since they would tend to work against the success of [the work] as a standardized product [49].

Thus, the authentic presence of the theatrical performer as an artistic individual is diminished in the new franchise productions of commercial theatre. The idea of an actor's theatrical presence is then analogous to Auslander's film projectionist in that the audience expects both the actor and the projectionist to be skilled, but not creative. Visual intimacy then becomes the only measure of presence that audiences come to theatrical events to experience. In effect the audience comes to see re-creations of nostalgic events, and within those events they perceive performances but not the presence of the performers. The image as commodity is supreme and theatre participates in the economy of repetition, not by being recorded and replicated, but by the mass production of the live event itself.

FIVE

Media as an
Overt Presence in Theatrical
Text and Production

Nineteenth-century definitions of presence that locate the physical existence of someone or something by describing its position in a particular place are no longer adequate in a world dominated by the cultural hegemony of the media. Internet connections provide live interface from different continents and local cable access makes it possible for anyone to be on television. Presence is no longer defined by geographical position or proximity but by a communal negotiation of what is culturally acceptable. In *The Prison Notebooks*, Antonio Gramsci argues: "The "normal" exercise of hegemony is characterized by the combination of force and consent, which balance each other reciprocally, without force predominating excessively over consent" (217). Gramcsi's insight on cultural hegemony is particularly evident in the relationship between a marginalized theatre and the more dominant media. Gramcsi's theories apply as we look at ways theatre practitioners have negotiated a place within the dominant discourse through an exploration of media as an overt presence in both texts and staged performances.

The advent of material that responded, incorporated, or deliberately addressed a media influence can be documented in theatrical productions early in the twentieth century. For instance, in Erwin Piscator's European 1924 production of *The Flags: An Epic Drama,* the history of the 1886 uprising of anarchists in Chicago, was depicted using projection slides and placards. Shortly thereafter, the *Living Newspapers*, produced in America by Hallie Flannigan for the Federal Theatre Project during the 1930s, was a reaction to and a demonstration of many of the communication technologies of the day. However, it was not until the late 1960s that television and film are referenced regularly in both theatrical content and form.

With the shift in political and social conditions in America and Europe during the late 1960s, a newly found social consciousness led to a reassessment of artistic practice. Artists and practitioners began to break down, or at least acknowledge, barriers between themselves and their audience. Theatre practitioners attempted to present issues and create visual forms that connected theatre back to ordinary human experience. While theatre artists like Joseph Chaiken and Peter Schumann responded with an organic approach to theatrical performance and sought to connect the audience with the social protest of the performer in a community of activists, others explored the ways in which theatre directly accessed this changing audience through technology. It became clear that both television and film were cultural material that could be mined for form and content by theatre professionals.

Theatre practitioners exploring television and film took their inspiration from various views of their effect on society. For example, Laurie Anderson's 1983 production *United States* represented America as a country flattened by the artifice of media forms. Standing in front of backdrops made of compressed screen images, Anderson demanded a respite from the exploitation of the pervasive media culture and its consumer-based mindset.

In 1982 Michael Smith explored the desire of performance artists for celebrity in the Whitney Museum's presentation of *Mike's House*. In this performance piece, Smith appeared on videotape as a situation comedy star working to get access to a television stage set of his own living room. Smith's dual role as live performance artist and television persona demonstrated for the audience the thin line between what is imagined and real in the creation of celebrity.*

Other producers like Elizabeth LeCompte's the Wooster Group mounted productions that used media to deconstruct conventional uses of time and space. One such production, *Brace Up!* (a 1993 adaptation of

---

Roselee Goldberg's seminal text Performance Art: From Futurism to the Present *discusses what she calls "The Media Generation" at length, including a detailed examination of performance artists Laurie Anderson and Michael Smith (152–9).*

Chekhov's *Three Sisters)* used television monitors and cameras to exceed the conventions of the proscenium arch. Breaking with the naturalistic tendency to demarcate the physical place of the play as separate from the audience, the production destroyed the spatial frame associated with realism by video taping the character of Natalia, who remained off stage for the whole production and appeared only through a video feed. Standards of time and culture were also altered and confused by a Japanese samurai film that played throughout the production.

In stark contrast to the work of LeCompte and Anderson, the 1996 revival of *How to Succeed in Business Without Really Trying* embraced media technology as an atmospheric tool that visually conveyed the new image-based nature of marketing companies. The Broadway revival updated the visual look of the original production by using technology designed by Multi-Image Systems, Inc., to construct a 17' by 24' video wall system used for the backdrop on this touring production. The thirty-two projection cubes that made up this system were modularly designed to move on automated cable systems during the show.*

Through an investigation of these examples and others, two themes are prominent in texts and productions that use media openly. These themes both support Gramsci's theory of negotiated space, in which the predominant conveyor of ideology attempts to force a discourse, and in which discourse is altered by the ways in which real human beings consent to that forced discourse. First, film and television are identified as pervasive entities through which authentic communication is subverted and material capitalism reigns. Second, the mass media are identified as the disseminator of cultural relevance for the disenfranchised. The first theme is well demonstrated by David Mamet's *Speed the Plow*; the second, by Adrienne Kennedy's *A Movie Star Has to Star in Black and White*. Both Mamet in *Speed the Plow* and Kennedy in *A Movie Star Has to Star in Black and White* grapple with the pervasive media presence by using media overtly in the discourse of the plays. Characters speak about film, and act as film characters, in an effort to understand themselves. In Mamet's play, the characters reflect on the presence of the media in their lives, while the protagonist in Kennedy's play simply accepts its presence and incorporates it into her own life. Settings for both plays reflect both the media industry and its influence on spaces outside that industry. The themes of both plays simultaneously reject and embrace a media influence. The reader-

---

Multi-Image Systems, Inc., documents their work on the project on their website, http://www.-multi-image.com/projects.

spectator of these plays is asked to evaluate the power of mass media as an overt force, whose effects are discussed and interpreted in the play.

Mamet's *Speed the Plow* is one example among many that depict the media industry as a pervasive cultural power through which a hegemonic, capitalist influence is purveyed. As in David Rabe's *Hurly Burly,* the Hollywood of *Speed the Plow* is a gritty world moving at an insane pace. Multimillion-dollar decisions are made by deft but callous middle-management moguls who sacrifice civility to have their name above the title of a blockbuster film.

Set in Bobby Gould's nondescript office, an office that could be anywhere in the movie business, two midlevel executives, Bobby Gould and Charlie Fox, stumble into a project that will make them rich and powerful — a prison buddy picture which includes a package deal with a headlining director. All they have to do is maintain the controlling rights to a film treatment for twenty-four hours, when they can pitch their idea to the head executive. The success of their venture is complicated when Bobby's temporary office assistant presents him with a second film treatment to pitch to the executive producer. This second script, which he has asked her to read as a courtesy to his boss, is an artistic narrative about radiation. Her deal with Bobby includes an offering of sex and companionship and a chance to recoup what has been lost in the art of the deal. Mamet makes it clear that both films will have a cultural impact for the benefit or the detriment of a mass audience.

Written during Mamet's first foray into filmmaking, the play is less a study of the three characters than a searing view of an industry. Mamet describes the cooperative and mutually beneficial relationship between the producer and the consumer, saying, "As the media gets more and more powerful, film as mass entertainment, which is to say solely as marketing of the consumer product, that tradition gets much, much stronger. The job of mass entertainment is exactly the opposite of the job of art — the job of mass entertainment is to cajole, seduce and flatter consumers to let them know that what they thought was right is right, and that their tastes and their immediate gratification are of the utmost concern of the purveyor" (Covington, *Salon* interview).

Mamet's sentiment plays out in the relationships between the characters presented — a newly appointed head of production, Bobby Gould, and his long-time associate, Charlie Fox, both of whom are clearly aware of their own power in the complicit relationship between producer and spectator. They represent themselves as "two whores" (26). Gould says, "I'm a whore and I'm proud of it, but I am a secure whore" (26). Later in the play when Karen asks Gould if the film they are about to pitch to their boss is a good film, he replies:

GOULD: It's a commodity ... and I don't know if it is a good film.
KAREN: What about art?
GOULD: I'm not an artist. Never said I was, and nobody who sits in this chair can be [41].

Later, he tells Karen that there is no need to examine a filmscript for its possible artistic or intellectual contribution to the viewer. Instead, says he, making a film is about providing a status quo for the spectator/consumer. He continues: "That's what we're in business to do. Make the thing everyone made last year. Make the image people want to see" (56).

While Gould and Fox embrace the marginal product that is created from industrial avarice, Karen does not acknowledge any connection to film commerce and its artistic corruption. She is a temp in the office and intentionally signals her lack of experience to the men. Karen continually reminds the two men of her temporary status as a secretary in the office and in the movie-making business. She says, "I'm just a temporary," and "This is just a temporary job," to which Fox accurately replies, "Everything is temporary until it's not" (28). But, in the end, Karen is no different than Gould and Fox in her own desire for power. She professes a connection to the intellectual film that Gould asked her to read and convinces him that the film could save the two of them from the depravity of the business: "It [the film text] says that you were put here to make stories people need to see ... that we could do something. Which would bring us alive. So that we needn't feel ashamed. (pause.) We needn't feel frightened. The wild animal dies with pride. He didn't make the world. God made the world. You say that you prayed to be pure. What if your prayers were answered? You asked me to come. Here I am" (60).

Karen speaks about art. She speaks about connection to something higher than the commodity. Nevertheless, Mamet shows that Karen's words are not the key to understanding her. Instead, he asks the viewer to look at her body. In the same way that Gould and Fox's prison filmscript signifies the prostitution of their own values for financial gain, Karen's body becomes a similar site of dubious commerce. Gould and Fox make a "gentlemen's bet" of $500.00 that Gould can "screw" her before the next morning. Gould says, "I can get her on a date ... I can get her to my house ... I can screw her" (38). Karen literally prostitutes her physical self to get the radiation script "greenlighted" by acknowledging the bet and then sleeping with Gould:

KAREN: I knew what the deal was. I know you wanted to sleep with me.
  You're right, I came anyway; you're right.
GOULD: ... to sleep with you ...
KAREN: Didn't you?
GOULD: No ...
KAREN: Why lie? You don't have to lie [38–9].

In the original 1988 production at the Lincoln Center Theatre, Mamet extended the imagery associated with Karen's physical presence by casting Madonna in the role. Madonna, fresh from her *Like a Virgin* world tour (1985) and various other appearances, played up the sexual iconography that she was known for as a pop star.

As represented by Mamet, Hollywood is a powerful company town that shapes its base spectators by controlling what they see and hear; it is a town where profit reigns over art, sex is a commodity, and the products produced (movies) have significant social impact for good or for bad. All of these views are presented as simple facts; none are challenged or questioned within the text.

The stereotypical nature of these opinions is common to representations of mass-media industries in almost all places, including in the mass media itself. That this view is also found in theatrical texts is not surprising. What is significant is that this demonization of the mass media as the enemy to authentic communication is occurring in a venue that so often views itself as the purveyor of authentic communication — the American theatre. This difference in location elevates the dialogue into attempted social commentary, whereas the dialogue would instantly be read as satire if it was found in a film.

The stereotype of the cultural power of the mass media can alternatively be seen as an access point to cultural relevance for the disenfranchised. This is clear in Adrienne Kennedy's *A Movie Star Has to Star in Black and White* (1976). The main character of Ms. Kennedy's play, a young African-American woman named Clara, allows famous Caucasian film stars to represent her life. These stars play the roles of Clara and her family but are dressed for their roles in the identifying costumes of three prominent motion picture productions from the 1940s and 1950s. Clara is a writer who has immersed herself in the movies to escape her own sad existence. However, she remains on the sidelines of her own life, confined to the words that emerge from her typewriter while the audience sees and hears her words spoken by the iconic men and women of the silver screen. Bette Davis, Jean Peters, and Shelley Winters speak for Clara, giving her words the weight and power associated with their on-screen images.

Kennedy's description of the setting and staging emphasizes the importance of the film stars as they appear on stage in Clara's imagined world. Clara describes the characters as "Leading Roles" (80), which are played by actors who look exactly like each film star. The persona of the actor-character that is reflected in the play's notes depicts the seriousness with which the characters assume their roles: "These movie stars are romantic and moving, never camp or farcical, and the attitudes of the supporting players [the real people in Clara's life] to the movie stars is deadly serious" (80). The play is framed by the appearance of the Columbia Pictures logo, a lone white woman draped in silk and bathed by a high key light, who appears center stage at the beginning and end of the production. Clara is simply described as "a Negro woman of thirty-three wearing a maternity dress [who] does not enter the room but turns away and stands very still" (81).

Initially Clara does not appear on stage with the characters; she is placed off to the side with her typewriter, on which she types as she observes the characters speaking her words. Eventually she appears on stage intermingling with the movie stars, but never speaking to them or interacting with them. Clara's own aural descriptions of her writing and her brief conversations with her mother and her husband are disjointed, nonlinear commentaries that make little sense when singled out. But her thoughts and stories are clear and vibrant when spoken through the film actor. Clara recognizes this and comments on the irony: "Ever since I was twelve I have secretly dreamed of being a writer. Everyone says it's unrealistic for a Negro to want to write. Eddie says I've become shy and secretive and can't accept the passage of time, and that my diaries consume me and that my diaries make me a spectator watching my life like watching a black and white movie. He thinks sometimes ... to me my life is one of my black and white movies that I love so ... with me playing a bit part" (99).

Clara chooses to play a "bit part" because she believes that the film-like enactments of her life merged with scenes from the films* provide a more clear vision of herself than her own words do. Clara becomes the protagonist in her own story only when her feelings are expressed through the various film stars. Scenes in which the actor-stars play Clara are framed and edited to guide the viewer to an understanding of Clara's perspective, a perspective that would not be clear in a simple enactment of her own

---

Kennedy's film characters are taken from the motion pictures Now Voyager *(Warner Bros., 1942),* Viva Zapata *(Twentieth Century–Fox, 1952), and* A Place in the Sun *(Paramount Pictures, 1951).*

life. Kennedy uses visual scenes from the classical Hollywood films to cue the viewer's aural and visual attention to connections between the enacted experience of the film personas and Clara's real life. These connections identify Clara's intense emotion even when she cannot express or demonstrate it herself.

The film stars speak to her husband and parents telling stories of unwanted pregnancies and unsuccessful suicides that she would not choose to reveal, all the while visually portraying dramatic sequences from their own filmed melodramas. Movie music from each star's film plays throughout, cueing the audience to the emotional sensation of the movie and equating the significance of the film moments that parallel moments in Clara's life.

These forced connections between the women are used throughout the play, but the strongest example of the mass-media icons giving a marginalized life cultural relevance takes place in the final moments of the play when Clara speaks about her brother's near-fatal accident. The scene begins with Clara and Shelley Winters speaking in unison from separate portions of the stage about her brother's possible brain damage. Together they cry out, "All we know is that his brain is possibly badly damaged" (102). The stage directions indicate a sudden shift of light in which Shelley Winters "stands up and falls into the water. She is in the water, only her head is visible, calling silently...." Movie music begins to play and the stage directions indicate a film-like crosscut to Clara, who continues to speak: "The doctor said today that my brother will be paralyzed. After he told us, my mother cried in my arms. We were standing on the steps, and she shook so that I thought both of us were going to fall headlong down the stairs" (103). The stage directions describe the visual images that accompany this speech: "Shelley Winters drowns. Light goes down on Montgomery Clift as he stares at Shelley Winters drowning. Lights on Clara. Movie music. Darkness" (103). The visual image, Shelley Winters drowning, cues us to Clara's emotional state at the news of her brother — a mental drowning. Clara's state of mind is clarified only through the drowning, and the significance of the loss is tied to the loss of a movie icon.

Once the film star cannot speak or move on her behalf, Clara is also gone and the stage is dark. In essence, Clara ceases to exist without the iconic images she uses to represent her in a performance of her life. Kennedy's depiction of Clara negotiating a space for her own voice through the female film icons is a powerful reminder not only of the media's dominant role in Clara's life but its dominant presence in the work itself. Clara's desire to cite the iconic women in the telling of her story becomes what Judith Butler would call an "assumption," or an utterance that is simultaneously an interpretation of the norm (for Clara) and an opportunity to expose the norm as a privileged interpretation (for Kennedy).*

Clara's actions in Kennedy's play are based on specific knowledge of the films that are used in the play and the cultural power of each film's representative women. The film presence of the actor-characters becomes a tool in which the African-American character and the African-American writer assume the cultural power of the Caucasian film icons in order to tell their own stories.

This dual role that the film stars' presence serves is also key to the audience's understanding of the play. For the spectator to believe that this young, poor, disenfranchised African-American woman is the central figure in the play, the audience must understand the cultural power of the film icons that represent Clara throughout. Jeanie Forte says the key to Kennedy's work is the "images and associations, registering as an experience of the consciousness affected by representations in literature, pop culture and film" (Bryant-Jackson and Overbeck 159). But Kennedy's representation of Clara's consciousness depends on more than a textual representation of Clara's consciousness as it is affected by cultural iconography. The visual images and associative connections must be familiar to the audience as well.

To understand Clara, we must be familiar with her film representatives and their cultural clout. Kennedy therefore depends on what film scholar Richard Dyer calls the "star phenomenon,"† or the spectator's foreknowledge of everything that is publicly available about the star. The play is not only about the perceived reality of the protagonist; it is also depend-

---

In her seminal work, Bodies That Matter, Judith Butler discusses the extent that "I" is secured by its sexed position. She says, "This 'I' and its 'position' can be secured only by being repeatedly assumed, whereby assumption is not a singular act or event but rather an iterable practice. If to 'assume' a sexed position is to seek recourse in a legislative norm, as [Jaques] Lacan would claim, then 'assumption' is a question of repeating that norm, citing, or miming the norm. And citation will be at once an interpretation of the norm and an occasion to expose the norm itself as a privileged interpretation (108). While Butler is making this argument as it relates to the discursive limits of sexuality and the sex act, I feel is pertinent here as it applies to any alterity that is being negotiated within a predominant space.

†*Richard Dyer discusses the "star phenomenon" in his work "Heavenly Bodies: Film Stars and Society," which reads: "The star phenomenon consists of everything that is publicly available about the stars. The star's image is not just his or her films but the promotion of those films and the star through pin ups, public appearances, studio handouts as well as interviews, biographies and coverage in the press of the star's private life. A star's image is also what people say or write about him or her, as critics or commentators, the way an image is used in other contexts such as advertisings, novels, pop songs, and finally the coinage of everyday speech" (60).*

ent on the perceived reality of the audience member. The spectators' acceptance of Clara's reality depends on their own abilities to make associations with the visual images that she chooses to represent her, and so the reception of the play also becomes a site of negotiation in which the predominant power of media must be discussed and evaluated.

Mamet and Kennedy purposefully address film as an all-encompassing entity through which their characters' authentic communication is shaped. More importantly, both playwrights assume that their audiences have an understanding of the medium that they attempt to expose. The blatant use of media as narrative content is ultimately an acknowledgment of media's cultural effectiveness. The hegemonic power of the prevalent media is evidenced in continued negotiation of force and consent in theatre texts and the subsequent stagings of those texts.

Such is the case of the Amerindian Project. In 1992–93 Coco Fusco and Guillermo Gómez-Peña conducted an international tour in which they presented themselves as "undiscovered Amerindians" from an island in the Gulf of Mexico. This satirical ethnographic performance installation, which took place at respected museums and other intellectually inscribed venues, was an attempt to examine the dynamics of traditional ethnographic display as a form of intercultural performance.* Fusco and Gómez-Peña posed as newly discovered indigenous people who were exhibited in a cage with objects from their own environment. Subjected to invasive public observation in which crowds watched as the couple displayed the intimate details of their supposed primitive life and embraced their new environs by accepting, examining, and then incorporating magazines, a television set, and prepackaged food items into their daily routine behind the cage.

The Amerindian Project overtly incorporates a media presence into its staged presentation of the couple in the cage. Early in the documented project a television appears in the cage. The television is centrally located within the cage and eventually plays a prominent role in the "education" of the indigenous pair. Initially the couple ignores the television set, but eventually they watch the moving images, respond physically and verbally to them and finally the performers/Amerindians imitate what they see on

---

*While researching the project Fusco and Gómez-Peña traced the origins of ethnographic exploitation of indigenous people from Columbus who brought Arwak Indians back to Spain to the circus/freak show phenomenon of the late nineteenth and early twentieth centuries. Their intent with the project was not to fool people with their performance but to recognize previous exploitative acts of ethnographic display as part of performance history. For more information on Fusco's project, see her own description of the event at http://www.moma.org/onlineprojects/ conversations/trans_cfusco.html.

the screen. Each item in the cage setting is used during the installation and many demonstrate "progress" on the part of the couple in using these objects, but the deliberate use of the television and the constant focus on its presence could be viewed as a clear attempt to communicate the difference between the exhibit and the spectator. The central placement and scripted use of the television makes the set more than a visual property within the cage. The calculated use of the television becomes the signifier of the difference between the spectator's world and the exhibited world. The spectators' embrace of television's cultural power in their own life is key to their perception of the exhibit's authenticity and to the Amerindian's alterity. The overt use of the television then is the key to the success of the presentation.

While the overt presence of the television is intentionally used by Fusco and Gómez-Peña, a second media form, the camera documenting the event, also affects the performance's production and reception. During the course of the project, Fusco and Gómez-Peña collaborated with filmmaker Paula Heredia to document the performances on videotape.* The filmed project, known as *The Couple in the Cage,* captures their work as well as the performance of the spectators at the event. The intended purpose of Heredia's camera is to compile documentary footage of the event and the spectators' responses to the event.

The presence of the camera and the spectators' knowledge of the camera's use shape the performance and its reception, and at some points draws focus away from the project itself. Heredia's camera, which is used as an observation tool and an interview tool, in some ways acts as a barrier to capturing an authentic response from the spectator. Because of the spectators' foreknowledge of the camera's function (as reporter or presenter or manipulator), the spectators who are observed or interviewed become self-conscious; some even perform for the camera. In one segment of the film, children swing on the Amerindians' cage, preening and posing for the camera, and instead of capturing their response to the installation, the camera captures their own performance. Likewise, people who are interviewed on camera are far more interested in projecting an image of themselves than they are in describing their reaction to the exhibit. Responses to Heredia's basic questions are guarded and seem to take effort. The camera, which is not intended as an overt presence, affects the outcome of the project because it alters the spectators' reception of the event.

The 30-minute documentary film, The Couple in the Cage: A Guatinaui Odyssey, was selected for the 1993 New York Film Festival Video Visions program and won the Best Performance Documentary Award at the Atlanta Film and Video Festival in 1994.

In some respects the most significant media presence affecting the Amerindian Project was absent from the physical installation. Fusco and Gómez-Peña never attempted to make connections between their project and the historical representation of otherness in the media or elsewhere; they were simply interested in the dynamics of public ritual and its generation of a context of place and time for its participants. With the Amerindian Project, they assumed that they would shape the spectators' responses through their performance.

What Fusco and Gómez-Peña found was that the spectator arrived at the event with preconceived ideological perspectives influenced by their own interaction with the world and that most of their responses were shaped by visual images that they had encountered before they participated in the installation. Fusco summarized her view of these influences: "I think that the confusion that our presence generated was really an educational experience for us. We had no idea that the power of certain institutional frameworks could have to encourage people to project certain kinds of fantasies onto us."*

The interactive dynamic in the ethnographic performance experiments of Guillermo Gómez-Peña allows for a productive spectator whose thoughts and actions drive the performance away from prescription to a place where real questions about identity, culture, and performance can be addressed together. What Gómez-Peña stumbled upon was a spectator-driven narrative — one that was created in part prior to the production and was based on the spectators' negotiation of institutional frameworks and personal experience. A large part of that spectator experience is obviously coming from their exposure to the media.

Through the examination of the participatory spectator it is also possible to consider the significance of what happens in the liminal† boundaries or the negotiated space between the colonized theatre and the colonist media as productive and informative contributions to our understanding of theatre practice. Postcolonial theorist Homi Bhabha describes this liminal space as "interstitial" space, or an intersection between different entities in which hybrid forms of the two entities developed through the

*See the Coco Fusco online interview previously cited.

†The term liminal as I use it here is not the ritualized "limins" described by Victor Turner and appropriated for performance by Richard Schechner. Instead I am drawing on the definitions of the term described by the postmodern Marxist Fredric Jameson and postcolonial theorist Homi K. Bhabha. Bhabha describes the liminal setting between boundaries as a place where negotiations occur between the colonist and the colonized. According to Bhabha, a hybrid identity is negotiated mutually through the uneven struggle between the two entities.

coexistence of each domain can form and exist, and sometimes restructure the traditional organization of power. According to Bhabha: "In between spaces provide the terrain for elaborating strategies of selfhood — singular of communal — that initiate new signs of identity, and innovative sites of collaboration, and contestation, in the act of defining the idea of society itself" (1).

It is possible then that the mind and body of the theatre spectator is one such site — a hybrid subject of innate ritual and the cultural training of the media in which the form and content of two mediums, theatre and media, compete and collaborate to form unique receptive interactions with individual texts and their performances. Here in this hybrid space the participatory spectator prefigures a new type of performance that develops out of the interaction between the two mediums.

SIX

Media and the Performing Body

In 1999 the country music celebrity Garth Brooks released a new conceptual album where he posed as an alter ego — Chris Gains. Brooks's intent with the release of the album was to promote the character that he had created for a film that was simultaneously under development. The film, entitled *The Lamb,* followed a down-and-out rock star (Chris Gains) through the development of his career. Brooks was set to play the leading role. As part of the promotion for the film he began to record music as Chris Gains. This led to public appearances and the release of an album in the guise of the character. Brooks as Chris Gains sported a new look and persona. Disregarding his established personality conventions as an energetic, flamboyant, man-of-the-people celebrity, Brooks reinvented himself in an unconventional way. As Chris Gains, he presented himself as angst-driven, introverted, and aloof. The character was slimmer, had black hair, and pronounced cheekbones. More important, the music of Chris Gains was distinctly different from Brooks's traditional vocal stylings.

The release of Brooks's album *In the Life of Chris Gains* was met with critical and popular confusion. While some critics admired Brooks's vocal range, most fans were frustrated by his seeming attempt to leave behind the music and personality conventions that they were attached too. Initial postings on a Garth Brooks fan website raise questions of authenticity. Liz Orean writes: "My husband and I are arguing about this topic.

I'm lost. He says Chris Gains *IS* Garth Brooks. I don't believe that! Can you PLEASE clear this ongoing fight!" (Brooks forum, online).Other postings indicate frustration with the industry and the artist. Steve J. Rogers writes:

> A lot of it [the lack of success and fan frustration] can be blamed on the serious backlash Garth got from the fans, media, and others in the industry, who were already in the belief that artists like Garth ... were trying to move far away from "traditional country music" with more 90's era pop sounds....
> To them this was Garth Brooks trying to put out a straight pop album but under a different name so he can tell the country music industry and fans "Hey I'm still Country Star Garth Brooks" while at the same time being this Chris Gaines character to the rest of the music industry. So it clearly wasn't accepted and received well at all [Brooks forum, online].

Finally, a disgruntled fan with the screen name Skywise points out that Brooks's departure from his accepted conventional norm is the problem with the staged event: "Part of it was Garth's thinking that [Chris Gains], which was a radical departure from his normal "persona" would even fly — a good concept — bad execution all around" (Brooks forum, online).

The project clearly demonstrated Brooks's limitations as a crossover artist. His dramatized act of appropriation required his base audience to embrace an alternate music culture in addition to the substituted performance persona. In affect it invalidated the audience's initial preference for Brooks as a cowboy-hat-wearing country star. The new audience that Brooks was attempting to reach out to also felt alienated because the persona he appropriated is often presented as "being true to yourself as an artist," or as being resultant from actual life experience rather than simply choosing to put on a new costume. Neither audience, in the end, could remove the cowboy-persona from the artist because of his familiarity.

As the familiar and established persona, Garth Brooks had played before seven hundred and fifty thousand people in New York's Central Park. He had been named country music entertainer of the year and been awarded multiple gold and platinum albums. His established country music persona was marked by success. In contrast, Garth Brooks as Chris Gains lacked the cultural power necessary to rally his base audience around the persona, and he also lacked the cultural capital to assemble a new critical or popular base.

It seems that Garth Brooks's attempt at a new persona lacked mobilizing power. Pierre Bourdieu describes this as the lack of ability to "mobilize the authority accumulated within a field" (649). While he is primarily concerned with linguistic exchange, Bourdieu has facility in the discussion surrounding the power of public persona and Brooks's ill-attempted appropriation of another cultural identity. He addresses the fluctuating efficacy of discourse in *The Economics of Linguistic Exchange*: "[I]ts power to convince depends on the authority of the person who utters it.... A person speaks not only to be understood but also to be believed, obeyed, respected, distinguished" (653).

Brooks's lack of success in creating a new public persona raises several questions about audience acceptance of performing bodies as vessels of appropriate cultural representation. Specifically, how does the performing body gain cultural efficacy? How does a performing body effectively appropriate forms and conventions that society will believe in? And what makes audiences embrace or identify with a performance in contemporary America? I would argue that the performing body gains cultural efficacy in contemporary performance spaces by offering its audience something familiar and representative of that audience's own world.

Judith Butler has described the human body as "a historical situation [and] ... a manner of doing, dramatizing, and reproducing a historical situation" (521). If this is accurate, then the best examples of representational bodies, or theatrical bodies must reflect the concerns, forms, and functions that are familiar to their contemporary audiences to be successful and to maintain authority.

CONTEMPORARY PERFORMANCE BODIES

Richard Schechner in *Performance Studies* outlines five areas of contemporary performance. He suggests that the complete list of performance modes is comprised of typical styles that have existed for over one hundred years, many even centuries old. For Schechner each performance event is a reiteration of one of these modes. Schechner bases these categories of performance on congruence with daily life, types of actions presented, the state of mind of the performer, and the importance of objects within the performance matrix. Schechner describes contemporary performance classification as:

1. *Realistic acting*, which assumes that the emotions of the characters are like those of real people. Realistic acting shifts and changes as social life shifts and changes.
2. *Brechtian acting*, a supplement to realistic acting emphasizing the meaning of the drama and the individual agency of the performer. The

Brechtian actor works from an objective place where the actor can comment on the action of the play though direct means and by gesture. In Brechtian acting the illusion of reality is bared and the performance becomes an interrogation of the character's actions and a demystification of the events of the play.

3. *Codified acting,* which depends on semiotically constructed gestures, movements, songs, costumes, and makeup that are set by tradition and passed down from teacher to teacher. Audience members must understand the specific vocabulary and grammar of the codified system to fully understand the expressions of the performance.

4. *Trance acting,* which is when performers are taken over by nonhuman beings and enact actions not of their own but of the spirits or Gods who possessed them. Trance acting is directly opposite of Brechtian performance because it focuses on the surrender of mind and body to the all-powerful forces of the trance. The actor maintains no critical distance and may not even remember what occurred during the period of the trance.

5. *Performing objects as performance,* a technique utilizing puppets, masks, and other objects that are infused with life by the body of the actor.

While contemporary theatres employ all five of these performance styles, commercial theatre most often employs realism (regularly incorporating Brechtian theories in the realistic performance) and codification. Commercial theatre's use of realism and codification over the other forms of performance is grounded in an effort for the commercial theatre to market itself to contemporary audiences. These two forms are most popular because they each allow for explicit and clear communication between the performer and the audience. Both forms are useful to the contemporary commercial theatre because both acting forms demand a clear connection between the performing body of the actor and the audience. Realism allows for internal and experiential connections, and codified performance requires a communication of codes and physical signifiers. Each form allows for meaning-bearing structures that aid the performer in uniting with audiences. Realism is steeped in thematic meaning based in emotional, social, political, or personal commentary. In contrast, codification is infused with physical and outwardly aesthetic meaning-making techniques.

These two performance systems offset each other in many ways. Realism focuses on the emotional body in which the actor primarily develops his or her performance from the inside, using the mind and the heart as performance tools. Practitioners of realism use emotional and mental techniques to explore character subtext and inner life as a part of their acting pedagogy. Conversely, the codified performance focuses on the outside body, or the physical and mechanical aspects of performance. Codifying actor training consists of rigorous attention to physical strength, flexibility, and muscle control.

In many respects the dichotomy between these two performance styles used on the contemporary, commercial stage is a reflection of the contemporary world itself. On one hand realism values and embodies public and private connections through emotion; and on the other hand, codified performance embraces the mechanical or the technical, moving the performing body closer to the plastic or the technological aspects of contemporary human existence. In this case the performing body becomes evidence of particular external focus and physical intensity.

While both forms require an exertion of the body, it is important to note that in a contemporary setting each type of performance demands an extension: a connection to something in the real world that allows contemporary spectators to make sense of the production, to value the production. In fact, in either case the production mode is only successful as it communicates with the audience through lenses — specifically content and form — that they are comfortable with and can embrace internally in some way. This need for immediate resonance with the audience only allows for two types of performing bodies: (1) A nostalgic performing body that connects to the audience through purposeful associations; and (2) A mechanical performing body that connects to viewers through visceral convergence.

STAGING THE NOSTALGIC BODY

Theatre performers accomplish clear communication using realism because the performance body is simulating "real life," engaging with the viewing audience at an emotional level. Realism at its best captures an emotional reality that resonates with the theatre-going population. Themes portrayed in realism grapple with human existence. The traditional approach to realism, beginning in the work of Konstantin Stanislavski, explores humanity in both public and private spheres. The goals of the performer using realism require the actor to find situations in his or her life that correspond to the characters and events portrayed on stage. For example, The New School, a proponent of realism in acting, requires actors to experience and experiment with Stanislavski's acting technique — emotional recall. Emotional recall requires actors to call on memories that they personally experienced when they were in a similar circumstance to that of the character they portray. The realistic actor is also responsible for showing those feelings to spectators in a believable way.

Contemporary realism demands an emotional investment from the spectator. The spectator must draw on their past knowledge and their past experience to make sense of the performance. Performances with these conventions demand that audiences connect personally to the reality of the performance. While this might happen through a connection of the work to the audience's own recollections, it is more likely that the spectator will connect with the staged performance if the relationship is more public. Contemporary works often reflect on or repeat familiar ideas, feelings, and messages or connect to other performances the spectator is familiar with. This style of interaction might be viewed as a product of nostalgia. The performance and the performing bodies in such works often become offerings of nostalgia.

British director John Doyle's 2005 revival of Stephen Sondheim's *Sweeny Todd* is precisely that type of offering of nostalgia. This re-envisioning of the musical is a fascinatingly stripped-bare production. The story remains true to the original *Sweeny Todd* with its dispossessed barber who seeks vengeance on all of London with the aid of his oppressed landlord. However, Doyle's staging and direction of the horrifying Victorian melodrama are starkly different from the celebrated original 1979 production.

The *Sweeny Todd* stage of John Doyle is minimally dressed — chairs, instruments, and a large curio cabinet filled with shabby relics from a London flea market pervade the confined space. The space also doubles as an asylum for the mentally insane and as Sweeney's dilapidated London suburb. The director's signature is an experiment with actors and musicality. Because of this both the libretto and orchestration are completely pared down. A ten-member ensemble performs all of the roles and plays all of the instruments on stage. These ensemble actors, which included Patti LuPone as Mrs. Lovett and Michael Cerveris as the lead character, Sweeny Todd, were more than just characters, they were also the musicians — LuPone played a tuba and Cerveris a guitar. The duet between the young lovers Anthony and Johanna was marked as much by their cello duet as it was their subtle acting performance. The audience watches Anthony and Johanna fall in love through their contemporaneous playing of the cello.

The performers are scenerists, too — the movement of the set is completely actor driven and executed. Performers manipulate chairs and the coffin to become portions of the setting or to aid in new definitions of space. The coffin is used both physically and metaphorically to represent death — the death of Sweeny's patrons and eventually the death of the main characters.

For all intents and purposes this is a new *Sweeny Todd*, reinvented for a contemporary audience and a contemporary world. The critical commentary surrounding the production certainly recognizes the unique achievement of the staging and performance quality. The production is described by the *New Yorker* as "luminous and sort of a landmark" (Lahr, online). The actors' performances are described as "potent because of the production's bare-bones simplicity" (Teachout, online). Clive Barnes of the *New York Post* says Sarah Teasdale's orchestration "has jettisoned Jonathan Tunick's original orchestrations and translated the score in a totally different, equally effective way" (online). Each review suggests innovation and originality in the production's quality.

Ironically, much of the discourse surrounding the musical also provides another vision of the stage performance and the performing bodies. While most theatrical reviews find the production remarkable, these discussions also seem to find a difficulty in identifying its unique nature without comparing it to, or at least referencing, other works of art. For example, Michael Criscuolo's description of the production alludes to other films, plays, music videos, and even the original performance production of *Sweeny Todd* in his description, saying:

> British director John Doyle's production re-imagines *Sweeney* as if Marat/Sade had been turned into a musical and made to resemble a Nine Inch Nails video — more than enough to strike fear into the heart of purists who remember Harold Prince's original Broadway production (now legendary in Broadway lore) and its subsequent televised version. Where Prince's version was epic and operatic, employing a cast of nearly 30 and an orchestra almost as large, Doyle's heavily deconstructed version turns *Sweeney* into a claustrophobic potboiler and pares down the cast to ten actors, all of whom double as the orchestra [Criscuolo, online].

In other reviews, Doyle's staging is described as "transparently ripping off Peter Weiss's Marat/Sade — and its works" (McCarter, online). Performers are described as "Brechtian, [but] not of the Grand Guignol variety," and LuPone herself is described as "positively Weimar" (Lahr, online).

The picture created by critical writers of *Sweeny Todd* depicts the performance as viable only as it is connected to other works of art. The musical itself cannot be described without connecting it to another entity, without referencing a like force. In this way contemporary theatrical production and the presentation of actors' bodies becomes a referential or associative process — always compared to the past or filling in for the past. Understanding in such a production is primarily achieved through the lens of referential identity. Judith Butler similarly describes the performing body in her work *Bodies That Matter*. She depicts the performing body as always referential — always a citation of another body or performing subject. For Butler: "Performativity is ... not a singular 'act' for it is always a reiteration of a norm or a set of norms, and to the extent that it acquires an act-like status in the present, it conceals or dissimulates the conventions of which it is a repetition" (12).

Theatre such as this may seem innovative when staged, but that innovation is a mask concealing the conventions from which it borrows. John Doyle's *Sweeny Todd* is just one example of Butler's thesis playing out in contemporary theatre. Recent observations of theatrical staging and performing bodies indicate that most productions are shaped by similar citational connections or by references to other works of art or commerce.

Consider, for example, the promotional conventions of many of our contemporary productions. The print and billboard advertisements for the Eric Idle–produced musical *Spamalot* read: "*Spamalot*: A New Musical Lovingly Ripped Off from the Motion Picture *Monty Python and the Holy Grail*." Promotional material for the 2006 production of Richard Greenberg's play *Three Days of Rain* capitalized on Julia Roberts's megastar celebrity rather than the successful playwright's contribution to the work.

These promotional, critical, and theoretical discourses provide some insight into contemporary performance. In general, performing bodies have become solely referencing bodies. The theatrical staging of these bodies is built through conformity to codes already established as the norm, even in cases like John Doyle's inventive version of *Sweeny Todd*. The performance is marked by its adherence to norms and conventions that are comforting or familiar to its audience. These codes and norms between performer and audience grow out of encounters with the world. They are combinatory in many senses, relying on audience members' past knowledge — of performance, of character, of celebrity, of associative connection to contemporary culture. In this sense commercial theatrical performance becomes a nostalgic vessel, a vessel that produces what audiences are expecting to see and hear. The expectations, norms, and conventions — the very grammar through which contemporary theatre is produced and understood — are established in an overwhelming number of instances through media forms.

Jean Baudrillard describes nostalgia as "[m]elancholy for societies without power" (Natoli 372). Certainly this sentiment applies to theatrical performance. Theatre long ago ceded its cultural capital to mass media forms. Theatrical performance, therefore, must reflect and even cite other forms to remain culturally viable — that is, to have power. Financial or critical viability in most commercial theatre settings depends on a connection that audiences understand. In many instances this connection is made to mediatized entities. In creating these citational connections, theatre acts as a vessel of nostalgia. The performing body becomes a nostalgic container that portrays the symbols that are projected in the mass media.

As commercial theatre borrows signifiers from media forms, these signifiers are projected onto the staged theatrical performance as well as the performing body. Contemporary bodies staged in commercial theatres become nostalgic media bodies. For example, performers in Disney musicals, such as *Tarzan* (2006) or *Beauty and the Beast* (1994–present) are imbued with the characteristics of the movie musical. As mentioned above, Julia Roberts's 2006 Broadway debut in *Three Days of Rain* (2006) is certainly permeated with her media persona. Even new works produced on Broadway for the first time cater to the communal extension of the electronic media in the casting of their productions.

Producer Eric Idle's description of the casting process for *Monty Python's Spamalot* (2005) demonstrates this point clearly. When asked about casting the slapstick Monty Python version of King Arthur and his Knights of the Round Table on their quest for the Holy Grail, Idle quips: "Who is going to play these parts? That's the issue. We're looking for six major funny people and two major funny women. They play the bulk of everything. So, you're looking for a Cleese type, a Gilliam type, a Jones type, a Palin type and a Graham Chapman type" (Hernandez, online).

Idle's specific reference to the film and television personas hints at the necessity of nostalgic connection. Even in the actual casting the producers relied on name recognition, casting Hank Azaria *(The Simpsons, Mad About You*, etc.) as Sir Lancelot, David Hyde Pierce (*Frasier*) as Sir Robin, and Tim Curry (*Rocky Horror Picture Show*, etc.) as King Arthur. Although each of these performers has credentials on Broadway, they are most recognized for their extensive resumes in film and television. We make the nostalgic connection between the performers and their previous roles. The performance itself is automatically imbued with our nostalgia for past performances and past characterizations created by these actors. Roger Aden describes the efficacy of this type of nostalgic communication: "Nostalgic communication provides individuals with a means of symbolically escaping cultural conditions that they find depressing and/or disorienting. Using communication to move through time allows individuals to situate themselves in a sanctuary of meaning, a place where they feel safe from oppressive cultural conditions" (Aden, 21).

In contemporary theatre the nostalgic performing body provides a "sanctuary" for the viewer by offering a continuity of identification. The origins of the word "nostalgia" can be traced back to the seventeenth century when Johannes Hofer produced his *Medical Dissertation on Nostalgia*, which was a psychological explanation of "homesickness" (Colley, 2). This sense of "home" is central to the explanation of nostalgia, as is the interpretation of "home" as a place that is familiar, comforting, and beckoning. This invitation to "return home" is an unequaled cultural force that is well known as a highly effective and persuasive marketing and advertising tactic.

The examination of nostalgia in consumer research and advertising concentrates on this active understanding of and positive reaction to the past, characterized by Andrzej Gasiorek in a paper titled "The Politics of Cultural Nostalgia," where he describes "a form of parodic nostalgia [that is created] by combining a powerful desire to return to a superseded past with a wry awareness not only that such a return is impossible but also that the imagined past was not quite so hallowed as the myth-making mind would wish" (56).

This "wry awareness" is at the root of an understanding of nostalgia as a tool used by advertisers to sell products and also used by consumers to enhance the experience of the purchase. It is the same tool used by theater and media producers to promote their productions and also used by theater and media spectators to enhance their experience of viewing. It is the subconscious "inside information" that locates the spectator in a place of privileged social identity. It is the "inside joke" that signifies to the audience members that they are "in the loop." Thus nostalgia becomes the primary signifier that audience members can feel comfortable and "at home" within their culture because they know the language, and more importantly, they know the codes.

The spectator's role in such a system of communication through codes of identity, nostalgia, and perception has become more individually interpretive in nature even though the vocabulary of culture signifiers has become increasingly more universal. The dialectic that underpinned the nineteenth and a large part of the twentieth century has given way to a quagmire of knowledge that denies understanding while promoting communication. Communication now is not about understanding; rather, it is about exchanging information. Spectators, therefore, have been expertly schooled in the processing of information — we sort the junk mail from our mail, the spam from our e-mail, the news from the speculative opinion on the web page, and so on. This type of constant processing of information has become so much a part of our cultural experience that it is impossible for us to check these habits at the door of the theatre.

Audiences go to theatrical events today looking for information — nostalgic references, cultural codes, and societal signifiers. In an essay on theatrical interpretation, Marvin Carlson provides a template for the examination of theatre as a collection of codified signifiers. Carlson's vision of the establishment and communication of art hinges upon his vision of a "local habitation" or, in other words, the subconscious identification of common signifiers within a given community. This local habitation is the sum total of a community's cultural exposure. It is this knowledge through common experience that gives both the artist and his audience the tools to communicate in a common language. In this way Carlson asserts any given society's ability to define, interpret, and comprehend its own art forms. He states: "However general may be the 'airy nothing' with which the poet begins, when it is brought into the world of objects, given a name and a situation, then that process must inevitably be conditioned by the artistic tools of the artist's own culture and by the ways the culture defines and interprets artifacts. Thus the work of art may be considered a manifestation of cultural experience, a way of being in the world" (111).

The concept of local habitation provides rich connections between signifiers and codes found in mass media and new theatrical interpretations of commercial events. The performative signifiers found in theatre and purely commercial events are the same because the creators of both types of events are striving to speak the same language. In other words, those who wish to connect with spectators (for an artistic purpose, a commercial purpose, or any other purpose) must use the language or semantics of contemporary spectatorship. In western culture, that language is dominated by the semantics of mediated messages. Because spectator reception flows through this common language, cross-reading between events becomes the norm. Spectators wonder what it means — they look for, and perceive, theatrical narratives, themes, and meaning in the purely commercial. Also, spectators wonder what they're being sold — they look for, and perceive, commercial and political purposes in artistic expressions.

The best example of this new phenomenon of reading meaning into commercial events is the increased theatricality found in contemporary fashion shows. Fashion shows are purely commercial events where fashion producers display their wares for fashion consumers (mostly procurement officers for large retailers). Yet the presence of culture codes and signifiers has increasingly led audiences to interpret these commercial events as theatrical — having emotive and communicative elements that engage the spectator. By closely examining the fashion catwalk's emergence as a theatrical venue, we will be more able to see how commercial messages are placed and perceived in theatre that exists in a media environment.

FASHION AS THEATRE

It is not beyond our cultural experience to view comparable elements of both the fashion and the theatre worlds as unified theatrical and cultural signifiers: i.e., designer/director = sender; catwalk/stage = context; model/actor = message; consumer/ audience = receiver (Jakobsen 350–77). Given similar codified dimensions, the audience readily defines and accepts fashion as performative, and the relationship between fashion and theatre can best be examined through codified terms.

For example, John Galliano's 1999 spring-summer fashion collection illustrates the increasing trend toward theatricality on the haute couture runway. Galliano's concept for the presentation of his clothing designs was a historically informed rehearsal space. Leaning heavily on historical allusion, Galliano provided the model-actors with an environment that referenced the intimate atmosphere of Isadora Duncan's school in Grunewald, Germany. Some of the models assumed historically specific roles: Isadora Duncan and Martha Graham. Others portrayed nameless characters such as a dance teacher, a piano player, and an ingénue. Models performed "limbering up" exercises and other signifiers of a dance rehearsal. Spectators seated on the perimeters of this theatrically created dance space listened to languid rhythms and observed tableaus of pre-performance. Such uses of theatrical expressions as a means to promote a commodity are a common fact of the contemporary high fashion stage.

At one time, the audience for this new fashion theatre was limited to those whose primary interest in fashion was strictly economic, and even today a first-hand gaze at contemporary fashion spectacles is limited to the famous and the wealthy. However, fashion performances have now become readily available to consumers through magazines, television, and even the Internet. The press of the world rushes to the catwalks of Milan, Paris, and New York, not only to observe and critique fashionable clothes that will never be worn by most of the viewing public but also to specifically report on the messages delivered by the designers. The interpretive coverage that fashion shows regularly receive from mass media can be seen as common examples of how the fashion world has been redefined as a new theatrical experience. High-quality fashion shows no longer act as elongated advertisements for a product or a designer. Instead the industry has co-opted a nouveau-theatricality that incorporates thematic directors' concepts, elaborate gestes, and performer-audience spatial relationships into spectacle driven productions. Structural comparisons between the high fashion catwalk and accepted theatre signifiers create a post-modern fashion theatre that moves beyond the economic roots of pure fashion into a forum for cultural expression and identification.

Both the theatrical stage and the catwalk can enhance the communication between the sender and the receiver through physical manipulation of palpable elements. Each event requires the interaction of body and space. Each event employs the deliberate use of lighting, sound, and space to create an emotional ambiance to intensify the narrative. Musical scores are often an integral part of the narrative concept of each event. Indeed, the common tasks between the theatre director and the fashion designer with regards to adopting elements of spectacle into the scenic presentation of each event renders them practically identical in their function and capacity as an art director. This change in the production and reception of commercial fashion industry events was not innovated into existence by a few individuals; rather, it evolved ubiquitously throughout the industry because it is surrounded by a mass media environment, and therefore (just as theatre) must adopt the communicative conventions of the dominant culture language — mass media.

The use of lighting, music, and space is essential in the determination of the theatrical or nontheatrical meaning placed on the designer's human parade. Each component contributes an additional layer of meaning to the clothing and the designer's concept of the show. The selection of lighting, music, and space determines the level of theatre the designer chooses to present to the audience. Light, space, and music are used to theatrically enhance or juxtapose the message of the clothing in the show. The intensity of the lighting can lend a soft or harsh atmosphere to a collection. The use of music can determine whether the collection is contemporary, reflective, or futuristic. Similarly, a collection of bridal dresses shown in a cathedral setting can assume a different tone than if they were shown in a public toilet.

Alexander McQueen's 1998 spring-summer narrative collection is considered one of the most dramatic shows ever staged. Art director Simon Costin utilized theatrical techniques to create an evolutionary fashion show. The concept was based on a section from the film *2001* where astronauts first discover the ancient monolith on the moon. McQueen describes the show in terms of its theatrical conception and dramatic evolution: "I wanted the people to feel that they were entering an unearthly, almost religious space where an enormous amount of energy was contained, but ... it had to feel potentially dangerous" (Tucker, 41–42).

The show used a forty-ton Plexiglas water tank as a runway. The large tank was lit from below by one thousand individual fluorescent tubes that produced a golden glow in the performance space which illuminated models in pure white costumes. McQueen and Costin also installed a rain machine that sprayed the models and the clothing at various times throughout the show. During the three-minute interval between costume presentations, Costin introduced a negative visual element that reversed the atmosphere presented in the first portion of the show. In a moment of silence when the stage was empty of bodies and clothing, the tank, which was originally translucent, was pumped full of black ink. The whole structure took on an entirely different pathos as billowing black clouds slowly obscured the light coming from below. The dramatic change was further reinforced by the appearance of the models who were now dressed in dark and forbidding colors.

The fashion show becomes theatre because it incorporates traditional physical conventions to create the space between the performance and the observer. In epic tradition, the audience at a fashion show is rarely incorporated into the "performance" space. The fashion spectator is an observer that is forced to make decisions about what he or she sees (Do I agree or disagree with the message? Am I offended by the content of the show? Does the show represent a product that I value?). These decisions represent a theatrical type of involvement on the part of the audience. Specifically, the high-fashion experience is the type of theatre that is rapidly growing in popularity: a montage of images and an arrangement of signifiers that allow the observer to determine meaning in what he or she sees and hears.

This is precisely the formula that Cirque du Soleil has used to garner international acclaim. Beginning in the early nineteen-eighties Cirque du Soleil began to experiment with the idea of a new human circus. Their work focused on a theatrical mixing of circus and street performance arts. The group toured through the United States and Europe presenting visual and aesthetic displays that emphasize the tactile, kinetic, and proximic possibility of the human body. Currently the theatrical company presents their work in eight theatrical venues around the world, each exploring the exquisite capacity of the human body as it encounters and experiences the plastic and spatial world. Each of these powerful spectacles draws hundreds of thousands of people yearly to the performance venues.

The thematic elements of each of Cirque du Soleil's performances are usually delivered as a parade of cultural signifiers that allows for individual interpretations. For example, on Cirque du Soleil's website, a description of the opening scene of Cirque du Soleil's production *Mystère* reads: "The adventure begins with the Big Bang, symbolizing primitive man embarking on a never-ending journey. The opening also juxtaposes the characters and contexts in a way that creates the timelessness of *Mystère*: the primitives on the drums, the Renaissance Archangels and the ultra-modern decor coexist seamlessly" (Mystere Online). The presence of the cultural signifiers (primitive drums, Renaissance Archangels, and modern décor) is obviously a choice made by the creators of *Mystère*, but the manner in which they are to "coexist seamlessly" or why they are to do so is a matter left entirely up to the spectator to determine. The only direction given to the spectator is the expectation that all of these elements should coexist. The connection is entirely the spectator's to make.

In theatre such as this, meaning comes entirely from referential associations of visual signifiers and extra-textual information. The actor becomes contributory rather than central to meaning-making and communication. The director's concept dominates the production, and the actor's contribution is equal to, but does not exceed, that of all the other elements of the event, such as the costumes, lighting, and music.

Again, the example of theatricality in contemporary fashion shows is illustrative of our cultural acceptance of actors who participate as visual elements rather than emotive sources of meaning and communication. In his book *Fashion as Communication*, Malcolm Barnard describes signified meaning in fashion as the product in people's heads: "Meaning is thought of as being the product of what is in people's heads, their intentions. Thus if the wearer gives a garment a particular meaning, the meaning of the garment may be said to be the product of the wearer's intentions. According to this argument, the beliefs, hopes and fears of the wearer are expressed through their use of the garment" (72).

This popular-culture based desire for meaning becomes theatre when we consider the feasibility of the model as a mimetic actor. The model sends a specific message that reflects the concept of the individual designer in each fashion show; the consumer audience in turn receives the intended meaning and has some response (a purchase and possibly a change in consciousness).

The continual transformation of the haute couture model into the mimetic representation of the designer's creative thought has all the trappings of Brecht's alienation effect. Brecht's discussion of the actor's place in the alienation effect illuminates the idea of model as actor:

> For the actor it is difficult and taxing to conjure up particular inner moods or emotions night after night; it is simpler to exhibit the outer signs which accompany these emotions and identify them. In this case, however, there is not the same automatic transfer of emotions to the spectator, the same emotional infection. The alienation effect intervenes, not in the form of absence of emotions, but in the form of emotions that need not correspond to those of the character portrayed [94].

Like the Brechtian stage actor, the model assumes a geste that evokes the creator's theme. The model-actor develops outer signs that form a persona-character that exposes the designer's narrative. Utilizing these conventions of the theatre (gesture, blocked movement, and visual symbols), the actor draws in the audience to experience his or her projected emotions rather than the emotions of the designer. The actor connects and disconnects his or her own personality to the persona enacted on stage. The theatrical semiotic location is created because the consumer-audience determines an alliance to the material.

Such performance is also acceptable to the contemporary theatre audience because of the codified signifiers that lead to extra-textual projection of meaning by the audience onto the actor. These codes are universally disseminated through mass media. Access to the performance, therefore, is incumbent upon the audience's access to mass media. In this way, mass media information, cultural codes, and signifiers are not just a chosen element of contemporary theatre — the cultural vocabulary of mass media is a compulsory element of all performative expression. Performing bodies are becoming less outwardly emotive in their function on today's stage. Performing bodies are becoming *technological bodies*— mechanisms that emotions and meanings can be projected onto. Spectators generate these projections as they gather information from the codified signifiers provided by the entirety of the production. The technological body is a receiver of meaning or a device for the display of meaning.

It is easy to see fashion models as technological bodies when they are thought to convey meaning in the context of a fashion show, even though their outward expressions are often of detachment or disinterest. However, it is the same for stage actors on contemporary stages, even though their training is rife with emotive techniques. The simple fact is that all performing bodies placed before an audience are technological bodies because they cannot escape the projected meaning that comes from spectators educated by a mass media culture to gather information from culture codes and society signifiers. Thus, performances that are deemed successful in today's climate of information saturation are often codified performances that allow the maximum amount of connection to the maximum amount of people.

STAGING THE TECHNOLOGICAL BODY

Rooted in eastern performance techniques that draw on ancient religious rituals, codified performance relies on a clear communication of symbolic forms and content that is presented by the actor and received by the audience. The actor's body becomes the focus of performance. Technical mastery of the coded movements is essential to providing a significant performance.

Audiences connect with codified performance because codified structures are clearly embedded in other aspects of their lives. Richard Schechner points out: "Most rituals — secular as well as sacred — some popular entertainments and sports employ codified movements. To perform a marriage, execute a ballroom dance, or shoot a basketball requires mastering codified behavior" (156).

Schechner reminds us that codified events (sports, concerts, ceremonies, and etc.) are incomprehensible to those who don't know the codified movements of the event. In fact codified events, according to Schechner, owe their particular power to engage audiences to the combination of codified and improvised behavior. The basic moves are codified to allow people to know what is going on and to appreciate expertise or incompetence. At the same time, brief and flexible movements of the performing body can allow for variance and new combinations of the form.

Contemporary Western theatre began to produce theatre influenced by Eastern methods of codified performance in the beginning of the twentieth century. For example, Antonin Artaud based many of his ideas for the "Theatre of Cruelty" on a revelation that he had while watching Balinese dancers perform ritual dances at the Colonial Exposition in 1931. Bertolt Brecht developed his methodology for the alienation effect through observation of codified performances by the Chinese actor Mei Lanfang. Vsevolod Meyerhold's theory of biomechanics, which relies on an actor's focused study of the mechanics of the body, is also an influence on the work of Western productions by Peter Brook, Ping Chong, Richard Schechner, and other contemporary Western directors.

Beyond these, it is the work of British director and philosopher Edward Gordon Craig that specifically addresses the value of symbolic performance as a vehicle for communication. In 1908 Craig began to write about a transformative view of performance in which the actor becomes puppet-like, symbolic rather than emotive. His writing about the actor's body appears in essays written for his theatre journal *The Mask*, as well as other publications. In *On the Art of the Theatre*, Craig depicts a new theatrical form in which the "objective of the theatre is neither intellectual, nor emotional but is the evocation of aesthetic pleasure derived from the presence of imaginative beauty" (295–96). For Craig, contemporary theatre was a unified representation of a single artistic imagination, and the stage was "an atmosphere not a locality" (31) that harmonized with the place imagined in the artist-director's mind.

Craig describes his disdain for contemporary actors in essays about his ideal of the "total theatre." According to Craig in the 1958 reprint of *On the Art of the Theatre*, the actor is governed by the tenants of naturalism and realism and is limited to the potential and the purposes of the director's imagination. Craig describes the actors' bodies as carrying "the proof in his own person that as the material for the theatre [they were] useless" (31). Instead, the ideal performing body to Craig was a perfect instrument — symbolic in form and function.

Craig's musings about the place of the performing body in artistic work led him to consider the elimination of living bodies altogether. By 1905 Craig had introduced the concept of the "uber-marionette," an automaton that served the purposes of the artist's theatrical design. Initially Craig decried the modern actor's portrayal of thoughts, saying, "For his thoughts (beautiful as they may be) may not match the spirit of the pattern which has been so carefully prepared by the director" (167). Craig valued a mechanical being that could be controlled by the director. In his essay "Gentlemen, the Marionette," Craig describes the function of the actor as uber-marionette: "There is only one actor — who has ever served as true and loyal interpreter of the Poet [director]. This is the marionette" (Gentlemen, 207). Thus, the performer as marionette became an inanimate object to be manipulated and controlled by the poet.

Charles R. Lyons describes Craig's motives for the marionette, saying: "[Craig] saw the marionette as the symbol for the perfectly disciplined actor. The marionette, as a figure which holds neither animation nor personality apart from that given to him by the stage-director, would provide a flexible and calculable material for the design without obtruding upon it" (263).

Despite great general respect for Craig's powerful scenic designs and his intriguing commentary on the art of directing, his suggestion of an aesthetic theatre which turned itself away from the emotive actor was much maligned by other scholars of his day. But Craig was a visionary of sorts. Today his description of a total aesthetic theatre that incorporates an actor who is stripped of the conventions and codes of realism and naturalism has come to fruition in the work of human circuses produced in sports arenas, media programming, and large commercial theatrical venues, and teaches us to value the meanings embedded in formal systems over the content of emotive systems.

Key examples that demonstrate this communal fascination with physical contortions of the human body include the media fascination with the Olympics, professional sports, and the explosion of Internet pornography. Worldwide Wrestling Entertainment is also a prime example of this fascination with codified performances of the body. The WWE is a publicly traded company that promotes codified professional wrestling with a yearly revenue of four hundred million dollars. Each of these spectacular events focuses on the body as an object of physical display and versatility. In each of these cases the performing body conveys appropriate codified behavior to interest and inculcate large audiences (mediated audiences as well as live) to value the production forms and narratives that are clearly not a part of reality. These performances instead focus on codifying the extremities of the human form and the physical experience. Karl Toepher explains the contemporary fascination with this manipulation and codification of the body, saying:

> The spectacle of the body twisting into "unnatural" configurations invariably haunts the spectator, for it appears as if the contorted body transcends either a normal threshold of pain or an acceptable juxtaposition of body parts.... Contortionism therefore constructs a complex, contradictory image of the body as a site of extreme pliancy, extreme strength (or boldness), and extreme vulnerability, and it is this tension between extremes of physical expression that accounts for the visceral excitement of the spectator [104].

In Toepher's description, the encounter between the performing body and the viewing body is a site of extremity that leads to a palpable internal reaction from the audience. There is no emotional connection of ideas in this type of codified experience. Rather, the visceral experience connects the performer and the spectator. The spectator, innately aware of the confines and requirements of the human body, is awed by the exploration of the physical expression, and therefore is drawn into the experience because of his or her own awe. Knowledge of the codes and conventions of the entertainment allow the audience to feel safe, and the physical, almost always collective, exploration of those boundaries engages the audience in the performance.

Like Worldwide Wrestling Entertainment, contemporary commercial theatre has also capitalized on this type of performative expression. Most notably is the work of Cirque du Soleil, a company that creates corporeal experiences designed for the commercial stage. Cirque du Soleil and two of the companies' directors, Robert Lepage and Franco Dragone, have brought Craig's concept of the uber-marionette to life. Their productions focus on connecting with spectators through the physical performance inherent in the other performative venues mentioned above.

These theatrical exhibitions are unique to other theatrical experiences because of the intense focus on corporeal performance as an aspect of the spectacle. The body is a mechanized part of the performance; it is central yet interchangeable between various performers with virtuosity in execution being the only common element. The performance planning and execution forgoes individual emotive skills inherent in other performance styles. Individual human content is vetted from the presentations and the performing body becomes a controlled and integrated, even mechanized, tool of the director. The performing body is a component of the show much like the lighting or the sound elements of the production.

The body in Cirque du Soleil is a site marked by physical strength and virtuosity. Performances require the actor to execute contortions, acrobatics, and dance and water ballet skills. But in the context of the production these are not equated with individual performance. By accomplishing the requirements of the physically technical and mechanized performance, individual actors' bodies may test the personal limits of physical exertion, beauty, and facility in rehearsal, but in performance the body is consumed into the production and becomes a part of a larger whole. The body in Cirque du Soleil productions represents archetypal themes rather than specific character emotions and traits. Individuality is replaced by the presentation of archetypal ideas, and the human body becomes solely a reflection of those ideas.

In one example, *La Reve* (The Dream): *A Small Collection of Imperfect Dreams*, the production focuses on humanity's imperfect but beautiful capacity to survive. Human strengths, weaknesses, pain, pleasures, and temptations are all depicted in the ninety-minute performance, but individual characters do not have a connecting narrative line. The performance, which is directed by former Cirque du Soleil artistic director Franco Dragone, is performed nightly for large audiences at the Winn Las Vegas Hotel. The arena stage seats audience members in close proximity to the action. There is no seat more than forty feet away from the stage. Audience members are able to see every aspect of the world simultaneously.

Performers are alternately submerged in water or hoisted into the air. The actors perform on a series of platforms, which alternately rise high into the air allowing for intense segments that include stunning feats in the form of aerial ballet. Actors also plunge deep into the water, performing synchronized Busby Berkeley, aqua-musical-like movements and choreography. The bodies are constantly exposed to the elements. Performing bodies encounter, among other things, wind, lightning, and floods.

Performers execute a variety of identifiable archetypes. These range from ethereal godlike figures that seem to control the actions of the collective performers to buffoons who remind the audience of humanity's imperfections. The core performance explores physicality and requires the audience to connect to the theatrical work through their engagement with the produced and manipulated construction of the human form.

In a theatrical review of an early Cirque du Soleil performance in the 1990s, Stephen Barker asserts that the very nature of this performance style alters the way that contemporary audiences receive the body. He says:

> What is most fascinating about the Cirque du Soleil's "Nouvelle Experience" is that it guides us to the essential element of spectacle, to the grotesque and the beautiful, the marvelous and the disturbing. The Cirque presents and represents a direct assertive, and interrogative theatricality designed simultaneously to assert and undermine a kind of searing flight, a diversion of energy away from thought, self-consciousness, and reflections. It is a pyrotechnical *kirkos* of struggle against the limits of performance capabilities and the spectator senses in which looking is accomplished with different eyes, wonderfully wrenched out of complacency, stretching the imagination further than it has gone or indeed may want to go toward an unknown, unexpected, dangerous and exciting limit [Barker 245].

Barker astutely observes that the very nature of the performance requires the audience to engage differently, to look *with different eyes* as they view this style of performance text. His words obviously suggest that there is a shift in the way spectators view performing bodies. The new requirements established for spectator engagement — that are introduced by mediated means and demonstrated by codified theatrical performances and performing bodies — are borrowed from and learned by our direct engagement with media forms. This shift in spectator perception allows for a new contemporary performing body that combines the emotional connection of the nostalgic body and the physical prowess of the mechanical body. This body moves beyond the emotions of the nostalgic body and the traditional ritual associated with the mechanical body. This new performing body employs the formal elements of nostalgia and technique to create a performing body that is technically adept and physically polished, but is only one part of the larger commercial production. This performing body combines nostalgic representations of the past but is solely iconic in presentation. It is the nostalgic-mechanical body — the technological body.

It is precisely this type of body that is the focus of Disney's *Tarzan* production on Broadway. Nancy Coyne, principal partner of the marketing firm Serino Coyne, obviously believes that the Broadway theatre audience is ready to accept such a view of the performing body. Speaking of the marketing strategy for the show she says: "I think one of the things we're going to be trying to emphasize is the athleticism of the experience, sort of the extreme sport of the show" (Kuchwara 1). Such an emphasis for a $15,000,000 Broadway production indicates that the technological body that has been a mainstay on the stages of Las Vegas for ten years is now the prominent, if not preeminent, form of presentation and reception of the actor on the American stage.

SEVEN

Theatre and the Grammar of Media Technology

Commentators on contemporary American society easily identify media's cultural colonialism. Those who comment on the American theatre landscape in general are no exception. The position of mediatized messages as a dynamic cultural element makes it a nearly irresistible subject for observation and commentary. But the true test of a theory of mediated cultural homogeny is through analysis of theatre events where media is not the subject.

Even when the media is not the topic of discussion, media-derived structures permeate the cultural language of theatre. The recognition of media in theatre is the core of this study: media not only as an overt or implied presence in the American theatre, but as an internal mechanism, or influence, that acts as a dynamic cultural structure that shapes the projection and reception of meaning. The language of theatre has assimilated a new media vocabulary and grammar into itself. This grammar, born of technology, cannot be labeled as deleterious to the art form, just as it cannot be said definitively that opera is best in Italian or inferior in German. What can be said is that there is a new language being spoken on American stages. A key example of this is Anna Deavere Smith, who strongly embraces theatrical representation but nevertheless demonstrates the penetrative power of media structures. Smith embraces the forms in her work, incorporates the technology in her productions, and capitalizes on her own exposure in the mass media.

Anna Deavere Smith privileges language often to the exclusion of the visual medium. Her critically recognized one-woman series, *On the Road: A Search for American Character*, is based on an oral tradition of story-telling that she learned from her paternal grandfather. By her own account: "In Baltimore when I was growing up, my paternal grandfather was my biggest influence. He was a talker who told me that if you say a word often enough it becomes you.... My interest in language probably has some roots in that" (Stayton 74).

Smith, a Stanford professor and professional actress who began the *Search for American Character* series in 1982 at the Cleare Space in New York City, is most famous for her documentary-style performances in which she depicts divisive cultural events from various angles.

Smith initiates each project by going to the site of a controversial event. She solicits interviews with people who participated in or were affected by the event and then documents the responses of these real people from various economic and social strata by tape recording them. She uses a tape recorder rather than a video recorder. She continues her focus on the verbal intricacies of each interviewee's language as she reviews the compiled audio material and selects portions of their words from these tapes for her performance. To her, rehearsal is a repetition of each individual's performed language in which the character's words are mimicked with exactness and her movement is a remembered representation based on what she hears over and over again. She describes the work, saying: "The point is to repeat it until I begin to feel it and when I begin to feel his song and that helps me remember more about his body" (quoted in Martin 57).* She mimics the aural interview. Her inflections and rhythms match those of the person she interviews because the aural interview is a material possession that can be repeated and studied, the physicalization of the interviewed carries less authority because it exists only in her memory and is therefore represented, embellished, and influenced by her study of the spoken word. Smith's performance of the compiled interviews in the plays *Fires in the Mirror* and *Twilight Los Angeles* also gives primacy to language. Both plays are based on the social and cultural unrest that lead

---

Anna Deavere Smith describes her character work on Leonard Jeffries in an interview with Carol Martin. According to Smith, her style of character development moves away from the more conventional psychological realism in which the actor works to embody the character by identifying likenesses between the character and the performer. Instead her approach is to simply repeat what the individual she interviewed says until she remembers the way they moved in the interview. For a detailed explanation see "The Word Becomes You," in The Drama Review *37: 4 Winter 1993. p. 45–62.*

to division among groups of people. Smith interviews individuals from a variety of racial and social groups and then uses the interviews as the basis for her staged performance art. *Fires in the Mirror* concerns a civil disturbance between Lubavitcher Jews, African Americans, and Caribbean Americans in Crown Heights Brooklyn. The events described in the interviews for *Fires in the Mirror* took place in August of 1991. The rioting was spurred by a traffic accident in which seven-year-old Gavin Cato was accidentally killed by a vehicle from a procession of cars occupied by leaders in the Lubavitch community. Rioting between the racial factions led to the death of Yankel Rosenbaum, a twenty-nine year old Hasidic Jew. *Twilight Los Angeles* is based on the uprising in South Central Los Angeles that followed the acquittal of four Caucasian policemen for the beating of an African-American, Rodney King, on April 29, 1992.

In the original stagings of both plays, Smith is the only person on stage and she chooses to repeat the stories told to her verbatim. There was little spectacle in her staged performance pieces. Using minimal props and sets, Smith's live performances were a verbal polyphony of voices merged with her own. Smith was the visual focus, and she became what she describes as a "re-teller," (re)presenting their stories through the ethnographic lens of her own voice. For Smith, her representation of the human experience was grounded in the words they speak. She differentiated her theatrical documentary style from that of filmed documentaries, saying: "Theatre is action, but in the beginning was the word. And the word was all. And speech is action, but it's not movies where you see images. The way action happens in the theatre is through the propulsion of words. The text is spoken to move the action forward. You get information about what happened before and what's going to happen, and people cause action with each other through their words" (quoted in Lewis 58). And yet despite the lack of a prevalent media presence, media practice infiltrated Smith's work.

SMITH'S USE OF MEDIA IN PERFORMANCE PRESENTATION

Smith's interest in conducting interviews and then representing the interviews as performance material began as an exercise first for herself and later for her students at Stanford University. She began her study of character, and her quest for what lies between the nouns and verbs, in front of the television. She describes the transition moment in her career as happening while watching Sophia Loren and Joan Rivers on the *Tonight*

Show in 1979. She noticed that each guest's ability to embrace or reject the rhythms of the language affected the whole structure of the show: "I started watching interview shows on television looking for these places where the rhythm of the show would fail, or when a person's language would fail. Originally I was just like the paparazzi ... watching interview shows and tape recording them and sitting up all night transcribing them" (Stayton 73).

In the early stages of her project Smith determined that her work was language based, that listening was the key to character. What the example above demonstrates is that, even from the earliest stage of her project, Smith drew insights from the visual as well as the verbal. In Smith's description of the early development of the project she describes herself as "looking" and acknowledges the use of videotape as a tool of discovery. Smith's work, though language based, is dependent also on visual tools. This is evident through exploration of Smith's use of media form and content in her three most recent productions in the *Search for American Character* series.

Smith uses media as a spectacle that comments on or enhances the verbal text, as a tool to convey the context of the whole series (e.g., televised excerpts from *Fires in the Mirror* and *Twilight Los Angeles*), and as content (e.g., her most recent addition to her theatrical series, *House Arrest: An Introgression*, which focuses on the power of the media in American politics). *Fires in the Mirror* employs black-and-white photographs featuring the two groups of people represented in the conflict. The journalistic photographs serve as visual evidence of the events represented verbally through the performed interviews. *Twilight Los Angeles* is Smith's first play to use video imagery: archival television footage is interspersed between monologues and is equal in importance to any of the spoken words of the script. Smith counterposes television news footage of the event with the performed individuals represented in the play. In her opinion, "media was almost like a character during the riots. People relied on the media for information. Those who couldn't get any other help used media as a vehicle for communication" (Stayton 72). In *House Arrest: An Introgression*, media images are used to connect and contextualize historical events. For example, the Zapruder film of President Kennedy's assassination plays out on large screens as twelve actors reenact President Lincoln's assassination on stage. The use of media materials augments the verbal message and connects the two events together during the performance. In many cases Smith allows the director of the production to determine how media will be used and in what form it will contribute to the production message.

Smith has demonstrated her willingness to invest her work, and her own performance of that work, with the increased cultural significance that distribution to a mass audience provides. Twice Smith has used television to present portions of her *On the Road* series for the Public Broadcasting System. *American Playhouse* presented *Fires in the Mirror* in 1993. In April 2002, ten years after the videotaped assault on Rodney King, PBS aired Smith's *Twilight Los Angeles* on *Stage and Screen*, a televised series that presents theatrical productions. The televised productions in each instance altered the theatrical elements of the original stage version.

The television production of *Fires in the Mirror*, directed by George C. Wolfe, is a carefully crafted bridge between Smith's theatrical format and the tools of television. Wolfe takes care to capture the essence of Smith's theatrical performance technique. The camera is unobtrusive, and Smith's physical body is presented from a theatrical distance that allows the viewer to see nuances of the face and body of the performer without the filmic fetish of invasive close ups. Minimal sets and costumes are used that copy those of the live production. However, there are several elements that mark the performed material as televised rather than theatrical.

The *American Playhouse* version of the same taped performance is edited for time and the episodes are rearranged. The televised performance is augmented with black-and-white photographs and videotaped footage of the events depicted in the play, and text appears on the screen to identify the characters and their setting. These additional elements are clarifying tools that undoubtedly replaced a theatrical program book. Smith addresses the difference between theatre and television in the early moments of the presentation when she frames the performance experience with commentary about the event she portrays, her performance technique, and the socio-political implications of the performance piece. Janelle Reinelt describes the televisual framing device as journalistic and connects the performance codes utilized in the initial sequence with those used in television news programming. In regards to Smith's framed commentary, Reinelt believes: "Codes specifically identified with television dominate the video by structuring the authority of the performer as similar to a journalist or a documentary filmmaker. Smith's role might be likened to that of an anchorperson who reports the news in a mixture of subjective and objective relationships to reading the news" (612).

Reinelt's observation is significant because it points out one dramatic alteration in the televised performance. Smith's theatrical technique is marked by her ability to represent the people she interviews physically and vocally and still remain present herself. In the theatrical version of the play,

Smith's own voice is heard alongside that of the interviewees because there is no verbal or visual commentary outside of the performed monologues. This duality is not captured on tape because Smith brackets the performance with journalistic commentary where she becomes an observer rather than a participant. She marks herself as outside of the experience by indicating her presence only as an observer in the early moments of the program. In some respects the televisual performance unintentionally changes the focus of Smith's play from an intimate exploration of individual experiences to a peopled display of social ills as represented by a commentator akin to television's reality or journalistic programming. More important, the televised version of Smith's work alters the precepts of Smith's performance technique because Smith — the observer — negates the authenticity of Smith — the participant — within the performance. In her attempt to make her technique clear to the television audience she subverts the patterns of her live performance work.

Smith's collaboration with a media presence is more intentional in the *Stage on Screen* performance of *Twilight Los Angeles*. PBS describes the performance as "a filmed adaptation" of Smith's play, and the performance is laden with documentary film footage of the Rodney King beating used in the staged play as well, but also included filmed footage of subsequent events (such as the police brutality trial and the subsequent riots, including the Reginald Denny beating) and Smith reprising her role of interviewer when Mark Levin records Smith's journey back to Los Angeles to re-interview key people that participated in her project in 1992.

The film, directed by Mark Levin (the 1998 winner of the Sundance Film Festival Grand Jury Prize for his film *Slam*), depicts Smith's performance as a secondary voice supporting the visual events that are depicted alongside her performance. Levin's project is in fact more about Anna Deavere Smith and her interaction with the media event of the Los Angeles riots than it is a screen version of the play.

Levin's project is structured like a filmed documentary. Smith's performed monologues are woven between visualizations of the events her characters describe. Monologues are not juxtaposed to each other in the same way that they are in the staged play. Instead, they become verbal support for the visual documentation that Levin selects for the film. The archival film footage includes national and local political figures. Live footage of Maxine Waters's impassioned response to the riots is substituted for Smith's portrayal of Congresswoman Waters. Additional filmed footage of the interviewees is also provided. A filmed interview with community activist Gina Rae, aka Queen Malkah, is followed by Smith's portrayal of the same woman during the riots. In one segment Smith's physical body is actually merged into the visual material that Levin collected. We see a close-up of Smith's head (as Josie Morales, one of the eyewitnesses to the Rodney King beating) move across footage of the beating as if she were an eyewitness to the officers' crime and then through the filmed footage of the police officers' trial and the news of their acquittal. This movement directs the viewer away from the verbal testimony to the visual interplay between the graphic design elements in the segment.

Levin continues to direct the television audience away from the performance of the play to a visual documentation by condensing and overlapping monologues. In Smith's theatrical work, the editing of material is done to serve each character. Attempts are made to keep the interviewees' words intact. In the filmed version, the portrayal of the interviews becomes a television sound bite. Character monologues are cut severely to allow time for lengthy film documentation, and interviews are spliced together to create a filmic pace. The result is a frenetic presentation of stereotypes that lack the duration to develop elements of the previous theatrical context and that instead establish a context that is solely visual. Instead of experiencing intimate observations about the riots in juxtaposition to other intimate portraits of the experience, the television viewer sees and hears a more choppy montage of Smith's characterizations combined with videotaped footage that supports what the characters say. The televised version of *Twilight Los Angeles* does not emphasize Smith's trademark performance style in which repetition is used to reinforce its own form and content.

Smith's most recent project shifts the use of media from form to content. In 1995, using a grant from the Pew Charitable Trusts, she began research on her "Press and the Presidency" project. The project, an attempt to discover the relationship between the media and the president of the United States, resulted in the performance of *House Arrest: First Edition* performed at the Arena Theatre in Washington, D.C.* The press is in attendance to the president as much as the Secret Service is, or even more. The Secret Service is really visible only if you see the president live, whereas most of us view the president as a product of the press and its camera lens (*Talk to Me* 100).

In preparation for *House Arrest*, Smith interviewed approximately four hundred people, including President Bill Clinton, many of his White Houses aides, dozens of the most important political commentators and

This is drawn from Smith's description of her own pre-production and production experience during the play in her book Talk to Me: Travels in Media and Politics.

pundits of the era, and even some minor government workers. Smith also sought out local residents of Washington, D.C. These interviews, combined with relevant governmental historical documents that were also performed verbatim, created a narrative about the media, the presidency, and the American people's perception of both.

Fourteen actors, who performed historical characters and the recently interviewed political figures, originally staged the play. They formed a fictional acting troupe whose primary responsibility was to discuss the infusion of truth into art. *House Arrest* was unique in its interaction with media because the project did not cover one specific event, as had Smith's previous projects discussed in this chapter. Like the media personalities and events it portrayed, the play was constantly in flux to stay contemporary with the media itself. The performed project was revised nightly, and as events in the press altered, the content of the show necessarily shifted. The performed event mirrored media events so closely that when the Monica Lewinsky affair broke out in the press, a reviewer for the *San Francisco Chronicle* described Smith's analysis of the president and the press in the play as "stale from familiarity and the intense press analysis" (Winn 48).

Ironically, in the presentation of ideas surrounding media and politics, *House Arrest* lost many of the unique theatrical qualities that Smith presented in her previous work, *Fires in the Mirror*. For instance, Smith's contextualization of the multiplicity of voices presented on television utilized the audience's visual memory of the event presented in theatrical form. The voices Smith portrayed in *Fires in the Mirror*, on the other hand, were largely unknown in the media; Smith's play filled in the missing portions of the story, even embellishing the visual images and sound bites. However, in Washington, D.C., the people she interviewed provided her with insights they shared on cable news interviews regularly. Anna Deavere Smith's interviews were only another place to repeat their stump speeches and have them disseminated.

Smith's own media celebrity also altered her ability to represent herself as the apparatus through which the interviews flowed. In the production of *House Arrest* and any current documentary elements in the *Search for American Character* series, Smith is recognizable from her mass-media performances. Smith's acting performances, first as the president's press secretary in the film *The American President* and then as a regular cast member on the television show *The West Wing* as the fictional president's national security advisor, have given Smith a small degree of name and face recognition.

SMITH AS AUTEUR

Anna Deavere Smith is a self-described reteller of truths, but an examination of her work and discussions surrounding it make it evident that the success of her presentation is based in artistic control of the words she repeats. Smith's authorial voice rings most artistically powerful in her editing of the material she performs. For her most prominent works, she completes over 150 interviews. When Carol Martin asked how she selected the people she interviews, Smith remarked, "I usually get a few contacts from the newspaper and then try to make my way into any institution, to somebody in authority ... eventually, I know very specifically what kind of person I want to meet so I know what kind of person I want to find" (quoted in Martin 46). This statement indicates that Smith is thinking about the performative aspects of her play before the interview phase is even beginning. Smith as director shapes the piece even as she gathers and records her text. Smith and her team of interviewers use similar questions for each interviewee, and the interviews are conducted at or near the site where the events she is interested in occurred.

In the second phase, Smith as editor makes additional authorial choices when she selects specific interviews and then cuts those interviews to meet time constraints and establish a dramatic flow. Smith is careful to protect the authentic voice of each interviewee (never excising an individual word or phrase), choosing to cut at natural breaks in conversation. Where Smith is most skilled and most cinematic is in the juxtaposition of the material she chooses. Emily Mann, the director of Smith's most prominent work to date, *Twilight Los Angeles*, at the Mark Tapor Forum in 1992 describes Smith's efforts as an editor in purely cinematic terms:

> If you were making a documentary film you'd be using much the same technique as she uses.... She takes shards of language, and then she juxtaposes them, orders them. Much of what she does in terms of creativity as a dramatist comes from this juxtaposition. She also has an uncanny ability to find the lifeblood, or the pulse point of a monologue. She might do 150 interviews, and she may use 40 or 30 or 25 and make her piece out of that. The writerliness of it comes from the editing and the juxtaposition. The editing becomes a very personal thing. She finds what those edits are, the order and the performance [Dawson 125].

Mann's description of Smith's efforts is significant because it draws parallels between Smith's work and descriptions of early film editing. Montage editing was developed in the Soviet experimental cinema of the 1920s and is primarily associated with the work of Sergei Eisenstein. Smith's editing technique precisely mirrors that of Sergei Eisenstein's montage editing. Eisenstein believed that collision and conflict were inherent in all visual signifiers and that through the juxtaposition of individual shots meaning could be created.

A key factor in montage editing is that through the choice of images presented a preferred reading can be inscribed on the audience. The non-linear process of montage moves beyond the guided articulation of a narrative (Nowell-Smith 202–3) but still introduces its ideological agenda through its visual syntax. While juxtaposed images associated with montage editing require the spectator to be a participant in the creation of meaning, the American classic Hollywood style of continuity editing works to seem invisible to the spectator. Specific devices used in continuity editing guide the spectator to believe that they are seeing continuous action. For example, the eyeline match and shot-reverse-shot pattern show us a character looking at something and then we see what the spectator views in the consecutive shot. This effect essentially stitches the gap between the character and what he or she sees. A second example is the 180-degree rule, an imaginary line that demarcates the various angles from which the camera can shoot to achieve believability in spatial relations from shot to shot. Montage editing, as Smith's own work employs in the theatre, gives more power to the spectator than continuity editing does.

Just like the early montagists, Smith chooses the material and its placement and intends that her audience will determine the ideological intent of her material through their own interpretations of these juxtaposed images. It is important to note that like the Soviet montage filmmakers, Smith does not intentionally guide the viewer to her own agenda through direct or personal comment, although she does introduce a preferred set of values through the juxtaposition and dramatic collision of the play's verbal semantics.

Smith's juxtaposition of voices introduces an ideological perspective about the events she covers. She reveals her own perspective in the ordering of her material precisely as a montagist does. This is evident throughout her work, but an example from *Twilight Los Angeles* clearly demonstrates the connection between Smith's style and that of the montage editor. *Twilight Los Angeles* dramatizes the events surrounding the Rodney King beating in southern California, including the subsequent police brutality trial, as well as the riot and the aftermath after the police officers' acquittal. At the play's midpoint Smith places three monologues together. The play text indicates that the monologue representing Tom Bradley, the former mayor of the city of Los Angeles, appears between the monologues of two Asian-

American men who experienced the riots firsthand. While Bradley is presented as polished, it is clear that his descriptions of the event are steeped in political jargon. He describes his preparation before the verdict and the subsequent riots:

> We learned that the verdict was coming in that afternoon. Um, we had four messages, depending on the verdict. If it was a guilty verdict, some guilty, some not guilty, we had a separate message. The one that I had put down as just a ... a precautionary measure, an acquittal on all counts, was something we didn't seriously think could happen, uh we had a message and it did happen. And so within a matter of an hour and a half we had that message on the air ... directly to the public, and it was essentially to call for ... to express my outrage at this verdict of not guilty for all these officers [*Twilight* 85–6].

In contrast, the two Asian men speak with authority about personal loss because of the rioting. Chung Lee, president of the Korean-American Victims Association, describes the events in Korean while his son translates in English: "I called my neighbor's store and the gentleman — uh, the man told me, 'Your store's been completely looted! Your whole stock is scattered all over'" (*Twilight* 83). And Richard Kim, an appliance storeowner, depicts the fear near the apex of the event: "[A] neighbor called and said you better come down here because there are hundreds of people and your store's being looted at this time. So we packed up our van, four people, five people, including myself, and we headed down there. I already knew people were carrying guns, already knew my mother was shot at that corner. So it was like going to war" (*Twilight* 87).

These contrasting monologues stand as verbal snapshots of these scenes. Their position in relation to each other creates an emotional collision where the audience is guided to a preferred opinion. The structural result is identical to that of a visual montage, and the audience is receptive to the message because they are subconsciously familiar with the form.

Smith's goal in her *On the Road* series was to be objective, that is, to include all voices that best represent the event, but it is in the selection and placement of each monologue that her authorial voice resonates. Through the collision of commentary in these three monologues, she provides a social and economic context for the event, identifies the political atmosphere in the city that fuels the rioting voiceless, and authenticates the experience of those most affected by the event through their competing discourse.

Many prominent documentary films are notable for their attempt to focus on the struggles of common people. In similar form, Smith positions herself with the general population of Los Angeles through her editing techniques, giving more space to firsthand accounts of the riots than to pundits and politicians. Smith often edits her material with collaborators, giving credit to director and friend JoAnne Akalaitis for the powerful shift in the performance text for *Fires in the Mirror,* in which the monologue from Carmel Cato, Gavin Cato's father who was originally slated to appear in the Crown Heights section of the play, is ultimately given the last word in *Fires in the Mirror.** She also gives credit to the team of dramaturges that helped shape the piece prepared for the performance of *Twilight Los Angeles* at the Mark Tapor Forum.† But regardless of this additional input, Smith guides the work with an authorial hand because she alone follows the process through as the interviewer, the editor, and the performer. Her desire to repeat is a new form of performance that is an effort to copy in the same sense that which the camera copies.

Smith describes her artistic technique and its theoretical underpinnings as a move away from psychological realism to a new performance style that embraces repetition. Smith's style differs from psychological realism in her rejection of the need for the actor to establish a connection between his personal psychological experience and that of the character. In psychological realism, the actor's physical and psychological presence is immersed and often masked by that of the character. Smith instead sees the actor's role as one of performed exactness — a replication of the individual interviewed. Her own participation is not masked behind the guise of character as it is in psychological realism, because she believes that the physical machinery conveying the character is apparent even as the character is apparent. Smith refrains from using emotional identification as an actor tool, and while her own physical and psychological being is obvious because she chooses to show the medium through which the material flows, she attempts to remain objective in her performance of each character.

In many ways her physical presence is like the documentary camera, she is an apparatus from which real-life sounds and images emerge. Smith,

---

Gavin Cato was the accident victim whose death spurred the contention between Hasidic Jews and African-Americans in Crown Heights. JoAnne Akalaitis helped make editing decisions during the production of Fires in the Mirror *that took place at the Public Theatre in New York in 1992.*

†*The dramaturges associated with the first production of* Twilight Los Angeles, 1992, *include Dorinne Kondo, a Japanese American anthropologist and feminist scholar; Hector Tobar, a Guatemalan-American reporter for the* Los Angeles Times; *Elizabeth Alexander, a professor at the University of Chicago; and Oskar Eustis, a resident director at the Mark Tapor Forum.*

like a camera, attempts to capture each individual's presence in time and space, seeking the authenticity of the original moment of the interview. In the introduction to the published version of *Twilight Los Angeles*, Smith describes her efforts to seek out and perform the presence of the people she interviews: "What most influences my decisions about what to include [in the performed play] is how an interview text works as a physical, audible, performable vehicle. Words are not an end in themselves. They are a means to evoking the character of the person who spoke them. Every person that I include in the book, and who I perform, has a presence that is much more important than the information they give" (*Twilight*, xxiii–xxiv).

Smith's interest in replication of human presence is not a new approach to performance but can be traced to the earliest discourses on performance practice. Plato and Aristotle both talk about reproduction or imitation as part of performance. In the *Poetics* Aristotle discusses the use of imitation from three modes: "For it is possible to imitate the same objects, and in the same media (1) by narrating part of the time and dramatizing the rest of the time, which is the way Homer composes (mixed mode), or (2) with the same person continuing without change (straight narrative), or (3) with all the persons who are performing the imitation acting that is carrying on for themselves (straight dramatic mode)" (Else's translation of Aristotle 18). Other practical attempts at historical accuracy are evident in the work of early nineteenth-century director and stage manager William Charles Macready, who consistently used historically accurate costumes and scenery in his productions; and certainly the theoretical discussion of Naturalism, as displayed on the late nineteenth-century stage, employs a desire for exactness in the authentication of man as he relates to environmental space and place. In his essay *Naturalism in the Theatre*, Emile Zola calls for the physiological representation of man: a man determined by the environment that produced him. According to Zola, truth on stage is born out of attempts to present art without spectacle: "I picture this creator [the dramatist of genius] scorning the tricks of the clever hack, smashing the imposed patters, remaking the stage until it is continuous with the auditorium, giving a shiver of life to the painted trees, letting in through the backcloth the great, free air of reality" (351).

While Smith's approach develops out of these theatrical traditions, her work also hinges on the twentieth-century ideological stance that expands out of the study of images created through mechanical reproduction. It is this connection between her replication process and that of mechanical reproduction that makes her work move beyond psychological realism and its mask of the performer. Consider Walter Benjamin's essay on "aura" and mechanical reproduction, as it relates to Anna Deavere Smith's process of reproducing interviews for the stage:

> [P]rocess reproduction can bring out those aspects of the original that are unattainable to the naked eye yet accessible to the lens, which is adjustable, and chooses its angle at will.... Photographic reproduction with the aid of certain processes, such as enlargement or slow motion, can capture images which escape the natural vision.... Technical reproduction can put the copy of the original into situations which would be out of reach for the original itself. Above all it enables the original to meet the beholder halfway.... The cathedral leaves its locale to be received into the studio of a lover of art; the choral production, performed in an auditorium or in the open air, resounds in the drawing room* [733].

Smith's work parallels Benjamin's description of mechanical reproduction; like the camera she captures the original interviews verbatim. Like the editor she chooses the interview material and the angle of its presentation. Finally, she also has the ability to adjust the context of the original interview material. She does this by contrasting it with other interviews. Using techniques similar to those of mechanical reproduction, Smith manipulates the focus of the audience to themes or subjects that she deems important and away from the interview itself. For example, competing narratives are purposefully placed together to incite emotion. Section titles of *Twilight Los Angeles* such as "The Territory," "War Zone," "Twilight," and "Justice" guide the viewer to a context for individual monologues as they are presented in groups. Smith's staged re-contextualization is certainly theatrical: she is the material presence that appears on stage, she uses minimal costumes and props, and she appears live on stage before an audience. However, the techniques she employs to achieve the theatrical event are analogous to mechanical reproduction. Smith's work (and theatrical works similar to hers) could therefore only be imagined in the twentieth century after the birth of mechanical reproduction.

ANNA DEAVERE SMITH'S USE OF CINEMATIC FORM

Smith's event-based work is often described as documentary theatre, a form of theatre in which primary source material is incorporated into

---

Walter Benjamin distinguishes mechanical reproduction from other forms of reproduction (painting, lithography, etc.) in his essay The Work of Art in the Age of Mechanical Reproduction. *For Benjamin the process of mechanically reproducing an art object or a natural phenomenon allows for a re-visioning of the original object.*

the dramatic play through a variety of means. Gary Fischer Dawson, a scholar who has written widely on documentary theatre in the United States, separates documentary theatre from kindred theatre forms — historical drama, epic theatre, and agit-prop — by describing the documentary as an evolving theatrical form that includes primary sources, is "microhistorical" and "content driven," is "persuasive," and "brings the private to the public" (12).

Dawson delimits three periods of documentary expression in America. First: *The Living Newspapers*— an early American expression of the documentary form that is often connected with political unrest, a documentary format that expressed the tension between the working class and the establishment through live performances depicting the "true" events behind newspaper stories. Plays in this category, like *Triple A Plowed Under* (1936), expressed the strong socialist agenda of the working class.

Second: A re-establishment of documentary theatre that began with *In White America: A Documentary Play* twenty-four years after the Federal Theatre Project was defunct. This period of expression is most known for a manipulation of primary source documentation to achieve a dramatic effect. In *In White America*, which is written chronologically, Martin Duberman depicts thirty scenes telling the history of African Americans from their forced journey from Africa to their struggle for civil rights in the 1960s. The play is the first in America to use historical documentation to attain historical authenticity. Although Duberman edited the documents for dramatic purposes, he published his documentation in its complete form within the playscript and asked performers to note the complete information in rehearsal for the performance. It is also included in the published playscript. Duberman's desire for authenticity through primary sources became the model for documentary theatre work from the 1960s through the early 1980s.

Third: A period of documentary form that evolved from the nonfiction work of Emily Mann in the early 1980s. Mann's work, which includes eyewitness accounts and testimonials from individuals that Mann interviews, moves from historical accounts to the personal experience. Works such as *Annulla*, an autobiographical play based on the words of Annulla Allen, and the Tony Award nominated *Having Our Say* are personal testimonies based on verbatim interviews conducted by Mann.

It is in this atmosphere of bringing the private to the public that Anna Deavere Smith's work was born. While Mann's focus is on the personal, Smith borrows and expands Mann's form into the social and the political. Dawson calls Smith's work "drama vérité" (132). Drama vérité is a new form of documentary theatre, which borrows from Mann and Duberman but is much closer to the work of documentary filmmakers like Vertov, Flaherty, and Grierson in its desire to present ethnographic pictures (descriptive, characteristic documentation of community or anthropologic realities).

Flaherty and Grierson were early documentary filmmakers. Robert J. Flaherty is most well known for his efforts to photograph the lives of Inuit tribes on film in the early 1920s. His hope was to capture idyllic images of a group of people never before photographed. We know now that his ethnographic efforts are suspect because much of his footage was restaged for the camera. In truth, the Inuit culture was far more modernized at the time of filming than is depicted in Flaherty's documentary footage. John Grierson is most well known for his depictions of the working class. Process and duration in lives of coalminers are presented in a film he produced, *Coalface* (1935). Grierson described documentary form as an instrument of information, education, and propaganda.

Drama vérité, as used by Dawson, is a play on words. Dawson is making a comparison between Smith's work and that of the Russian filmmaker Dziga Vertov. Vertov gained notoriety for his filmed edition of the Soviet newsmagazine *Pravda*. The title of the filmed version, *Kino-Pravda* or "film truth," later became a term used to describe a documentary style that featured real people in their natural settings. In *Key Concepts in Cinema Studies* Susan Hayward describes cinéma vérité as "unstaged, non-dramatized, non-narrative cinema. It puts forward an alternative version to hegemonic and institutionalized history by offering a plurality of histories told by the non-elite" (39).

Attilio Favorini* asserts "documentary engagement with public figures and high profile events brings the conventions of the 1960s 'direct cinema' into tension with the postmodern aesthetics of performance art" (xxxii). Theatre critic Vincent Canby concurs by describing *Twilight Los Angeles* (1992) as "a new kind of documentary theatre which has the immediacy of live drama and the fluidity of film" (Duberman 131).

Critical comparisons of Smith's performances to a film aesthetic are helpful in identifying the media presence in Smith's work. Side-by-side comparison of Smith's performance technique and the techniques of the previously described filmmakers yields many similarities. Three connections are most important: First, Smith's performance text of recorded

Attilio Favorini is the editor of Voicings, *the first anthology of documentary theatre published in the United States. The anthology was published in 1995.*

material captures real people in both public and private settings for an audience in much the same way that Vertov's formal style, cinéma vérité, captured the people of his time. Second, Smith's authorial voice is evident in the editing process, and those who work with her have described her selection of material in filmic terms. Finally, Smith considers her performance of the interviewees a repetition of the interview. Her desire to repeat creates a new form of realistic performance that is an effort to copy in the same sense that the camera copies.

CINÉMA VÉRITÉ AND ANNA DEAVERE SMITH

Dziga Vertov describes the relationship of his camera (and in extension, himself as the camera operator) to its subject in his writings on the cinema: "I am eye.... I am apparatus, maneuvering in the chaos of movements, recording one movement after another in the most complex combination.... My road is toward the creation of a fresh perception of the world. Thus I decipher in a new way the world unknown to you" (17–18). In Vertov's description of the camera at work, the camera/operator is the apparatus through which movements are captured and recorded for an audience. Vertov believed that it was only in the recording of a multitude of mundane events that a fresh perception of the world could be captured.

For example, in *Kinoglaz* (1924) Vertov depicts life in a Soviet village. The action is centered on a group of young pioneers who are constantly pasting propaganda on walls, distributing handbills, and extolling the virtues of buying from the cooperative. Vertov experiments with film's form, projecting in reverse the slaughtering of a bull and the baking of bread. In *Chelovek s kinoapparatom* (1929) a cameraman documents a day in the life of the Soviet Union. He goes so far as to document the filming of the documentary itself, and of the audience watching it. The filmmaker documents all process of filmmaking including shooting, editing, and projection.

Smith's performance of interviewed subjects is similar in many ways to Vertov's objective focus on filmic form. Her desire to capture and reproduce an authentic presence on stage is most evident in her form. Like Vertov's camera, she acts as the apparatus through which the event and the individuals move and speak. In live productions, Smith does not moderate or narrate for the audience but simply repeats her subjects' words verbatim. Charles R. Lyons and James C. Lyons describe Smith's material presence as "a visual and aural screen on which and through which different voices speak" (47). Richard Schechner describes the performer's process of incorporating the people she interviews into her own body as shaman-like: "Some shamans exorcise demons by transforming themselves in the various beings — good, bad, dangerous, benign, helpful, destructive.... Smith absorbs gestures, the tone of voice, the look, the intensity, the moment by moment details of the conversation but in so doing, does not destroy the others or parody them. Nor does she lose herself" (2).

Smith describes her process as an intervention that can reshape the way people experience the events of the world: "[O]ne kind of intervention is the intervention of listening. We can listen for what is inconsistent as we ask what is consistent.... The break from pattern is where character lives, and where dialogue, ironically begins in the uh, in the pause, in the thought as captured for the first time in a moment of speech, rather than in the rehearsed, the proven" (*Talk to Me* xxxix). Clearly it is Smith's desire, like Vertov's, to capture all that she hears for an audience.

MEDIA'S INFLUENCE ON SMITH'S PERFORMANCE EVENTS

The discussion of media's influence on Smith's work would not be complete without an acknowledgment of the news coverage surrounding the events that she portrays. Each of the three plays discussed in this chapter was initially conceived, written, and performed during the media storm surrounding the public events that Smith depicts. Analysis of the media coverage in Crown Heights and Los Angeles, conducted by the Joan Shorenstein Center on Press, Politics, and Public Policy at Harvard University, suggests that media framing shaped the perception of these events. This framing is a conceptual tool used by the press and the viewing public to construe, communicate, and evaluate information.*

Framing techniques are used to organize information into a story-line, by emphasizing some factual material and expressly ignoring other parts of the story to shape meaning. Carol B. Conaway contends that reporters relying on a racial frame heavily influenced the racial tone of the riots in Crown Heights and misconstrued other underlying events, which demonstrated that the conflict in Crown Heights was primarily over eth-

---

*William A. Gameson describes framing techniques in the following manner: "Frames for a given story are frequently drawn from shared cultural narratives and myths. Some stories resonate with larger cultural themes; this tunes the ears of the journalists to their symbolism" (see "News as Framing," American Behavioral Scientist, 33. 2, [November 1989] 157).

nic traditions rather than race (93–118). Likewise, technological tools and advances in media presentation heavily influenced the way the story was told in Los Angeles. News crews were often on the scene before police. Therefore they determined the way the story would be told, the people who would be filmed, and the duration that each story would play in front of the American public. For example, Erna Smith describes the influence of technology on the televised narratives that were told during the Crown Heights riots: "Because of the premium placed on action visuals and the advance planning and technological abilities of television news crews to react quickly to the initial outbreaks of violence, dramatic images of the assaults by young black men on white, Latino and Asian motorists ... and confrontation between police and demonstrators ... in downtown Los Angeles were shown repeatedly throughout the coverage" (13). This repeated coverage along with the nearly continuous live coverage of urban violence in the first two days of the riots led to an increase in television viewing levels from a 31.3 rating in May 1991 to a 40.3 rating during rioting one year later (*Broadcasting* 15).

Increased viewing of television during the riots and the framing techniques of the media representatives contributed to the climate in which *Fires in the Mirror* was originally produced. Additionally, both *Fires in the Mirror* and *Twilight Los Angeles* were presented near the geographical epicenters of the events portrayed in each play. Smith's first performance of *Fires in the Mirror* premiered at the Crossroads Theatre Company in New Brunswick, New Jersey, forty-five minutes from the New York borough where the disturbances took place. The performance took place less than a year after the rioting occurred. Members of the audience would have been familiar with the case from local television as well as extensive reporting in the *New York Times* and the *New York Post*.

The impact of television coverage on the Los Angeles production of *Twilight Los Angeles* is more evident in interviews conducted in regards to the closeness of the Smith's performance to the epicenter of the action it depicted and to the time that the event occurred.* Viewers of Smith's play comment on this in postproduction interviews about the play. These viewers of the theatrical event in June 1992 clearly connected their theatrical experience at the Mark Tapor Forum with the televised events that occurred the week of 29 April during that same year. A survey of theatrical reviews for the premiere production of *Twilight Los Angeles* compiled

*The site of the play was the Mark Tapor Forum, which is located at the heart of Los Angeles on Grand Avenue at Temple Street; the forum hosted the event in the aftermath of the riots.

in the *Theatre Journal* and edited by Susan Vaneta Mason provides some insight into the correlation between the viewers' theatrical experience and their perceptions of the media's representation of the riots:

- "Dramatically, the piece (*Twilight*) is remarkably passive. Many monologues are in the past tense, moments remembered, rather than relived. A video sequence enhances this tone of remembrance. Through multiple screens resembling a large window, the audience glimpses, as if from indoors, the Rodney King beating and the looting and the pillaging of the city." Edit Vilarreal, University of California at Los Angeles.
- "The Video did little for me with its by now numbingly familiar images." Sandra Tsing Loh, performance artist and writer, Los Angeles.
- "Unfortunately the economic girders that structure racial differences go unexamined. For example, *Twilight's* omission of any admitted looters from its cast of citizens created a glaring imbalance and weakened the influence of the piece. Looting involved more people in the disturbance than any other action, and it was watched by millions day and night on television news shows." Susan Suntree, East Los Angeles College.
- "When the performance opened with a slide projecting the name of the piece and its author on an overhead screen, I felt as if I was about to watch a television documentary." Joyce Guy, performance artist, Los Angeles.
- "How appropriate that in 'Hollywood' we observe collective, professional amnesia about the politics of the framed image. Consider, then the events of April 1992, as, among many other things, a local critique of representation, of how representations are organized and framed, of whose frames are celebrated as 'disinterested,' 'factual,' ... part of the challenge is selecting 'Stars' like Reginald Denny and 'bit players' like June Park.... Yet there is another challenge, one of ground or perhaps more accurately, one of grout: in what matrix are these voices embedded? What controlling intelligence, what politics has decided which voices and which shards of which voices to leave in and to leave out? Or are we simply to pretend that these voices, like those on the evening news, exist somehow outside of an organizing ideology." Judith Hamera, California State University, Los Angeles.

The reviewers connected their viewing experience in the theatre to their experience in watching television during the riots, making comparisons in form, content and execution of the material. This suggests that in many ways the reception of Smith's event-based work was dependent on a visual understanding of the events that the play is based on and which have been previously televised. Thus, despite her emphasis on language, Smith is complicit in encouraging visual memory as a component of production. Media scholar Tania Modeleski points out that as Smith's work gains notoriety, the communities she examines and then represents are larger and that there is an increase in characters that her viewing audience associates primarily with media representations (102). Characters include political leaders, religious leaders, film stars, etc. because of the types of events Smith chooses to represent.

The national publicity that the events receive before she uses the event for theatrical purposes is also a factor in Smith's representations of individual characters and the reception of those characters by a theatre audience who is familiar with the characters' public image. Finally, because of the influence of both televisual and filmic form on her theatrical technique, Smith's study of the verbal depends on the visual image's cultural efficacy.

In effect, Smith has given primacy to media's forms and content through her acceptance of media's indelible mark on her theatrical work. The mediatized presence throughout Smith's work, regardless of her desire to make it secondary or even absent in her writing and performance, clearly demonstrates how the media's structures can saturate theatre practice.

Eight

Reality and Spectatorship

A scholar on theatrical reception, Susan Bennett, says that scrutiny of the individual spectator and the collective audience must be investigated first from its social constitution. Speaking about the value of establishing a cultural context for individual audiences, Bennett asserts: "[S]tudies of the individual audience in their social, material, and historical specificities are an important contribution to how we understand what has gone on before and how we come to watch performance in our own contemporary moment.... [W]hat has emerged from ... study of the audience is the necessity to view the theatrical event beyond its immediate conditions and to foreground its social constitution" (211). Consequently, if media constitutes a part of spectators' experiences, then media will also determine their perception of what is real on stage. It is important then to examine mediatized spectators and consider the ways that media has influenced their reception of contemporary theatre.

Theatre Spectatorship and Culture

Writing about the impact that technology has on contemporary bodies, film scholar Vivian Sobchack describes "a moving image culture" in which film, television, and computer technologies have reshaped our mental and physical selves, offering the body alternative methods to physical representation. According to Sobchack, human encounters with media technology have transformed us as subjects because they allow the human body to explore the manipulation of time and space as each relates to our own bodies:

> Although relatively novel as "materialities" of human communication, cinematic and electronic media have not only historically symbolized but also historically constituted a radical alteration of the forms of our culture's previous temporal and spatial consciousness and our bodily sense of existential "presence" to the world, to ourselves, and to others. This different sense of subjective and material presence both signified and supported by cinematic and electronic media emerges within and co-constitutes objective and material practices of representation and social existence [67].

The compelling portion of Sobchack's depiction of media's effect on the contemporary mind and body is her suggestion that all bodies — whether directly or indirectly — are reshaped because the mass media has altered the way that individuals think about themselves in relationship to time and space. Although she recognizes the total historical impact of the media, she specifically suggests that the alteration in human perceptions of presence occurs with the invention of first film, then television, and finally digital technologies. It is in the combined use of these technology structures that individuals begin to perceive the body as a mediated being whose capacity for communication is extended by its ability to communicate and even manipulate its own material consciousness.

Evidence that corresponds to Sobchack's ideas of an altered audience perception because of the audience members' exposure to the media can be found in the structure of many contemporary plays that feature a manipulation of time and space. For example, *Take Me Out*, the 2003 Tony Award winner for best play, is told entirely in flashbacks. The play's narrator, the character of Kippy, is constantly crosscut between immediate and contemporaneous communication with the audience and participation in scenes that are to represent action occurring previously. Often these shifts between scenes would last only for a matter of seconds, demonstrating the audience's learned ability, and the author's faith in that ability, to perceive a significant change in time and place and back again solely from visual cues.

This shift in our perception of the body is even more enhanced when media technologies encourage spectators to see themselves as central figures in mediated narratives and their interactions as performative in some capacity. A prime example of this occurred in the fall of 2001 when Jonathan Lebed, a fifteen-year-old, was charged with Internet fraud. Lebed was accused of purchasing and promoting stock using what the Securities and Exchange Commission described as "multiple fictitious names." He had come to the attention of the SEC because of his successful web persona. Lebed's Internet guise included day trading, web-based business research, and the design and the promotion of Stock-dogs.com, a website he developed and operated to promote promising stocks. Using knowledge gleaned from the television business network, CNBC, and his own natural abilities, Jonathan Lebed had accrued $800,000, gaining the attention of the national media and the United States government because of his ability to create and maintain a persona of authority through the Internet.

In *Next: The Future Just Happened*, Michael Lewis chronicles Jonathan Lebed's experience as an Internet personality and his subsequent interactions with the SEC. He describes Jonathan's cyberspace impersonations as an attempt to "simulate an appearance [performance] on CNBC." For Lewis, Lebed's presentation of self via the Internet delineates the performative nature of interaction with media technology: "The whole point of Jonathan Lebed was that he had invented himself on the Internet. The Internet had taught him how hazy the line was between perception and reality. When people could see him they treated him as they would treat a fourteen-year-old boy. When all they saw were his thoughts on financial matters, they treated him as if he were a serious trader" (74).

In essence Jonathan began his interaction with technology as a receiver. He gathered information from television news programs, listened in on web-based business conversations, and observed the personas created by other Internet day traders in e-commerce chat rooms. But eventually Lebed used the medium to project a performance of his fictional self. His role as a receiver changed to that of a performer, and what began as reception developed into theatrical performance through his interaction with media technology.

Like Jonathan Lebed's negotiation of a theatrical performance space via the Internet, the performative nature of material consumption can be encouraged by media's form and content. Mediatized interactions become dramatic, theatrical performances when participants see their own bodies, and their virtual extension, as the sites of interpretation or reinvention. Media as an extension of the body is evident in everyday encounters that are aided by technology like shopping online from a home computer or corresponding instantaneously across large geographical regions via email. In these cases, technology works overtly to extend the material body into alternate dimensions of time and space, demanding a virtual alternative to material presence.

PERSONAL NARRATIVE, THE MEDIA, AND THE
PARTICIPATORY SPECTATOR

Most contemporary studies in theatrical reception are attempts to correct the idea that the theatre audience is a monolithic entity, of interest only in its passive relationship to the theatrical production. Theorists and practitioners have recently begun to examine the participatory nature of the audience. Theatre audiences are often described as active participants who enter the performance arena as dynamic contributors to the artistic goals of a theatrical production.

Jerome Rothenburg describes a post-modern performer-audience paradigm in which "the audience disappears as the distinction between the doer and the viewer ... begins to blur" (14). Feminist scholar Jill Dolan acknowledges the individual viewer's power to construct alternatives to the ideological underpinnings of the theatrical mainstream and the subsequent staged display in conventional theatrical productions. Speaking as a self-described spectator whose view is "personally, artistically and spectatorially ... closest to the view from elsewhere" (119), Dolan argues that the individual spectator can "subvert representation" (119) and draw conclusions not offered by the text or performance.

These contemporary constructions of the audience that help us to acknowledge the potential for active participation of the theatre spectator in the construction of the performed text are founded on the study of phenomenology, the philosophical position of reader-response theorist Edmund Husserl. Through the precepts of phenomenology we can contemplate the theatrical performance as it is experienced and conceptualized by the viewer. For example, the context in which the receiver views and comprehends the production is an equally valuable contribution to the performance as the work material produced by the theatrical events' creators. A phenomenological reading of theatrical reception acknowledges that the theatre experience is initiated and even guided by the sounds and images constructed in the play's creation and then encountered on the stage by the viewer. But in performance the creation of meaning occurs within the spectator. The spectator fills in the gaps of the theatrical presentation through their own unique world experience. Thus any given production is shaped by where and when the viewer sees the theatrical production, the individual viewer's anticipation or foreknowledge of the given theatrical event, and even his or her understanding of the syntactic, or sequential organization of the play itself. While the creators of a given theatrical event can address an ideal or intended reader in their planned structures, the real life spectator breathes unique life into theatrical production through his or her individual participation with the theatrical performance.

Drawing on studies in phenomenology and reader response theories, Susan Bennett contends that theaters' shift from the accepted matrix of production and reception to a more flexible idea of what theatrical performance and spectatorship might be has altered venues, companies, and methodologies. It is from within this latest notion of performance reception that I draw two important conclusions. First, Bennett describes the contemporary spectator as a "participatory spectator/actor" (19). The active participant is emancipated in and through the varied negotiations of this shift from matrixed theatre to an understanding of performance that includes alternatives to traditional theatre, including the audience's more familiar relationship to technological media. Second, while Bennett's "participatory spectator/actor" could simply be another manifestation of the audience's cerebral participation in a given production, I believe that she is describing the active participation of both the mind and the body of the spectator — in essence Bennett's concept of participation allows for audience participation that can be both subjectively and materially constituted.

Certainly there is a precedent for active spectator participation within the framework of historical production. In earlier chapters I describe the complicit relationship between the audience and the performer in the work of Julian Beck and Judith Molina, who sought a centrality in the audience-performer relationship that broke the confines between the stage space and the audience. But Bennett's concept of a "participatory spectator/actor" has encouraged both theatre scholars and practitioners to further consider the boundaries of participation as they relate to the temporal, spatial, and bodily investment of the collective audience as well as individual participants. Media technology's saturation of our society has made it possible for individual audience members to actively negotiate a material and subjective space in which they allow themselves to exist within a theatrical narrative. This existence extends from the staged theatrical narrative into performative acts within their own personal space.*

Although the participatory spectator that I speak of has much in common with Augusto Boal's "spectactor" in whom the traditional boundaries between the actor and the spectator are broken when the spectator comes to the stage and performs the role of the protagonist for a period of the action, I see the spectator's immersion in the narrative as extending beyond the performance but not in the intentionally politicized way that Bertolt Brecht describes in his discussion of epic theatre. Instead the spectator is a participant fully immersed in the text to the point that he or she seeks to expand the themes and structures of the text into his or her own life. In this case media's form and content can be a model for the participatory spectator.

For example, admirers of the 2003 musical *Hairspray* can create online interactions by accessing the official website. Spectators can look through a cast photo album, watch streaming video interviews with individual cast members, listen to music clips from the musical, access the fan newsletter and learn to dance the "Stricken Chicken" and the "Peyton Place," two dances from the musical, by interacting through the computer with animated versions of the stage characters.

The extended connection between the viewer and theatrical performance that I describe here is similar to the incorporation of television soap opera story lines and soap opera characters into real life conversations by working women in Birmingham, England, described by cultural anthropologist Dorothy Hobson in "Soap Operas at Work." Documenting conversations with female members of the working class who view soap operas, Hobson illustrates that interaction with media programming can extend past the initial viewing of the television program into real life. For example the women depicted in her study often revisit previously aired soap opera episodes and anticipate what might happen to favorite characters in future episodes during lunchtime conversations. The soap opera conversation is so integral to acceptance in the lunchroom space, according to Dobson, that women who did not watch soap operas were ostracized from the lunchtime dialogue. The pressure to be a part of the lunchtime conversation was so acute that some women began watching soap operas outside the workspace simply to participate in the lunchtime conversation. Dobson's study is particularly interesting because it demonstrates the individual spectator's desire to extend viewership past the original viewing time and space into the time and space that is considered real life.

Media entities also teach spectators that they can interact and even perform within a theatrical narrative and that these actions can extend beyond their passive interaction in the theatre into their own personal space. While the mass media certainly works to extend the narrative into the virtual bodies of the participants discussed above, it is also important to consider the possibility that theatre's participatory spectator learned this negotiation from their interactions in a media-saturated society and that the prototype for this contemporary participatory spectator is a media model.

Televisual and cinematic forms encourage spectators to see themselves as central figures in mediatized narratives that move beyond the view of technology as a tool of communication. Media technology assimilates the spectator into the narrative structure of the media text and also encourages viewers to insert themselves into their structures. Several popular films of the late twentieth-century model the intersection between film and reality, playing with the borders between the two worlds. In Woody Allen's *Purple Rose of Cairo* (1985), a movie character walks off the screen into the real world holding the film and his screen character in limbo until he makes a decision about whether he will return to the screen or stay in the real world. In the *Last Action Hero* (1993), Danny Madigan is transported into the film world of his favorite action hero through a magic ticket provided by his local theatre projectionist. Danny becomes a part of the film's action but an evil character from the film finds Danny's movie ticket and escapes into the real world.

Total Request Live, the Music Television Network's premiere television program, is a prime example of televisual interaction. Started in the late 1990s by MTV executives, *TRL* is a show designed to place the television viewer at the center of the program's narrative. The live call-in television program, hosted by Carson Daly and other hip, young hosts, has built a enormous fan base by allowing viewers to see themselves as the central navigators in its programming.

The premise behind *TRL* is that the average teenage consumer has a voice that should be heard. Like most talk shows, *TRL* premieres music videos, brings popular artists to its studio, and features the popular music of the day, but its most prominent feature is the music countdown. The countdown occurs daily in front of a live studio audience that is selected from the thousands of bodies who wait outside the program's Times Square studio, but television viewers can also vote by phone or email for their favorite band. The audience determines which videos will be played and whom the most-played recording artists will be.

The audience members control the narrative (which song gets selected or eliminated from the countdown), but they also appear in the narrative (either as live performers or virtual performers via the Internet). MTV executives have structured the promotion of the program so that the average viewer seems to get as much airtime as the popular musicians who appear on the program. Technology enhances the viewer investment and centrality. The website hosts message boards and chat rooms where devotees can express their opinions about the program, interact with other fans, and send and receive emails to celebrities that appear on the show. It also identifies live performances hosted by MTV where audience members who cannot appear live on the New York based program can interact with performers and *TRL* personalities in large cities across the nation.

Of particular note is the message board where young people create a persona that other viewers can view and interact with. The spectator/actor develops a persona that is authentic in the *TRL* community regardless of its authenticity in the body. Through an examination of the profile, other members of the community can access information about the age, location, and attitudes of the persona. They can also read about the persona's favorite bands, people that he likes to connect with in the *TRL* community, and keywords that will help other members of the community access postings on the message board.

The message board and the subsequent interaction between *TRL* viewers is important because it breaks away from the purposes of the program's original design and allows for a virtual theatrical performance by a viewer for other viewers and for MTV executives. The original design of *TRL* and its supplementary technology considered the *TRL* viewership only as a large consumer focus group from which information could be gleaned that would help the company to select, develop, and exhibit future products on MTV; instead the viewers extend themselves through technology, creating an alternate version of their material bodies for presentation to other viewers.

Interactive video games also aggressively extend the body into the virtual space. The live mediatized experience is regularly advertised in the gaming industry. Interactive first-person narratives developed by John Carmack's company, id Software, are at the core of video games like Doom, Doom II, and The Ultimate Doom. In 1991 the design team began producing storylines in which the spectator is incorporated into the virtual narrative and skilled players can alter the game itself. While the games include state-of-the-art graphics, Internet technology, and intricate technical design elements, the key component of each game is its "first-person universe" in which individuals play the game as themselves. An advertisement for part of the series, Ultimate Doom — Episode Four: Thy Flesh Consumed clearly advertises a live experience in the virtual world, saying: "The demons came and the Space Marines died. Except one. You are the last defense against these hell-spawned hordes. Prepare for the most intense mutant-laden, blood-splattered action ever! The texture-mapped virtual world is so real, you don't just play DOOM — you live it" (online).

This centrality of the player-spectator is not just advertised but is fundamental to the product. Encouraging the interactivity of the game, id technicians made Doom's source code available, allowing skilled players to become designers. The company allows these modifications, known as mods, to be distributed as long as the designers offer their modification free of charge to other enthusiasts. The fundamental nature of the program and the company is the virtual extension of the narrative.

Although the visual narratives of both *TRL* and id Software rely on different media structures to develop a centrally placed spectator who sees himself as shaping the narrative's form and content, each creates a space in which spectator becomes performer and creator of their own extended narratives. It is this interaction between the mediatized producers and consumer that establishes a pattern of interaction for the consumer who engages with other narrative texts, even nonmediated texts. In other words, our engagement with media structures in a virtual mediatized space is so common that the patterns of interaction developed there become a part of our interactions outside the virtual realm. Theatre spectators use these learned interactions with media as a template for their interactions with theatre texts and theatrical performances.

A prime example of this occurred in the early days of the Broadway musical production *Rent*. In 1996 the producers of the contemporary musical sought to engage a young audience that could relate to the theme and character situations developed in the musical. To this end, they reserved two rows of seats each night for young people in their teens and early twenties. These seats could be purchased for $20, one third of the price of the other seats available in the theatre. Fans who purchased these tickets received special access to cast and crewmembers and production materials.

New York–based fans of the musical would camp on Forty-first Street outside the theatre the night before the production to get these coveted tickets. Habitual audience members on the *Rent* ticket line became a community that mirrored the play itself. The commitment of these regular theatre-goers shifted to showing admiration for a particular *Rent* actor by sleeping under publicity photographs to attempting to represent themselves as "characters" that lead similar lives to the "bohemian" life represented in the stage performance. These participatory spectators created false identities, in which they represented their age, their sexual preference, their residency, and their family status as similar to those presented on stage.

Interviewed by Ira Glass, a correspondent for the National Public Radio program *This American Life,* these young spectators describe an atmosphere in which individuals, influenced by their desire for an authentic connection to the production, created their own personal narratives that extended aspects of the show into their personal performance on the line. The poverty, illness, and homelessness romanticized in the play became the focus of the interactions and performances outside the theatre too.

In the most extreme case, a young woman created a persona who was dying of autonomic neuropathy, a disease caused by damage to nerves supplying the internal body structures that regulate functions such as blood pressure, heart rate, bowel and bladder emptying, and digestion. The young women's performance was so convincing that cast members from the Broadway production and friends from the *Rent* ticket line regularly held prayer circles for her before and after the performance of the show. In the young woman's performance of "Stephanie," she often referenced moments from the play. She even designed her impending funeral to mirror the death sequence from the musical, asking the cast and other members of the *Rent* community to re-create the song "I'll Cover You" from the stage production.

The young woman also augmented her performance of the character "Stephanie" with a secondary Internet persona, "Monica," who kept the cast and fans informed about "Stephanie's" surgery, her deep depression, and her subsequent attempts to kill herself when she returned to Los Angeles. When the young woman's deceptions were discovered, she was ostracized by the *Rent* cast and the show's fans, but many admit that her actions were, like their own smaller performances, efforts to extend the performance beyond the time spent in the theatre into their own space, time, and location.

While the performative acts of the *Rent* fans are extreme examples of the spectator's desire and ability to extend theatre's narratives, other more practical examples give evidence of that same extension of the theatre product into the everyday. Most commercial theatres sell merchandise related to a show. But purchasable items like tee shirts and baseball caps are augmented by digital interactions that allow spectators to experience the show from their own homes. These small interactions demonstrate that through media, time and space can be altered to place the audience member at the center of the narrative. In some cases the interactions between a mediatized spectator and a theatre performance can alter the dynamic between the audience, the performers, and the text. Documented interactions between the theatre spectator and media texts, in many respects, place the virtual spectator at the center of the theatrical narrative, which extends beyond the play into the world surrounding the performance.

PERSONAL NARRATIVE, THE PARTICIPATORY SPECTATOR, AND INTERSTITIAL SPACE

Returning to Homi Bhabha's idea of an interstitial space, the theatre of a mass-mediated society is a theatre of negotiated meanings. Each per-

formance venue in the American theatre has become a hybrid performance site where the spectator brings a new empowerment to participate,
perform, and create meaning: "It is in the emergence of the interstices —
the overlap and displacement of domains of difference — that the inter-
subjective and collective experiences of ... community interest, or cultural
value are negotiated ... strategies of representation or empowerment come
to be formulated in the competing claims of communities where, the
exchange of values, meanings and priorities may not always be collaborative and dialogical" (2). This hybrid performance site is most interesting
as observed in the negotiated space between the spectators' phenomenological perceptions of performance and their bodily assimilation and
acceptance of media's content and constructs.

Hybridity between theatre and media that leads to performance is
especially evident in the performances of spectators at cult films in the
late twentieth century and beyond. In the identification with and worship
of film texts and personas, cult film enthusiasts act out the traditional role
of observing spectators but also become participating performers, at times
mimicking and even adding to the electronic narrative with their own
body in quasi-theatrical events.

Cult films, according to Timothy Corrigan, oppose the immobility
and passivity typical of most viewing practices. Corrigan suggests that,
instead of internal identification, a connection is formed through material associations, "material markers that give [the] ... image significance"
(96). In many cases the physical appropriation of the text by its audience
becomes more important than the electronic text itself. Key examples
embrace physical performance choices that are innately theatrical.

Interactions between the audience and the electronic text often
emphasize the primacy of the "performer"/audience relationship over the
relationship between technology and the text itself. The electronic text
simply provides the context for the material performance. The film space
is altered from its traditional mode of operation. Audience members do
not remain seated, lights do not completely dim, and the screen is often
blocked by the performance of the observers. The traditional film experience is subverted by the performance acts of the audience made of theatrical spectator-performer.

At such showings of the *Rocky Horror Picture Show,* audience members dress as the characters they see on the screen. They precisely perform
the characters' lines in front of the screen in synchronization with the film
or electronic version. Performers become the physical embodiment of the
screen image as they act out the film for other audience members, often

obscuring the screen during their performance. The viewing audience also collectively performs ritual activities. For example, early in the film audience members throw rice at other audience members dressed as the bride and groom in unison with the wedding scene in the film. When a rainstorm ensues on the screen, audience members squirt each other with squirt guns and bottles. Collective expressions are regularly shouted at the screen, and the entire audience sings and dances during the film's principal song, "The Time Warp."

The dominance of an active physical performance over a more passive interaction with the screen images is even evident on the cult film's website, which provides step-by-step instructions of various rituals for "virgins," or people who have not seen the film before and plan to be initiated into the customs of interaction by other spectators. Interactions between individuals, the collective audience, and the screen also demonstrate the primacy of audience performance with the text. These exchanges are simultaneously personal and collaborative, and the film text is paradoxically worshiped and deconstructed through audience participation. In *Creatures of the Night*, Sal Piro, an original instigator of the audience participation movement for the *Rocky Horror Picture Show*, demonstrates the spiritual and corporeal dynamic of the interface between the individual spectators and the audience collective in his recollection of the first floor show performances at the Waverly Movie Theatre in Greenwich Village:

> I began living the movie as it unreeled.... The first time I heard Louis Farese's voice speaking back to the screen, it was funny and I was delighted. Suddenly I was ten years old again, going with my mother to see *Snow White* and the *Three Stooges*. I remember that just as Snow White was about to bite into the poisonous apple, a voice from some-where in the movie theater warned audibly, "You'll be sooorry!" The whole theater rocked with laughter. As the film continued, I wanted to shout out something clever too, but I didn't have the nerve. But now, thanks to Louis and friends, it was all right to talk back to the screen. By the time I had watched *RHPS* twice, I knew by heart the places to yell lines and how to time them. By my third viewing, I was ready to try my hand at an original line. When Frank asked, "Whatever happened to Fay Wray?" I answered, "She went apeshit!" — exactly what the audience did when they heard me. This was the first of dozens of lines that I created. I not only invented lines; if I heard someone else's line and liked it; I kept it alive by integrating it with the rest of the litany. This is how the show "went public," people inventing lines and using the lines of others. An individual would yell a line; others would pick it up; then a whole group and eventually the entire audience would shout out the line together [*RPHS* online].

Cult films events like the *Rocky Horror Picture Show* have been described as "secular documents, celebrated as sacred texts by audiences and used as shared foci to collectively create rituals and belief systems" (Kincade and Katovich 191), and the space defined by the audience's physical response to the text has been called a private world in which components of the film are acted upon as if they were integral to a personal belief system and postmodern in the sense that the spectator's quotation of the film reveals society's inability to separate itself from its interface with film and its knowledge of film (Umberto Eco).

Corrigan's express connection between performance and consumption in *Films and the Culture of Cult* is key to understanding participatory spectator performance. He believes that "cult films become the property of an audience's private space, and in this assumption of public images as private space, these films become ... material acquisitions" (91). In other words, by participating in the performance acts surrounding the film, spectators negotiate their own prominence within the film's narrative. Spectators take ownership over the text and acquire the ability to play with the text, reframing the film text to meet the needs of their individual performance acts.

This appropriation of the texts alters much of the traditional filmic experience. While the film text itself remains stable, issues of the film's reception shift. Time, space, and even the rhythm of the visuals are influenced by the extra-textual interactions. Collective and individual vocal responses that overlap and augment screen dialogue challenged sound fidelity. In contrast to a passive response to the film's suture, in which that film viewer is stitched into the film text by the film's signifying codes (continuity editing, etc.) that position the spectator's gaze, this unique form of reception makes the film viewing a live event in which the spectator's performance is the primary focus of the experience.

The participatory performance of the cult film spectator is marked by its ritual nature. The live performance is protected. It is only for those initiated into the performative group experience. Physical interactions are ritualized performative expressions that are marked by the distinctive cadences of each private experience. The performances themselves access media texts in individual ways; and although the performance site clearly includes the film, every performance exists in its own time, space, and location. Participatory reactions are therefore subject to change based on the mythic structures forced onto the performance by the context in which the interactive event is performed.

For example, *The Rocky Horror Picture Show* performed at the River

Oaks Theatre in Houston, where the cast publishes a weekly four-page newsletter and sells handmade *RPHS* costumes in the lobby, is different than the Rocky Horror Internet Sect "The Wired and Untamed Things," a group of Rocky Horror devotees that performs each Friday night at midnight via "Internet Chat Relay" and "Real Audio/Shoutcast." The performers in this second group live across the United States and perform physically independent of other performers.

Although the official Rocky Horror Fan Club produces an authorized audience participation script and has published a "Rocky Etiquette Manual," performance sects are encouraged by the national organization to respect unique performative interactions.* These performative media interactions are personal acquisitions of the individual spectator made private by the collective reverence for the live experience associated with the film. In this way, each performance ritual associated with *The Rocky Horror Picture Show* is dependent on the unique cultural context associated with the individual group performance.

While the idiosyncratic contexts and individual applications of the cult film participatory experience demonstrate the possibility of individualized live performative interactions, other more commercial theatrical/media events extend the potential for performance into a larger arena. In these cases the performative interactions of the contemporary spectator with the media text are carefully planned, and the spectator is guided to appropriate interactions with the media text. Some live theatrical/media experiences even include a detailed preparation period in which the collective audience is taught interactions with the given media text. The material body then becomes an extension of the media's content and form, working in sync with the media text to produce a collective theatrical performance. The interactive components that exist in the cult film experience still have been co-opted in these events, but, instead of the cloistered environment of the cult experience, the capacity to perform is mass produced and democratic. All spectators take on a performance role and their interactions are learned together.

The most prominent of these interactive commercial enterprises is the Sing-A-Long company, an entity of Fox broadcasting, which premiered the first sing-along version of *The Sound of Music* in London's

---

*For example, the official Rocky Horror website encourages varied interactions with the film respecting the unique performance in each venue. Describing the atmosphere to first-time participants, James Norman, et al. say: "AP [Audience Participation Script] is NOT fixed from theater to theater and night to night. If you feel a new line coming on, YELL IT! A big part of keeping the show fresh is creating new lines with topical humor" (see http://www.rocky horror.com/virgknow.html).

Prince Charles Cinema during the summer of 1999 and began an international tour of the interactive show in 2000.* The interactive theatrical/ media event is designed so that spectators watch and interact with the original film in a large venue alongside other *Sound of Music* fans. The production includes pre-show events at which a host conducts vocal warm-ups, costumes are judged and spectator/performers are trained to use the "Magic Moments" packets that contain props that the audience wears, waves, and uses to interact with the action on screen. These packets are distributed to all at the door. All spectator/performers are initiated through this process into the vocal and physical interactions that accompany the screened film. For example, audience members are directed to boo the Nazis, hiss Baroness von Schroeder, bark at Rolf, and wave edelweiss when moved to do so by Maria and the von Trapp children.

The spectators then participate in the viewing of and interaction with the 1965 film. Digitized subtitles appear on each film print allowing the audience to sing along with the musical numbers. The audience for the event includes participants who are dressed as characters from the show or in costumes that reflect something from the show. The people are dressed in costumes that range in nature and in style. Some spectator/performers come dressed in traditional Austrian costume and others come dressed metaphorically. For example, someone might dress as "brown paper packages tied up with string," drawing the costume from a song in the musical.

Other spectators assume the role of observers, but each is nevertheless equipped with the "magic moments" packet. The digital subtitles, the magic moments packet, and the instructions that begin the show structure the audience's interaction. Distinctive performances from each material body are possible and are represented in the creative costumes worn by participants and modeled during the preshow activities. However, in many ways the event is not designed to encourage individuality — instead the live event is designed to mediatize a collective body. In some respects the individual material bodies involved in the event participate actively in the film's suture.

The gaze of the participatory spectator is not passive but is actively engaged in assimilating itself into the film's narrative, actively seeking the suture that was formerly disguised. Through their own performative acts, these individual material bodies become a part of the electronic simulation. Participation in the film's suture is no longer a passive recognition

---

The company has since produced similar sing-a-long events with an ABBA concert and the film versions of the musicals Annie *and* Joseph and the Amazing Technicolor Dreamcoat.

of the dominant point of view; it is an aggressive acquiescence. By singing alongside Maria and the children and shouting the guided phrases at the Nazis and the Baroness, the audience becomes a part of the film's narrative. The spectator becomes a live, physical representation of characters and even inanimate objects portrayed in the film's narrative.

In these active participatory, performative moments the spectator's representation resembles the imagined reality demonstrated on the screen. But the spectator's performance is not reality; it is a simulacrum of the narrative presented in the film's narrative that is playing out in front of the audience. The performance is participatory but in one sense an imitation of something else, and in the platonic sense not quite real. The live body participates willingly in the creation of a simulacrum of the film narrative. Ironically, reality plays out before the audience in electronic form and the performance of the tangible, physical bodies performing in the audience are simply replications of the media presentation.

SIMULACRA AND THE MEDIATIZED PARTICIPATORY SPECTATOR PERFORMANCE

Encounters with a theatrical/media hybrid performance are not limited to the examples of performance-augmented screenings of films that I have used. Spectator performance exists in venues extending from talk radio to online gaming and beyond. It can easily be said that performative interactions with the media have become so pervasive that material bodies now act as mediatized entities that replicate and extend the media's narratives into American homes and communities. The American people's desire to insert themselves into the narratives presented through media technology is evident in the design of planned communities like the Disney Corporation's "Celebration," where a homeowner's living space is designed to recall the image of utopian small town America and each owner willingly performs individual roles set forth in the town's conditions, covenants, and restrictions.

Celebration sits adjacent to Walt Disney World in Orlando Florida. It is designed to reflect the attitudes and personality of early Disney films and encourages community members to live a lifestyle in which they also reflect the ideas that Disney wistfully presents of a previous time period. Kathleen M. Hogan describes the community, saying:

> It is at this place, this crossroads of nostalgia and consumerism, where the truly fascinating event takes place. For to make this community a reality,

to make it look and sound as though it were a prewar Rockwellian dream-scape, Disney has introduced a government in which Celebration's citizens have no elected representation and a social system that leaves the town devoid of the very things that together form the essence of the dream for which its inhabitants are stretching out their arms. There is no town government, no churches, its citizens must follow an explicit set of codes that regulate everything from what kind of plants grow in their yards to how many people are allowed to sleep in a single bedroom. They have traded away their actual rights as American citizens for a fantastic version of American life.... Driving into Celebration is like driving into a dream, or onto a movie set [Hogan Online].

Celebration is a community designed to replicate the idealized image presented in Disney television and film. The residents of the community are participatory spectators who have embraced the narrative presented in film and are attempting to become a part of the mediatized narrative that the Disney Corporation is promoting. The consumer in this case purchases his or her own presence in the narrative by purchasing a home in Celebration.

Our purchases become recreations of the performances that we view electronically from the catwalks of Milan, Paris, and New York via cable television programs like E Entertainment Television's *Fashion File* and MTV's *House of Style*. For example, the purchase of a pair of beaded ankle wrap sandals created by Manolo Blahnik becomes a performative act through the consumer's choice to purchase and wear the product, or remake the product with their own resources. The appearance and description of shoes, clothes and other accessories like the Blahnik shoes on medi-atized programs in the private homes of middleclass consumers allows for a new space to develop that intertwines two previously cloistered worlds — the private home of the consumer and the previously remote haute couture.

This simulation of an imagined reality is not just a performance for others; it extends even further, onto our persons so that the purchase of shoes becomes evidence of a willing simulation of the mediatized presentation of consumable products. By purchasing and wearing the shoes the individual becomes a performative facsimile of the visual narrative presented by fashion models and celebrities through the electronic medium.

In similar fashion, the incorporation of media's narratives play a key role in the production and reception of the contemporary stage play. Producers often remake traditional theatre texts, designed specifically for theatrical production, into mediatized reproductions by casting iconic film and television stars in these commercial theatre productions. Theatre and film stars have always crossed the threshold between the two mediums;

however, this concept of transferring star power from television and film to the theatre has taken hold in the commercial theatre of the late twentieth century. Contemporary Hollywood film stars like Matt Damon, Gwyneth Paltrow, and Nicole Kidman have all appeared on stage during the early part of the twenty-first century. Disney Corporation's theatrical division has cast high profile media stars in leading roles in *Beauty and the Beast* and *Aida,* and the international tour of the Bob Fosse musical *Chicago* has promoted its lengthy run with television and film stars in the leading female roles.

Eve Ensler's play *The Vagina Monologues* demonstrates the power of associating a theatrical text with television and film stars. The play, which won a 1997 Obie Award, is internationally recognized, not for its acute observations about what it means to be female in today's world or the fact that the theatrical text is well respected as the centerpiece of the V-Day movement — a worldwide campaign to stop violence against women and girls. Instead, it was Ensler's promotion of the play and V-Day through the performance of the play by what Ensler calls her "vulva chorus," stars with iconic status like Oprah Winfrey, Alanis Morisette, Cate Blanchett, Winona Ryder, Susan Sarandon, Whoopi Goldberg, Marisa Tomei, Rosie Perez, Lily Tomlin, Kate Winslett, Melanie Griffith, and Calista Flockhart that thrust the play into the minds of contemporary viewers.

Because of the cast's star power, the play has become a part of popular culture. *Newsday* Author Mary Vobril describes the publicity surrounding the play: "[M]agazine covers, skyscraper spotlights, attention in the temples of pop culture — the play's name has come up on television's "Ally McBeal," "Sex and the City" and "Dharma & Greg"; it spawned a limited-run theatrical confection called "The Penis Responds," and a mention of "Monologues" has made it into the John Updike literary canon" (Vobril online). The play's audience is less likely to know the name of the play because of the critical acclaimed Ensler received at its inception than to recognize it because of its affiliation with media personalities. It is true that the audience's reception of the celebrity performances of the Obie Award winning play may sometimes be focused on the ideas presented in the play. However, it is more likely that the focus of the spectators is on the people who are playing roles.

This is not a new occurrence. Throughout history actor performances have been evaluated in terms of the actor's personality and presence on stage and the perceived persona off stage. I see this example as an extension of the spectators' association of a performance role or style with a particular actor. In this case the media allows spectators to imagine that they have greater intimate knowledge of an actor because of their access to the actor through media entities like talk shows, entertainment shows, and other promotional programming. However, the actual proximity associated with the actor and his or her audience prior to the twentieth century does not exist because of global technology communication. Because of this the spectator's information and the perceptions they draw from that information are all derived from the image they see in the media. When they finally see the actor on stage, all their associations are tied up in the image they have seen presented in the media prior to the stage performance.

Articles about *The Vagina Monologues* from both scholarly publications and news magazines consistently mention the play's success as it related to the star power of its performers. Interestingly, it is the mediatized body of the actress playing the role that has consumed popular interest. The actresses are associated with their popular roles on television and film and each performance brings the caché of that media persona. The association between the two forms is emphasized by the crossover promotion in the television shows of key performers where the characters that the actresses play on television mention the play in the cultural context of their fictional world. In that light the spectators can also actively access their own knowledge of the media persona's previous performance as they watch. So instead of seeing a Bosnian woman talk about being raped, they see Calista Flockhart from the television show *Alley McBeal* portraying the role of the Bosnian rape victim. While this activity does not effect the performance, it does alter the reception of that performance, and the actual text becomes less important to the audience than its association with who the performer is.

Media constitutes a part of any contemporary spectator's lived experience, and certainly media determines that spectator's perception of what is real on stage and what is perceived as real in the American cultural mind-set in media simulation. Accepting this, mediatized spectators clearly perform in new ways because of association with media technology. Through that association with the media the spectator learns to be a more active and more willing participant in narratives, even extending theatre narratives past the threshold of the theatre space into his or her own private space.

Performance, once relegated to the stage, is now part of the participatory spectator's interaction with most theatre texts. But theatrical presence that previously depended solely on the actual proximity between the actor and the spectator does not exist. Even when there is material interaction between the performer and the spectator, even if the theatrical event plays out in a traditional setting, it is most likely framed by some media experience. Therefore, the participatory spectator becomes the site of negotiation between the dominant media and theatre. It is in this live body that theatre must compete and collaborate to continue to exist. Because of interaction with media, the previously passive spectator has liberated the theatrical stage as it has forced theatre to embrace the new reality — a mediatized simulacrum.

Conclusion:
Towards Hybridity

The primary goals of my study are to establish the presence of mediatization, or media semantics, in American theatre and to present a methodology of reading theatre in order to identify this presence. To this end, I have examined the idea of *presence* in theatre past and present, *nostalgia* as a mass-marketed commodity, *media* as a subject for theatrical narrative, the forms of media communications as a new language of theatre, and new notions of *reality* and *spectatorship*. All of this is in support of my contention that a clear understanding of the contemporary American stage can only be achieved when the current, cultural mechanisms of communication, and therefore perception, are understood.

Jonathan Crary poses key questions for contemporary society in his seminal work on the nature and creation of visual observation, *Techniques of the Observer: On Vision and Modernity in the Nineteenth Century*. He asks two questions pertinent to the twenty-first century: "How is the body, including the observing body, becoming a component of new machines, economies, apparatuses, whether social, libidinal, or technological? [And] in what ways is subjectivity becoming a ... condition of interface between rationalized systems of exchange and networks of information?" (2). This study of the contemporary stage has been an attempt to answer these questions for a theatre community that is affected by its direct interaction with the popular media. In other words, I have worked to demonstrate how the semantics of the technology-driven mass-media have been assimilated into contemporary theatrical performance in American theatre.

This interest in a methodology that identifies the imprints of a media presence on theatre has led me to explore the media as an internal influence on the new language and structures of American theatre in terms of production and reception. My observation and documentation of these shifts

187

in theatrical production and reception because of media's influence demonstrates that theatre in general has intentionally become mediatized by adopting the semantics and the contexts of mass media as a method of both accessing and generating meaning. But this work also reveals the difficulty that even theatrical forums that seek to do otherwise nevertheless have in avoiding affiliation with media's content and form into their theatrical products.

Homi K. Bhabha addresses the nature of similar interactions between dominant entities and less dominant counterparts, saying: "Terms of cultural engagement, whether antagonistic or affiliative, are produced performatively. The social articulation of difference, from the minority perspective, is a complex, on-going negotiation that seeks to authorize cultural hybridities that emerge in moments of historical transformation" (2). With this in mind, it is important to consider the responsibility of theatre scholars, artists, and practitioners who create and observe theatre in this interstitial space. Clearly theatre and media overlap — often deliberately and sometimes by chance — and theatre scholars must investigate the current implications of that collective experience as well as media's future influence on the theatrical medium. Theatre artists and practitioners must also consider the efficacy of their work within this collective space.

This study is a recognition of this hybrid space in which theatre currently resides alongside media technologies. In this space theatre can be examined as it competes and collaborates with media's content and form. More important, theatre scholars could more fully examine the ways in which the exchange of priorities, ethics, and meanings of theatre are negotiated as theatre attempts to stage itself as a mediatized form between the borders of traditional theatre practice and conventional media models.

The changes I have documented in the provided examples are changes in production practices that aggressively seek to create meaning through the semantics of technology (namely, images, nostalgia, directed focus, and negotiated presence) and a change in reception from passive spectatorship to participatory spectatorship that draws meaning from experiences with technology. These changes stem from the hegemonic weight that the media has as a cultural influence.

These changes are clear in altered stagings of reality on the contemporary American stage. The contemporary theatre audience's acceptance of staged reality is governed by the constructs that are learned by the general populace through the assimilation of media's forms into their collective consciousness. That consciousness of the audience is now developed vicariously via mass communication. Presence takes on more meaning than proximity in this circumstance because the normal cultural experience for audience members is vicarious rather than personal in nature. Audiences, therefore, bring more to the theatre than an open mind and a warm body: they bring cultural data, mined from mediatized sources, which interface with culture data delivered from the stage. Meaning is generated in the negotiation between the two data sets, and the theatre becomes a hybrid space of negotiated meaning between the ideas projected from the stage by the performers and producers and the ideas projected onto the stage by the audience.

The accelerated nature of this negotiation is the difference in theatre from past to present. The participatory spectator is therefore not a byproduct, but a necessary element of current American theatre. The ritual of performative, theatrical communication is certainly ancient, but the language that is currently being spoken in American theatre is a new language of technology. In this new theatre meaning is dependent upon continual and rapid negotiation between projected meaning and perceived meaning, reality is dependent upon the spectators' participation, and presence is no longer dependent upon temporal or spatial relationships.

The most important feature that current American theatre can claim in common with its ancient ancestors is its willingness to address its audiences in the language of its originating culture. In this sense, theatre hasn't changed at all. What has changed is that the language that is spoken in America is the homogenous, visual, mechanical language of technology and mass-media. It is the language of mass-media communication that has prompted the American theatre to cultivate the participatory spectator. It is the language of mass-media communication that has prompted the American theater to create meaning through the visual semantics of technology. It is the language of technology and mass-media that has created a hybrid space in the mediated American theatre. It is the language of American culture, and therefore the language of the American stage, that has altered the boundaries between stage and audience, redefined the relationship between actor and spectator, and changed the nature of theatre for Americans.

Appendix A: Media Conglomerates in Theatre Production

Eight prominent media corporations are currently investing in commercial theatre productions. Below I include brief descriptions of each corporation taken from their corporate profile. I also list theatrical productions titles and the original beginning date for each production and the length of its theatrical run.

1. News Corporation (20th Century–Fox, Fox Films, Etc.)

New Corporation is a diversified international media and entertainment company with operations in eight industry segments: filmed entertainment; television; cable network programming; direct broadcast satellite television; magazines and inserts; newspapers; book publishing; and other. The activities of News Corporation are conducted principally in the United States, Continental Europe, the United Kingdom, Australia, Asia and the Pacific Basin.

20TH CENTURY–FOX THEATRICAL PRODUCTIONS

Past	Present	Planned
Big (1996)		*Ever After*
Is There Life After High School? (1982)		*Princess Bride*
The Supporting Cast (1981)		*Nine to Five*
Frankenstein (1981)		
The Red Cat (1934)		

20th Century–Fox Productions	*Date and Length of Theatrical Run*
Big [Original, Musical, Comedy] Based on the Motion Picture *Big*, a film by 20th Century–Fox Productions	April 28, 1996–Oct. 13, 1996
Is There Life After High School? [Original, Musical] Produced by Twentieth Century–Fox Theatre Productions, Inc.	May 7, 1982–May 16, 1982
The Supporting Cast [Original, Play, Comedy] Produced by 20th Century–Fox Productions	Aug. 6, 1981–Sept. 5, 1981
Frankenstein [Original, Play, Drama] Produced in association with 20th Century–Fox Productions	Jan. 4, 1981–Jan. 4, 1981
The Red Cat [Original, Play, Drama] Produced in association with 20th Century Pictures Corp.	Sept. 19, 1934–Sept. 1934

2. Disney Theatrical Productions

Disney Theatrical Productions, a unit of Buena Vista Theatrical Group, was formed in 1994 and operates under the direction of Thomas Schumacher. The company's inaugural production, *Beauty and the Beast*, is currently the sixth longest-running show in Broadway history. In May 1997, the Walt Disney Company completed restoration of the historic New Amsterdam Theatre on 42nd Street, reopening with the world premiere concert of Alan Menken and Tim Rice's *King David*. Later that same year, Disney opened *The Lion King*, which received six 1998 Tony Awards including Best Musical, as well as the 1998 Grammy Award for Best Musical Show Album. Now in its ninth sold-out year on Broadway, *The Lion King* can also currently be seen onstage in London, Amsterdam, Melbourne, Hamburg, Tokyo, Nagoya and throughout the U.S. by two touring companies.

DISNEY THEATRICAL PRODUCTIONS

Past	Present	Planned
King David (1997)	*Mary Poppins* (2006)	*The Little Mermaid*
Largely New York (1989)	*Tarzan* (2006)	
Total Abandon (1983)	*The Lion King* (1997–)	
Aida (2000–2004)	*Beauty and the Beast* (1994–)	
Hunchback of Notre Dame (Berlin, 1999)		

Disney Theatricals	*Date and Length of Run*
Mary Poppins [Original, Musical] Produced by Disney Theatrical Productions	Nov. 16, 2006–
Tarzan [Original, Musical, Comedy] Produced by Disney Theatrical Productions	May 10, 2006–
The Lion King [Original, Musical, Comedy, Drama, Puppets] Produced by Disney Theatrical Productions; Theatre Owned and Operated by Disney Theatrical Productions	Nov. 13, 1997–
King David [Original, Special, Concert] Produced by Disney Theatrical Productions; Theatre Owned and Operated by Disney Theatrical Productions	May 18, 1997–May 23, 1997
Beauty and the Beast [Original, Musical, Comedy] Produced by Walt Disney Productions	April 18, 1994–
Largely New York [Original, Play, Comedy] Produced by the Walt Disney Studios	May 1, 1989–Sept. 2, 1989

Disney Theatricals	*Date and Length of Run*
Total Abandon [Original, Play] A Perry Street Theatre production, developed with members of this production team, was funded by Walt Disney Productions	April 28, 1983–April 28, 1983
Swingin' The Dream [Original, Musical, Comedy, Variety]	Nov. 29, 1939–Dec. 9, 1939

3. Dreamworks

In 1994, Steven Spielberg, Jeffrey Katzenberg and David Geffen formed DreamWorks SKG. The company's animation division partnered with Northern California–based PDI to produce CG animated movies, beginning with *Antz* in 1996. The two companies went on to create critically acclaimed and successful animated movies, including *Shrek* and *Shrek 2*, which ended its theatrical run as the third highest-grossing domestic release of all time and the highest-grossing animated film of all time. Following the acquisition of PDI in 2004, DreamWorks SKG spun off its animation division in November of that year into a separate public company (DWA).

DREAMWORKS THEATRICAL PRODUCTIONS

Past	Present	Planned
		Shrek
		Catch Me If You Can

4. Metro-Goldwyn-Mayer

Metro-Goldwyn-Mayer Inc. is an independent, privately held motion picture, television, home video, and theatrical production and distribution company. The company owns the world's largest library of modern films, comprising approximately 4,000 titles, and over 10,400 episodes of television programming. Its film library has received 208 Academy Awards, one of the largest award winning collections in the world. MGM is owned by an investor consortium comprised of Providence Equity Partners, Texas Pacific Group, Sony Corporation of America, Comcast Corporation, DLJ Merchant Banking Partners and Quadrangle Group.

MGM THEATRICAL PRODUCTIONS

Past	Present	Planned
Chitty Chitty Bang Bang (2005)	*Dirty Rotten Scoundrels* (2005–present)	*Desperately Seeking Susan*
Sweet Smell of Success (2002)		*The Thomas Crown Affair*
Meet Me in St. Louis (1989)		*Mermaids*
Singin' in the Rain (1985–1986)		*Get Shorty*
All's Well that Ends Well (1983)		*Heartbreakers*
Seven Brides for Seven Brothers (1982)		*Rain Man*
		Midnight Cowboy
		The Pink Panther
		Weekend at Bernie's
		Moonstruck
		The Man in the Iron Mask
		A Shot in the Dark
		The Night They Raided Minksky's
		Where's Poppa?
		Marty
		The Adventures of Priscilla: Queen of the Desert (Coming to Australia)
		Legally Blonde

MGM On Stage	*Date and Length of Run*
Chitty Chitty Bang Bang [Original, Musical, Comedy] Based on the Motion Picture by MGM	April 28, 2005–Dec. 31, 2005
Sweet Smell of Success [Original, Musical, Drama] Based on the motion picture by MGM / UA Home Entertainment Group, Inc.	March 14, 2002–June 15, 2002
Meet Me in St. Louis [Original, Musical, Comedy] Based on the motion picture *Meet Me in St. Louis* by MGM	Nov. 2, 1989–June 10, 1990
Singin' in the Rain [Original, Musical, Comedy] Based on the film by MGM	July 2, 1985–May 18, 1986
All's Well That Ends Well [Original, Play, Comedy] Produced by MGM / UA Home Entertainment Group, Inc.	April 13, 1983–May 15, 1983
Seven Brides for Seven Brothers [Original, Musical] Based on the film by MGM	July 8, 1982–July 11, 1982
Dirty Rotten Scoundrels [Original, Musical, Comedy] Produced in association with MGM On Stage	March 3, 2005–

5. New Line Cinema

New Line Cinema is the oldest independent film company in the world. In addition to the production and distribution of theatrical motion pictures, it has divisions devoted to home entertainment, television, music, theater, licensing, merchandising and international marketing and distribution. Together with its subsidiary, Fine Line Features, New Line is a unit of Time Warner.

NEW LINE CINEMA THEATRICAL PRODUCTIONS

Past	Present	Planned
	Hairspray (2002)	*Saving Grace*
	Wedding Singer (2006)	*Secondhand Lions*
		Don Juan DeMarco

New Line Cinema	Date and Length of Run
The Wedding Singer [Original, Musical, Comedy] Produced by New Line Cinema	April 27, 2006–
Hairspray [Original, Musical, Comedy]	Aug. 15, 2002–

6. Paramount Pictures

On March 11, 1994, Paramount merged with Viacom Inc, under the leadership of Sumner Redstone, chairman of the board and chief executive officer. Today, Paramount Pictures, together with Paramount Television, CBS Television, Simon & Schuster Publishing, MTV Networks, Showtime Networks, Infinity, BET, UPN, Paramount Parks and Blockbuster Entertainment comprise the entertainment leader, Viacom Inc.

PARAMOUNT THEATRICAL PRODUCTIONS

Past	Present	Planned
Urban Cowboy (2003)	*Barefoot in the Park* (2006)	*The First Wives Club*
The Wild Party (2000)		
Saturday Night Fever (2000)		
A Funny Thing Happened on the Way to the Forum (1998)		
Seven Guitars (1996)		
Grand Hotel (1992)		
My One and Only (1985)		

Past	Present	Planned
Slab Boys (1983)		
Agnes of God (1983)		
The Roast (1980)		
King of Schnorrers (1980)		
The Price (1979)		
G.R. Point (1979)		

Paramount Pictures Corporation	***Date and Length of Run***
Barefoot in the Park [Revival, Play, Comedy] Produced in association with Paramount Pictures Corporation	Feb. 16, 2006–
Urban Cowboy [Original, Musical] Based on the film by Paramount Pictures Corporation	March 27, 2003–May 18, 2003
The Wild Party [Original, Musical, Drama] Produced by Paramount Pictures Corporation	April 13, 2000–June 11, 2000
Saturday Night Fever [Original, Musical] Based on the picture owned by Paramount/RSO	Oct. 21, 1999–Dec. 30, 2000
A Funny Thing Happened on the Way to the Forum [Revival, Musical, Comedy, Farce] Produced by Paramount Pictures Corporation	April 18, 1996–Jan. 4, 1998
Seven Guitars [Original, Play, Drama] Produced by Paramount Pictures Corporation	March 28, 1996–Sept. 8, 1996

Paramount Pictures Corporation	*Date and Length of Run*
Grand Hotel [Original, Musical, Drama] Produced by Paramount Pictures Corporation	Nov. 12, 1989–April 25, 1992
My One And Only [Original, Musical, Comedy] Produced by Paramount Theatre Productions	May 1, 1983–March 3, 1985
Slab Boys [Original, Play] Produced by Paramount Theatre Productions	March 7, 1983–April 17, 1983
Agnes of God [Original, Play, Drama] Produced by Paramount Theatre Productions	March 30, 1982–Sept. 4, 1983
The Roast [Original, Play] Produced by Paramount Pictures Corporation	May 8, 1980–May 11, 1980
King of Schnorrers [Original, Musical] Theatre Owned and Operated by Paramount Pictures Corporation	Nov. 28, 1979–Jan. 13, 1980
The Price [Revival, Play, Drama] Theatre Owned and Operated by Paramount Pictures Corporation	June 19, 1979–Oct. 21, 1979
G. R. Point [Original, Play] Theatre Owned and Operated by Paramount Pictures	April 16, 1979–May 13, 1979

7. Universal Studios

NBC Universal is one of the world's leading media and entertainment companies in the development, production, and marketing of entertainment, news, and information to a global audience. Formed in May 2004 through the combining of NBC and Vivendi Universal Entertainment, NBC Universal owns and operates a valuable portfolio of news and entertainment networks, a premier motion picture company, significant television production operations, a leading television stations group, and world-renowned theme parks. NBC Universal is 80 percent owned by General Electric and 20 percent owned by Vivendi Universal.

UNIVERSAL STUDIOS THEATRICALS

Past	Present	Planned
Suessical (2001)	*Wicked* (2003)	*Billy Eliot: The Musical*
Open Admissions (1984)	*Mamma Mia!*	*Cry Baby*
Doonesbury (1983)		
Nuts (1980)		
The Best Little Whorehouse in Texas (1982)		
Destry Rides Again (1960)		

Universal Studios Productions	*Date and Length of Run*
Wicked [Original, Musical] Produced by Universal Pictures	Oct. 30, 2003–
Seussical [Original, Musical, Comedy] Produced by Universal Studios	Nov. 30, 2000–May 20, 2001
Open Admissions [Original, Play, Drama] Produced in association with Universal Pictures	Jan. 29, 1984–Feb. 12, 1984
Doonesbury [Original, Musical, Comedy] Produced in association with Universal Pictures	Nov. 21, 1983–Feb. 19, 1984
The Best Little Whorehouse in Texas [Original, Musical, Comedy] Produced in association with Universal Pictures	May 31, 1982–July 24, 1982
Nuts [Original, Play] Produced in association with Universal Pictures	April 28, 1980–July 20, 1980

Universal Studios Productions	*Date and Length of Run*
Destry Rides Again [Original, Musical, Comedy] Produced by arrangement with Universal Pictures	April 23, 1959–June 18, 1960

8. Warner Bros. Theatre Ventures

Warner Bros. Theatre Ventures was inaugurated in May 2003, with the announcement of *Lestat*, an all-new musical from the legendary songwriting team of Sir Elton John and Bernie Taupin, based on Anne Rice's celebrated vampire Lestat, slated for a Broadway premiere in spring 2006. Theatre Ventures mines the myriad Warner Bros. Entertainment library titles and iconic characters that might lend themselves to theatrical presentation and instead of just licensing them to others, serves as the developer and producer.

WARNER BROS. THEATRICAL PRODUCTIONS

Past	Present	Planned
Bugs Bunny of Broadway (1990)	*Lestat* (2006)	*Grumpy Old Men*
Legs Diamond (1988–1989)	*The Color Purple* (2005–)	*Batman*
42nd Street (1980–1989)		
Her First Roman (1968)		
Billy Budd (1951)		
Janie (1942–1944)		
Jupiter Laughs (1940)		

Warner Bros.	*Date and Length of Run*
Lestat [Original, Musical, Thriller] Produced by Warner Bros.	April 25, 2006–
The Color Purple [Original, Musical, Drama] Based on the motion picture by Warner Bros.	Dec. 1, 2005–

Warner Bros.	*Date and Length of Run*
Bugs Bunny on Broadway [Original, Special] Produced by Warner Bros.	Oct. 4, 1990–Oct. 23, 1990
Legs Diamond [Original, Musical] Based on the movie *The Rise and Fall of Legs Diamond* by Warner Bros.	Dec. 26, 1988–Feb. 19, 1989
42nd Street [Original, Musical, Comedy] The use of all songs is by arrangement with Warner Bros.	Aug. 25, 1980–Jan. 8, 1989
Her First Roman [Original, Musical, Comedy] Produced in association with Warner Bros.	Oct. 20, 1968–Nov. 2, 1968
Billy Budd [Original, Play, Drama] Theatre Owned by Warner Bros.	Feb. 10, 1951–May 12, 1951
Janie [Original, Play, Comedy] Theatre Owned and Operated by Warner Bros.—*Replacement*	Sept. 10, 1942–Jan. 16, 1944
Jupiter Laughs [Original, Play, Drama] Produced by Warner Bros.	Sept. 9, 1940–Sept. 28, 1940
The Amazing Dr. Clitterhouse [Original, Play, Melodrama] Produced in association with Warner Bros.	March 2, 1937–May 1937

Appendix B:
Media Based Musicals

Includes an incomplete list of movie-to-musical material. The film industry and the commercial theatre have always shared texts. In this table I provide the film and the subsequent theatrical production. There are many more works in which the theatrical version is adapted for the screen. Those listings are out of the scope of my study and are not included in this table.

Movie Musical Title	Film	Broadway	Additional Information
42nd Street	1929, 1933	1980, 2001	The musical used original songs from the film owned by Warner Bros.
A Little Night Music (based on *Smiles of a Summer Night*)	1955	1973	Sondheim says the musical was "suggested" by the Bergman film
Ain't Misbehavin'	1941, 1974	1978, 1988	The film and the play are based on similar ideas. The film actually includes archival footage of the individuals performing their own music
Applause (based on *All About Eve*)	1950	1970	Based on the original story by Mary Orr
Beauty and the Beast	1991	1994	Disney's first movie-musical production
Big	1988	1996	Music was not a part of the original motion picture

Movie Musical Title	Film	Broadway	Additional Information
Big Deal (based on the film Big Deal on Madonna Street)	1958	1986	The Italian film is not a musical
Billy Elliot: The Musical	2000	2005	This musical premiered in London and has not been staged on Broadway
Calamity Jane	1953	2003	Premiered in London, and is in process for Broadway
Carrie	1976	1988	Based on the novel as well as the film
Catch Me If You Can	2002	in process	This production is based on the film and not the 1965 play of the same name
Chicago	1927	1975, 1996	Based on 1926 play, and the 1927 non-musical movie
Chitty Chitty Bang Bang	1968	2005	Richard M. Sherman composed the songs for the film and the musical
Cry-Baby	1990	in process	
Dance of the Vampires (based on The Fearless Vampire Killers)	1967	2002	
Desperately Seeking Susan	1985	in process	
Destry Rides Again	1932, 1939	1959	Also based on the original story by Max Brand
Dirty Dancing	1987	2006	Will premiere in London
Dirty Rotten Scoundrels	1988	2005	
Doctor Dolittle	1967	1998	Premiered in London, never came to Broadway
Donnybrook! (based on The Quiet Man, 1952)	1952	1961	
Ever After	1998	2007	

Movie Musical Title	Film	Broadway	Additional Information
Fanny (based on trilogy *Marius, Fanny,* and *Cesar*)	various	1954	
Footloose	1984	1998	
Get Shorty	1995	in process	
Gigi	1958	1973	Also based on novel by Sidonie Gabrielle Colette
Hairspray	1988	2002	
Hazel Flagg (based on film *Nothing Sacred*)	1937	1953	
Heartbreakers	2001	in process	
Here's Love (based on *Miracle on 34th Street*)	1947	1963	
High Society	1956	1998	Based on the film *Philadelphia Story* and the film musical *High Society*
Jerry Springer—The Opera	1991	2006	Based on the television show
Kiss of the Spider Woman	1985	1993	Also based on novel by Manuel Puig
Legally Blonde	2001	in process	
Legs Diamond (based on the movie *The Rise and Fall of Legs Diamond*)	1960	1988	
Light in the Piazza	1962	2005	Also based on book by Elizabeth Spencer, film not given credit, but has ties to Turner Entertainment
Little Shop of Horrors	1960	2003	
Little Women	multiple versions	2005	Also based on novel by Louisa May Alcott
Marty	1955	in process	
Mary Poppins	1964	2006	Will premiere in London

Movie Musical Title	Film	Broadway	Additional Information
Meet Me in Saint Louis	1944	1989	
Mermaids	1990	in process	
Metropolis	1927	1989	Premiered in London
Midnight Cowboy	1969	in process	
Monty Python's Spamalot	1975	2005	
Moonstruck	1987	in process	
Never Gonna Dance (from film *Swing Time*)	1936	2003	
Nine to Five	1980	in process	
Passion (adapted from Ettore Scola's film *Passione d'Amore*)	1981	1994, 2004	
Promises, Promises (based on Billy Wilder's film *The Apartment*)	1960	1968	
Rain Man	1988	in process	
Reefer Madness (satirizing 1936 film *Tell Your Children*, 2004 off-broadway musical)	1936	2004	
Return to the Forbidden Planet (based on Shakespeare's *The Tempest* and 1956 film *Forbidden Planet*)	1956		
Saturday Night Fever	1977	1999	
Seven Brides for Seven Brothers	1954	1982	
She Loves Me (linked to *The Shop Around the Corner*)	1940	1963	This is based on play by Miklos Laszlo, but is also linked to the film *The Shop Around the Corner* (1949)
Shenandoah	1965	1975	

Movie Musical Title	Film	Broadway	Additional Information
Shrek	2001	in process	
Silk Stockings (based on film *Ninotchka*)	1939	1955	
Singin' in the Rain	1952	1985	
Song and Dance	1983, 1984	1985	Based originally on a television program
Spider-man	2002	in process	Also based on the comic book
State Fair	1945	1996	
Sugar (from screenplay *Some Like it Hot*)	1939, 1959	1972	
Sunset Boulevard	1950	1994	
Sweet Charity (based on screenplay *Nights of Cabiria*)	1957	1966, 1986, 2005	
Sweet Smell of Success	1957	2002	
Tarzan	1999	2006	
The Adventures of Priscilla: Queen of the Desert (coming to Australia)	1994	in process	
The Color Purple	1985	2005	Also based on novel
The First Wives Club	1996	in process	
The Full Monty	1997	2000	Does not credit the film in promotional materials but is clearly linked to the film in terms of content
The Goodbye Girl	1977	1993	
The Graduate	1967	2002	This play features Paul Simon's music, made popular by the original film

Movie Musical Title	Film	Broadway	Additional Information
The Grapes of Wrath	1940	1990	Also based on John Steinbeck's novel. The play includes incidental music
The King and I (movie *Anna and the King of Siam*)	1946	1951, 1977, 1985, 1996	Also based on book *Anna and the King of Siam* by Margaret London, but film is viewed as an influence
The Lion King	1994	1997	
The Little Mermaid	1989	in process	
The Lord of the Rings	2001, 2002, 2003	2006	Opened in Toronto, and is based on the books and not the recent films
The Man in the Iron Mask	1998	in process	
The Night They Raided Minksky's	1968	in process	
The Pink Panther	1963	in process	
The Princess Bride	1987	in process	
The Producers	1968	2001	The hit musical has also been remade into a new film starring the Broadway cast
The Red Shoes	1948	1993	
The Thomas Crown Affair	1999	in process	
The Wedding Singer	1998	2006	
Thoroughly Modern Millie	1967	2002	
Urban Cowboy	1980	2003	
Victor/Victoria	1982	1995	Does not credit the film in promotional material but both starred Julie Andrews and features some of the same music
Weekend at Bernie's	1989	in process	

Movie Musical Title	Film	Broadway	Additional Information
Where's Poppa?	1970	in process	
Whistle Down the Wind	1961	1998	Premiered in London
Woman of the Year	1942	1981	

Bibliography

Aden, Roger. "Nostalgic Communication as Temporal Escape: When It Was a Game's Re-Construction of a Baseball/Work Community." *Western Journal of Communication* 59 (1995): 20–38.

Adler, Steven. *On Broadway: Art and Commerce on the Great White Way*. Carbondale: Southern Illinois University Press, 2004.

Adorno, Theodore, and Max Horkheimer. *The Dialectic of Enlightenment*. Trans. John Cumming. New York: Herder and Herder, 1972.

Allen, Robert C. *Vaudeville and Film: 1895–1915, a Study in Media Interaction*. New York: Arno Press, 1980.

American Playhouse: Fires in the Mirror, Crown Heights, Brooklyn and Other Identities. Dir. George C. Wolfe. Writer, perf. Anna Deavere Smith. Video Cassette. PBS, 1993.

Ang, Ien. *Watching Dallas*. London: Methuen, 1985.

Aristotle. *Poetics*. Trans. Gerald Else. Ann Arbor: University of Michigan Press, 1995.

Auslander, Philip. *Liveness: Performance in a Mediatized Culture*. New York: Routledge, 1999.

Barber, Benjamin. *Jihad vs. McWorld*. New York: Times Books, 1995.

Barker, Stephen. Rev. of Cirque du Soleil. *Theatre Journal* 44.2 (1992): 235–237.

Barnard, Malcolm. *Fashion as Communication*. New York: Routledge, 1996.

Barnes, Clive. "A Cut Above: Delightfully Odd Todd." Rev. of *Sweeny Todd*. Dir. John Doyle. *New York Post*, 4 Nov. 2005.

Barnes, Clive. Rev. of *The Graduate*. *New York Post*, 5 April 2002, late ed.

Baudrillard, Jean. *For a Critique of the Political Economy of the Sign*. Trans. Charles Levin. St. Louis: Telos, 1981.

Baudrillard, Jean. "The Precession of Simulacra." *A Postmodern Reader*. Eds. Joseph Natoli and Linda Hutcheon. Albany: SUNY Press, 1993.

Baudrillard, Jean. *Simulations*. Trans. Paul Foss, Paul Patton, and Philip Beitchman. New York: Semiotext(e), 1983.

Benjamin, Walter. "The Work of Art in the Age of Mechanical Reproduction." *Film Theory and Criticism*. Eds. Leo Braudy and Marshall Cohen. New York: Oxford University Press, 1999, 731–51.

Benjamin, Walter. "The Work of Art in the Age of Mechanical Reproduction." *Illuminations*. New York: Harcourt Brace Jovanovich, 1968.

Bennett, Susan. "Comment." *Theatre Journal* 51. 4 (1999): I.

Bennett, Susan. *Theatre Audience: A Theory of Production and Reception*, 2d ed. New York: Routledge, 1997.

Bentley, Byron. "No Time for Playwrights." *Theatre Arts* (December 1955): 31–32, 95.

Berson, Misha, ed. *Between Worlds: Contemporary Asian American Plays*. New York: Theatre Communications Group, 1990.

Bhabha, Homi. *The Location of Culture.* London and New York: Routledge, 1994.

Birranger, Johannes. "Contemporary Performance/Technology." *Theatre Journal* 51. 4 (1999): 361–381.

Blau, Herbert. *Blooded Thought: Occasions of the Theatre.* New York: PAJ Publications, 1982.

Boal, Augusto. *The Theatre of the Oppressed.* Trans. Charles A. and Maria-Odilia Leal McBride. New York: Theatre Communications Group, 1979.

Bourdieu, Pierre. "The Economics of Linguistic Exchange." *Social Science Information* (1977): 649–653.

Brecht, Bertolt. "The Modern Theatre Is the Epic Theatre." *Brecht on Theatre: The Development of an Aesthetic.* Ed. and trans. John Willett. New York: Hill and Wang, 1964, 73.

Brewster, Ben, and Lea Jacobs. *Theatre to Cinema: Stage Pictorialism and the Early Feature Film.* Oxford: Oxford University Press, 1997.

Broadcasting (20 May 1947): 28.

Brockett, Oscar G., and Robert Findlay. *Century of Innovation: A History of European and American Theatre and Drama Since the Late Nineteenth Century,* 2d ed. Boston: Allyn and Bacon Press, 1991.

Brook, Peter. *The Empty Space.* London: MacGibbon and Kee, 1968.

Brooks, Mel, and Tom Meehan. *The Producers.* New York: Round Table Press, 2001.

Brooks, Tim, and Earle Marsh. *The Complete Directory to Prime Time Network and Cable TV Shows 1946–Present.* 6th ed. New York: Ballantine, 1998.

Bryant-Jackson, Paul, and Lois More Overbeck. *Intersecting Boundaries: The Theatre of Adrienne Kennedy.* Minneapolis: University of Minnesota, 1992.

Buchanan, Leigh. "A New Staging Ground." *WebMaster Magazine* (May–June 1996): 31–35.

Bunn, Robert. "Masters of Grace: Austin Bunn Interview, the Digital Effects Team That Created Philip Glass and Robert Wilson's Newest 3-D Spectacle." *Monsters of Grace.* 22 February 2005, www.kwcc.com/works/sv/mog.html.

Burian, J.M., ed. *The Secret of Theatrical Space.* New York: Applause Theatre Books, 1993.

Burian, Jarka. *The Scenography of Joseph Svoboda.* Middletown, Conn.: Wesleyan University Press, 1971.

Butler, Judith. *Bodies That Matter: On the Discursive Limits of Sex.* New York: Routledge, 1993.

Butler, Judith. "Performative Acts and Gender Constitution: An Essay in Phenomenology and Feminist Theory." *Theatre Journal* (December 1988): 521.

Canby, Vincent. "In Glenn Close, 'Sunset Boulevard' Finds Its Megastar." *New York Times Theater Reviews.* New York: Times Books, 1996. Rpt. of 19 Dec. 1993, review.

Carlson, Marvin. *Theatre Semiotics: Signs of Life.* Bloomington: Indiana University Press, 1990.

Case, Sue-Ellen. *The Domain Matrix.* Bloomington: Indiana University Press, 1996.

Charlie. "Rate Las Vegas" online posting. 12 Dec. 2005. Rate Las Vegas Archives 10. Jan. 2006, www.ratevegas.com/blog/2005.

Chin, Daryl. "The Digital Dividend." *Location One.* 10 Aug. 2003, accessed at www.location1.org/ossa/index.html.

Chong, Ping. "Kind Ness." *Plays in Progress.* New York: Theatre Communications Group, 1986.

Chong, Ping. *Nuit Blanche.* California: The VRI Theatre Library: Series One, Contemporary Scripts, 1996.

Coe, Fred. "Televising Shakespeare." *Theatre Arts* (April 1955): 56, 96.

Cole, Toby, and Helen Krich Chinoy. *Directors on Directing.* Indianapolis: Bobbs-Merrill Company Inc., 1963.

Colley, Ann C. *Nostalgia and Recollection in Victorian Culture.* New York: Palgrave, 1998.

Conaway, Carol B. "Crown Heights: Politics and Press Coverage of the Race War That Wasn't." *Polity* 32. 1 (Fall 1999): 93–118.

Cooke, Kevin, and Dan Lehrer. "Who Will Own the Information Highway." *The Nation* (12 July 1993): 38.

Copeland, Roger. "The Presence of Mediation." *The Drama Review* 34. 4 (1990): 28–44.

Corrigan, Timothy. "Film and the Culture of Cult." *Wide Angle* 8. 3–4 (1986): 91–99.

Cosgrove, Denis, ed. *The Iconography of Landscape: Essays of the Symbolic Representation, Design and Use of Past Environments.* Cambridge: Cambridge University Press, 2000.

Couple in the Cage: A Guatinaui Odyssey. Dir. Paula Heredia, Coco Fusco. Perf. Coco Fusco, Guillermo Gómez-Peña. Distr. Third World Newsreel, 1993.

Covington, Richard. "Salon Interviews David Mamet" (1997). 10 August 2003, accessed at www.salon.com/feature/1997/10/cov_si_24mamet.html.

Cox, Gordon, and David Rooney. "B'way Opens Screen Door." *VFilm Weekly.* 12 Sept. 2005. 14 Feb. 2006, variety.com.

Craig, Edward Gordon. *On the Art of the Theatre.* London: Brownes, 1911.

Craig, Edward Gordon. *On the Art of the Theatre.* London: Heinneman, 1958.

Craig, Edward Gordon. "Gentlemen the Marionette." *The Theatre–Advancing.* London: Constable, 1921.

Crary, Jonathan. *Techniques of the Observer: On Vision and Modernity in the Nineteenth Century.* Boston: MIT Press, 1999.

Criscuolo, Michael. "Sweeny Todd Review." Rev. *Sweeny Todd.* Dir. John Doyle. 10 Nov. 2005. 15 Jan. 2006, nytheatre.com.

Crowe, Cameron. *Conversations with Wilder.* New York: Alfred A. Knopf, 1999.

Davidson, Justin. "Are You Ready For Digital Opera?" *Los Angeles Times*, Calendar section, April 12, 1998.

Davis, Fred. *Yearning for Yesterday: Sociology of Nostalgia.* New York: Free Press, 1979.

Dawson, Gary Fischer. *Documentary Theatre in the United States: An Historical Survey of its Content, Form and Stagecraft.* Westport, Conn.: Greenwood Press, 1999.

Debord, Guy. *The Society of the Spectacle.* Trans. Donald Nicholson-Smith. New York: Zone Books, 1995.

Dolan, Jill. *The Feminist Spectator as Critic.* Ann Arbor: UMI Research Press, 1988.

Domet, Sarah. "The Drama of Everyday Life: One Nation Under Television." American Drama Online. Accessed 15 March 2003.

Duberman, Martin. *In White America: A Documentary Play.* New York: Samuel French, 1964.

Dunlap, Orrin E. *The Future of Television.* New York: Harper & Brothers, 1942.

Dyer, Richard. "Heavenly Bodies: Film Stars and Society." *Film and Theory.* Eds. Robert Stam and Toby Miller. Malden, Mass: Blackwell Publishers, 2000.

Eco, Umberto. "*Casablanca:* Cult Movies and Intertextual Collage." *Travels in Hyperreality.* Trans. William Weaver. New York: Harcourt Brace Jovanovich, 1983, 197–211.

Eddy, Micheal S. "Smaller, Brighter, Quieter, Cheaper." Entertainment Design, 1 May 2002. 20 Dec. 2005, http://bg.entertainmentdesignmag.com/microcities/magazine.com.

Edgarton, Gary. *Film and the Arts in Symbiosis.* New York: Greenwood Press, 1988.

Eloueini, Ammar. "Abstract Machines." *Architectural Design: Architects in Cyberspace II* 68. 11–12 (1998): 61–65.

Favorini, Attilio. *Voicings.* Hopewell, N.J.: The Echo Press, 1995.

Federal Communications Commission Report No. DC 96–81 (August 1996). Accessed at www.fcc.gov, July 10, 2002.

Fiske, John. *Television Culture.* London: Methuen, 1997.

Fornes, Maria Irene. *Fefu and Her Friends.* New York: PAJ Publications, 1990.

Freeman, Mike. "Riots Boost May Ratings in Los Angeles." *Broadcasting* (June 1, 1992).

Freidburg, Anne. *Window Shopping: Cinema and the Postmodern.* Berkeley: University of California Press, 1994.

"Fremont Street Experience Light and Sound Show is a Modern Technological Marvel." 10 July 1995. 24 Jan. 2006, www.a2zlasvegas.com/fse/fse04.html.

Frome, Shelly. *The Actors Studio: A History.* Jefferson, N.C.: McFarland, 2001.

Gameson, William F. "News as Framing." *American Behavioral Scientist* 33. 2 (November 1989): 157.

Gasiorek, Andrzej. "The Politics of Cultural Nostalgia: History and Tradition in Ford Madox Ford's Parade's End." *Literature & History* 11 (2002): 52–77.

Gaver, Jack. *Curtain Calls.* New York: Dodd and Meade, 1949.

Gerould, Daniel C. *American Melodrama.* New York: Performing Arts Journal Publications, 1983.

Glass, Ira. "Hoaxing Yourself." *This American Life.* WBEZ, Chicago. Transcript. National Public Radio. 17 March 2000, accessed at www.thislife.org.

Goldberg, Roselee. *Performance Art: From Futurism to the Present.* New York: Henry Abrams, 1988.

Gomery, Douglas. *Shared Pleasures: A History of Movie Presentation in the United States.* Madison: University of Wisconsin Press, 1992.

Gould, Jack. "Matter of Form." *New York Times,* 31 Oct. 1948, 11.

Gramsci, Antonio. *Selections from the Prison Notebooks.* Trans. Quintin Hoare and Geoffrey Nowell Smith. New York: International Publishers, 1971.

Grossman, Jan. "O kombinace divadla a filmu" [*The Combination of Theatre and Film*], *Lanterna Magika.* Ed. Jiri Hrbas. Prague, 1968.

Hairspray Website. 22 May 2003, accessed at www.hairsprayonbroadway.com/.

Hall, Stuart, et al. *Culture, Media, Language.* London: Hutchinson, 1981. Rpt of *Encoding/Decoding in Television Discourse,* 1972.

Hayward, Susan. *Key Concepts in Cinema Studies.* London: Routledge, 1996.

Heilpern, John. "How a Stinker Becomes a Winner Becomes a Loser (and Ends Up the Biggest Winner on Broadway)." *Talk,* June–July 2001.

Hernandez, Ernio. "Creator Eric Idle Talks of Monty Python's *Spamalot* Quest from Film to Musical." 01 March 2004. 10 Jan. 2006, www.playbill.com/news/article/84680.html.

Higson, Andrew. "The Concept of National Cinema." *Screen* 30. 4 (1989): 68–93.

Hirsch, Foster. *A Method to Their Madness: A History of the Actors Studio.* New York: W.W. Norton, 1984.

Hobson, Dorothy. "Soap Operas at Work." *Remote Control: Television Audiences and Cultural Power.* Eds. Ellen Seiter, et al. London: Routledge, 1989, pp. 150–67.

Hogan, Kathleen. "Celebration." May 2003, accessed at xroads.virginia.edu/~MA98/hogan/celebration/main.html.

Holbrook, Morris B. "On the New Nostalgia: 'These Foolish Things' and Echoes of the Dear Departed Past." *Continuities in Popular Culture: The Present in the Past and the Past in the Present and Future.* Eds. Ray B. Browne and Ronald J. Ambrosetti. Bowling Green, Ohio: Bowling Green State University Popular Press, 1993, p. 75.

Holland, Bernard. "Critics Notebook: Part Glass, Part Wilson, Part Film, Part Opera." *New York Times,* April 17, 1998. Monsters of Grace. 22 Feb. 2005, www.kwcc.com/works/sv/mog.html.

"How to Succeed in Business Without Really Trying." Multi-Image Systems Inc. 2 Aug. 2002, accessed at www.multi-image.com/projects.

Hunter, Christopher. "From Cultural Hegemony to the Culture of Code." Presented at the International Institute of Communications Annual Conference, September 2000.

Hyman, Collette. *Staging Strikes: Workers Theatre and the American Labor Movement.* Philadelphia: Temple University Press, 1997.

id Software promotional materials (1999). May 2003, accessed at www.idsoftware.com/games/doom/doom-ultimate/.

Jackson, Wendy. "*Monsters of Grace*: High Tech Meets High Art." *Animation World* (May 1998). Monsters of Grace, 22 Feb. 2005, *www.kwcc.com/works/sv/mog.html*.

Jakobson, Roman. *Style in Language*. Ed. T. Sebeok. Cambridge: MIT University Press, 1960.

Jameson, Frederic. *Postmodernism, or the Cultural Logic of Late Capitalism*. Durham: Duke University Press, 1991.

Jensen, Amy Petersen. "Contemporary Theatre Design Survey." Questionnaire, Brigham Young University, Aug. 2005.

Johnson, Darek. "The Las Vegas Fashion Show; LEDs and plasma panels enliven IMAX Theater–style merchandising." 10 June 2002. 20 Jan. 2006, www.signweb.com/moving/cont/fashionshowb.htm.

Johnson, David. "The Next Generation of Projection Design." Entertainment Design, May 1, 2003. 22 Aug. 2005, http://bg.entertainmentdesignmag.com/microcities/magazine.com.

Kennedy, Adrienne. "A Movie Star Has to Star in Black and White." *In One Act*. Minneapolis: University of Minnesota Press, 1988.

Kincade, Patrick, and Michael A. Katovich. "Toward a Sociology of Cult Films: Reading Rocky Horror." *Sociological Quarterly* 33. 2 (Summer 1992): 191–209.

Krause, Rosiland, and Hal Foster. "Introduction." *October* 77 (1996): 3.

Kuchwara, Michael. "From 'Phantom' to 'Wicked,' Nancy Coyne Knows the Art of Selling Broadway." Associated Press International, 17 Aug. 2005, p. 1.

Lahr, John. "Music Men: A Hit, A Miss and Moola." Rev. of *Sweeny Todd*. Dir. John Doyle. *The New Yorker*, 14 Nov. 2005.

Lampert-Greaux, Ellen. "Victorian Secrets." Entertainment Design, 1 Jan. 2005. 12 Jan. 2006, http://bg.entertainmentdeignmag.com/microcities/magazine.com.

Lassell, Mark, ed. *Disney on Broadway*. New York: Disney Editions, 2002.

Laurel, Brenda. *Computers as Theatre*. Boston: Addison-Wesley Longman Co., Inc., 1991.

The League of American Theatres and Producers. "Broadway's Economic Contributions to New York, 2004–2005 Season" Research. 01 April 2006. 20 April 2006, www.livebroadway.com/econ.html.

The League of American Theatres and Producers. "Grosses by Date" Research, 01 April 2006. 20 April 2006, www.livebroadway.com/bwygrosses.asp.

The League of American Theatres and Producers. "Grosses by Show" Research, 01 April 2006. 20 April 2006, www.livebroadway.com/bwygrosses.asp.

The League of American Theatres and Producers. "Grosses by Theatre" Research. 01 April 2006. 20 April 2006, www.livebroadway.com/bwygrosses.asp.

The League of American Theatres and Producers. "Season by Season Stats" Research. 01 April 2006. 20 April 2006, www.livebroadway.com/bwystats.html.

The League of American Theatres and Producers. "Who Goes To Broadway: The Demographics of the Broadway Audience, 2004–2005 Season" Research. 01 April 2006. 20 April 2006, www.livebroadway.com/audience/html.

Leiter, Samuel L. *The Encyclopedia of the New York Stage, 1940–1950*. Westport, Conn.: Greenwood Press, 1996.

Lewis, Barbara. "The Circle of Confusion: A Conversation with Anna Deavere Smith." *Kenyon Review* 15. 4 (1993): 54–64.

Lewis, Michael. *Next: The Future Just Happened*. New York: W.W. Norton, 2001.

Liebes, Tamar, and Elihu Katz. The Export of Meaning: Cross-Cultural Reading of *Dallas*. New York: Oxford University Press, 1990.

Londrè, Felicia Hardison, and Daniel J. Watermeier. *American Theatre from Pre-Columbian Times to the Present*. New York: Continuum Publishing, 1998.

Lull, James. *Media, Communication, Culture: A Global Approach.* New York: Columbia University Press, 2000.

Lyons, Charles R. "Gordon Craig's Concept of the Actor." *Educational Theatre Journal* 16. 3 (1964): 258–269.

Lyons, Charles R., and James C. Lyons. "Anna Deavere Smith: Perspectives on Her Performance within the Context of Critical Theory." *Journal of Dramatic Theory and Criticism* 9. 1 (1994): 43–66.

Mamet, David. *Speed the Plow.* New York: Methuen, 1998.

Manovich, Lev. "The Poetics of Augmented Space," 2002. 10 Jan. 2005, www.manovich. net/DOCS/augmented_space.doc.

Martin, Carol. "Anna Deavere Smith: The Word Becomes You." *The Drama Review* 37. 4 (1993): 45–62.

Mason, Susan Vaneta. Rev. of *Twilight Los Angeles.* Playwright, Anna Deavere Smith. Mark Tapor Forum, Los Angeles. *Theatre Journal* 46 (1994): 111–19.

McCarter, Jeremy. "The Gore Campaign, Sweeny Todd, and See What I See Pump Some Much Needed Blood into an Anemic Season." Rev. of *Sweeny Todd.* Dir. John Doyle. *New York Magazine,* 7 Nov. 2005.

McCree, Junie. "A Vaudeville Luncheon in Three Acts," *American Variety Stage: Vaudeville and Popular Entertainment, 1870–1920,* in the Library of Congress American Memory Collection. 30 January 2002, accessed at http://memory.loc.gov/ammem/vshtml/ vshome.html.

McKinley, Jesse. "Having Reshaped Broadway, Disney Readies a Second Act." *New York Times,* 29 November 2003.

McLaughlin, Robert. *Broadway and Hollywood: A History of Economic Interaction.* New York: Arno Press, 1977.

McLuhan, Marshall, and Quentin Fiore. *The Medium is the Massage.* New York: Random House, 1967.

Modeleski, Tania. *Old Wives Tales and Other Women's Stories.* New York: NYU Press, 1998, pp. 57–76.

Morley, David. *The Nationwide Audience.* London: British Film Institute, 1980.

Morley, David, and Kevin Robbins. *Spaces of Identity: Global Media, Electronic Landscapes and Cultural Boundaries.* London: Routledge, 1995.

Museum of Modern Art: Conversations with Contemporary Artists. "Coco Fusco." 10 Sept. 2002, accessed at www.moma.org/onlineprojects/conversations/cff.html.

Music Television Video: Total Request Live (July 1999). 12 May 2003, accessed at www.mtv.com/onair/trl/votevideo.jhtml.

Musser, Charles. *The Emergence of Cinema: The American Screen to 1907.* New York: Charles Scribner and Sons, 1990.

"Mystere-Cirque Du Soleil Official Website-Show." CirqueduSoleil.Com. 12 Dec. 2005 <http://www.cirquedusoleil.com/CirqueDuSoleil/en/showstickets/mystere/Mystere-acts8.htm>.

Neiman Marcus Catalogue (2003). 15 June 2003, accessed at www.neimanmarcus.com/ store/catalog/.

Nelson, Steve. "Broadway and the Beast: Disney Comes to Times Square." *TDR* 39 (1995): 71–85.

Nowell-Smith, Geoffrey. *The Oxford History of World Cinema.* Oxford: Oxford University Press, 1996.

O'Quinn, Jim. "Getting Closer to America." *American Theatre* 13. 8 (1996): 18–20.

Perry, George. *Sunset Boulevard: From Movie to Musical.* London: Henry Holt and Co., 1994.

Pinhanez, Claudio. "Computer Theater." MIT Media Laboratory. Accessed 2 February 2003 at http://web.media.mit.edu/~pinhanez/isea/isea.html.

Pinhanez, Claudio. "It/I." MIT Media Laboratory. Accessed 2 February 2003 at http://web. media.mit.edu/~iti/.

Piro, Sal. *Creatures of the Night: The Rocky Horror Experience.* Livonia, Mich.: Stabur Press, 1990.

Playbill Online (2002). 10 June 2003, accessed at www.playbill.com/index.php.

Pontbriand, Chantal. "The Eye Finds No Fixed Point on Which to Rest." Trans. C.R. Parsons. *Modern Drama* 25. 1 (March 1982): 154–162.

The Producers on Tour Website. National Press Agents: Tanya Grubich, Molly Haydon, 2 July 2002. 31 July 2003, accessed at www.producersontour.com/flash.html.

Reich, John. "Stage Plays for Television." *Televiser* (Jan.–Feb. 1946): 11. *Television: The Business Magazine of the Industry* 11. 4 (Nov. 1948): 4.

Reinelt, Janelle. "Performing Race: Anna Deavere Smith's *Fires in the Mirror.*" *Modern Drama* 39 (1996): 609–17.

Rich, Frank. "Conversations with Sondheim." *New York Times Magazine*, 12 March 2000, pp. 40, 88.

Riding, Alan. "Filmmakers Seek Protection from U.S. Dominance." *New York Times*, February 2003, late ed., section E3.

Riverport Communications. *The Planet Garth Forum.* Jan 2006. 23 Jan. 2006, www.planetgarth.com/forums/showthread.php?t=122589.

Rocky Horror Picture Show Website (1996–2000). 18 May 2003, accessed at www.rockyhorror.com/.

Rosen, George. "Julius Caesar." *Variety* 9 (March 1949): 33.

Rothenburg, Jerome. "New Models, New Visions: Some Notes Toward a Poetics of Performance." *Performance in Postmodern Culture.* Eds. Michael Benamou and Charles Caramello. Madison: Coda Press, 1977, 11–18.

Rushkoff, Douglas. "Frontline: Merchants of Cool." Public Broadcasting Service online, PBS. 9 Sept. 2002, accessed at www.pbs.org.

Sandberg, Marion. "Hollaback Girl." *Live Design* 39.12 (2005).

Schechner, Richard. "Anna Deavere Smith: Acting As Incorporation." *The Drama Review* 37. 4 (1993): 63–64.

Schechner, Richard. *Performance Studies: An Introduction.* London: Routledge, 2002.

Schelling, F.W.J. *The Ages of the World.* Trans. Frederick De Wolfe Bolman. New York: Columbia University Press, 1942.

Schiller, Herbert I. *Communication and Cultural Domination.* New York: International Arts and Sciences Press, 1976.

Sing-a-long Website (2000). 4 May 2002, accessed at www.singalonga.com/flash_index. htm.

Smith, Anna Deavere. *Fires in the Mirror: Crown Heights, Brooklyn and Other Identities.* New York: Anchor Books, 1993.

Smith, Anna Deavere. "Not So Special Vehicles." *Performing Arts Journal* 17 (1995): 77–89.

Smith, Anna Deavere. *Talk to Me: Travels in Media and Politics.* New York: Anchor Books, 2000.

Smith, Anna Deavere. *Twilight Los Angeles, 1992.* New York: Anchor Books, 1994.

Smith, Erna. "Transmitting Race: The Los Angeles Riot in Television News." Research Paper R-11. *The Joan Shorenstein Barone Center for Press, Politics and Public Policy* (1994): 1–16.

Sobchack, Vivian. "The Scene of the Screen: Envisioning Cinematic and Electronic Presence." *Film and Theory.* Eds. Robert Stam and Toby Miller. Malden, Mass.: Blackwell Publishers, 2000.

Stage on Screen: Twilight Los Angeles. Dir. Mark Levin. Writer, perf. Anna Deavere Smith. Video Cassette. PBS, 2001.

Stayton, Richard. "A Fire in a Crowded Theatre." *American Theatre* 10.7–8 (1993): 20–22, 72–75.

Stewart, Kathleen. "Nostalgia — A Polemic." *Cultural Anthropology* 3. 3 (1988).

Struppek, Mirjam. "Urban Screens: Discovering the Potential of Outdoor Screens for Urban Society." 20 Jan. 2005, www.urbanscreens.org.

Swardson, Anne. "French Groups Sue to Bar English-only Internet Sites." *Washington Post*, 24 Dec. 1996: A1.

Teachout, Terry. "Fresh Blood on Broadway." Rev. of *Sweeny Todd*. Dir. John Doyle. *The Wall Street Journal*, 4 Nov. 2005.

Thompson, John B. *The Media and Modernity: A Social Theory of the Media*. Cambridge: Polity; Stanford: Stanford University Press, 1995.

Thompson, John B., ed. *Language and Symbolic Power*. Cambridge: Polity; Cambridge: Harvard University Press, 1991.

Toepfer, Karl. "Twisted Bodies: Aspects of Female Contortionism in the Letters of a Connoisseur." *TDR* 43.1 (1999): 104–136.

Toltan, Dinah. "Out of the Blue." *Graphic Exchange* 14. 4 (Fall 2005). 26 Jan. 2006, *www.gxo.com/Fall05/ACROBAT5/download.php?f=gX144bOutoftheBlue.pdf*.

Tucker, Andrew. *The London Fashion Book*. New York: Rizzoli International Productions, 1998.

Turner, Victor. *From Ritual to Theatre: The Human Seriousness of Play*. New York: PAJ Publications, 1982.

Valle, Phillip. "The Digital Frontier: On the Virtual and Material." *TYA Today* 16. 2 (2002): 12–14.

Vardac, A. Nicholas. *Stage to Screen: From Garrick to Griffith*. Cambridge: Harvard University Press, 1949.

Vertov, Dziga. *Kino Eye: The Writings of Dziga Vertov*. Ed. Annette Michealson. Trans. Kevin O'Brien. Berkeley: University of California Press, 1984.

Virillio, Paul. "We May Be Entering an Electronic Gothic Era." *Architectural Design: Architects in Cyberspace II* 68. 11–12 (1998): 61–65.

Vobril, Mary. "Breaking a Taboo." *Newsday*, 7 February 2001.

Wickstrom, Maurya. "Commodities, Mimesis, and *The Lion King*: Retail Theatre for the 1990s." *Theatre Journal* 51. 3 (1999): 231–360.

Willet, John. *The Theatre of Erwin Piscator: Half a Century of Politics in Theatre*. New York: Holmes & Meier Publishers, 1979.

Wilson, Robert Forrest. *Crusader in Crinoline*. Westport, Conn.: Greenwood, 1972.

Winn, Steve. Rev. of *House Arrest. San Francisco Chronicle*, 6 November 2000: B1.

Winship, Lindsay. "The Digital Age." *Stage Directions* 18.12 (2005): 18.

Zola, Emile. "Naturalism in the Theatre." *The Theory of the Modern Stage*. Ed. Eric Bentley. London: Penguin Books, 1968, 351–73.

Index